Research in Psychotherapy and Counselling

Research in Psychotherapy and Counselling

Ladislav Timulak

Los Angeles • London • New Delhi • Singapore • Washington DC

Ladislav Timulak © 2005, 2008

First edition published by Triton in 2005

This new edition first published in 2008

SAGE Publications Ltd
1 Oliver's Yard
55 City Road
London EC1Y 1SP

SAGE Publications Inc.
2455 Teller Road
Thousand Oaks, California 91320

SAGE Publications India Pvt Ltd
B 1/I 1 Mohan Cooperative Industrial Area
Mathura Road
New Delhi 110 044

SAGE Publications Asia-Pacific Pte Ltd
33 Pekin Street #02–01
Far East Square
Singapore 048763

Library of Congress Control Number: 2008920626

British Library Cataloguing in Publication data

A catalogue record for this book is available from the British Library

ISBN 978-1-4129-4578-3
ISBN 978-1-4129-4579-0 (pbk)

Typeset by C&M Digitals Pvt Ltd, Chennai, India
Printed in India at Replika Press Pvt Ltd
Printed on paper from sustainable resources

Dedicated to my parents and Katka, Adam, Dominika and Natalia

Contents

Acknowledgements

This text is based on the book *Současny výzkum psychoterapie* (Timulak, 2005), which was written in Slovak and then translated into Czech. The text of this book was first translated by me and my friends and colleagues, Matus Biescad, Julia Halamova, Sona Chamrazova and Jana Hanulova. I would like to thank them for this contribution. The translation was then edited, revised and updated by me. Helpful comments from the reviewers of the book (Mick Cooper, Georgia Lepper, Robert Elliott and John McLeod) were then incorporated, as well as the suggestions of Alice Oven, editor at Sage. I would like to acknowledge their contribution as well. The whole text was then language edited by Beth Humphries and then thoroughly copy-edited by Sarah Bury for whose help I am thankful. I would like to thank Dr David Hevey for help with the Glossary. I would also like to acknowledge the support of my wife Katka Timulakova and to my mum for all the help she provided to both of us, which allowed me to focus on this work.

The work was also supported by following grants: the Trinity College Benefaction Fund and the Provost's Academic Development Fund and grant VEGA 1/4520/07.

Introduction

Psychotherapy and counselling research is one of the areas that contributes to the development of psychotherapy and counselling.[1] Psychotherapy and counselling research is interesting in that it is not in a laboratory that it is first conducted before it is brought to practice; instead it is practice itself that informs what should be studied (McLeod, 2003). Apart from direct research, psychotherapy and counselling also benefit from basic research in psychology and related areas. Counselling and psychotherapy are also informed by related scientific disciplines, such as philosophy and other human and social sciences and medical, biological and interdisciplinary sciences such as neuroscience (Grawe, 2007). Counselling and psychotherapy are to a great extent also formed by practitioners' clinical experience of working with clients, as well as by practitioners' personal development experience and supervision.

Research in psychotherapy and counselling tries to come to an understanding, by the use of rigorous methods, of what is happening in therapy that leads to client changes in the direction of improved mental health. Like every research, psychotherapy and counselling research is extraordinarily complex. Rigorous investigations attempt to employ critical and reflective processes that will enhance our understanding of psychological therapy. However, critical thinking also reveals many limitations of studying psychotherapy. Awareness of the historical and social context that influences research activity is part of this critical process.

When talking about psychotherapy and counselling research, we must not forget that the investigation of human beings is always influenced by the worldview of the investigator. What is relevant to study is up to the investigator. Similarly, the investigator's view on what constitutes the core of human beings determines the nature of the investigation. The researcher asks only those questions that he or she needs to understand and considers

---

1 I will use the terms counselling and psychotherapy interchangeably throughout the text. Similarly, the words client and patient. Generally, I use each of them in the context in which it is most often found (e.g. primary care counselling, psychoanalytic psychotherapy).

valuable. Researchers' own perspectives on what constitutes people's well-being will inform their understanding of the tasks and goals of psychotherapy and counselling. In this, the researchers' position is not so different from that of practising therapists, who often differ significantly in their views on what the tasks and goals of therapy should be.

The worldview that shapes the delivery and goals of therapy does not preclude therapists from sharing their experiences of and reflections on therapy. The same applies to research. Researchers as well as therapists of different orientations and persuasions can learn from empirical findings that were gathered in the studies of 'other camps'. However, what they should bear in mind is that this therapy and investigation was conducted in a certain paradigm, which they need to translate to their own. The paradigmatic differences may sometimes preclude openness to the findings from some research studies or therapies. It is a reality that for years has been part of the field of psychotherapy and counselling.

Despite the differences, it is quite likely that therapists and researchers of different orientations ask similar questions and that their conceptualizations of psychotherapy and its goals do not differ dramatically. This is probably more visible in recent years, when integration in psychotherapy and counselling has been quite popular. Furthermore, the *empirical* nature of research in psychotherapy invites researchers and consumers of research findings to use the findings to enrich their understanding of therapy beyond the ideology they employ.

The positive side of psychotherapy research is that it can inform the understanding of therapy as well as therapeutic practice. The negative side is that it can be misused in ideological battles between different psychotherapy camps. This text hopes to encourage readers to be aware of psychotherapy research and critical of its limitations and potential misuse.

Theoretical Orientation of this Book

This book attempts to look at psychotherapy and counselling as *generic* curative activity, as proposed by some well-known psychotherapy researchers, such as Klaus Grawe (2004) or David Orlinsky and Kenneth Howard (1986). This conceptualization of psychotherapy cuts through different theoretical approaches, in the best tradition of psychotherapy research, as it attempts to discover universal mechanisms of psychotherapeutic endeavour and change. Understanding psychotherapy as a generic and relatively unified activity fits well with the empirical nature of research in psychotherapy and counselling, as well as with my own persuasion that there are universal principles that can be applied within different therapeutic contexts (which are often shaped by one's own personal history and professional training and experience).

Despite the fact that I have my own preferences in what I offer to my clients in my work and views on what constitutes human well-being, I have an interest in how, in general, psychotherapy is being researched, and what the findings are. This allows me to adapt and use in my practice findings gathered in contexts that are often different from my own way of conducting therapy. It also allows me to search within an enormous area of psychotherapy research studies for answers to questions that I encounter in my practice. I constantly experience excitement when I conduct research or read research studies that creatively attempt to uncover pure psychological mechanisms and principles of therapeutic change.

Two Reasons for Researching Psychotherapy and Counselling

There exist two main reasons for empirical investigations of psychotherapy. The first is to *inform therapeutic practice*. Research tries to bring knowledge that either confirms how psychotherapy is practised or points to the need to alter existing therapeutic practice (when alterations become significant, new approaches to therapy can be born). Practitioners may use research as a resource that is quite similar to everyday practice, when one works in an exploratory and collaborative manner with the client, constantly checking whether the chosen strategy works. The main advantage of research, as opposed to everyday practice, is its rigor and the otherwise inaccessible outside perspective it gives. This advantage can be incorporated by the therapist in his or her own reflective process when conducting therapy with a particular client.

Apart from the fact that psychotherapy and counselling research informs everyday practice, research can also serve as a *justifier of the therapeutic endeavour*. Psychotherapy research rigorously assesses the benefits of psychotherapy for clients as well as broader society. Different stakeholders want to be assured that their resources are not wasted if they are invested in psychotherapy and counselling. From this perspective it is important that psychotherapy research is also conducted (or reviewed) by investigators who represent stakeholders who have a healthy scepticism towards the usefulness of psychotherapy and are open to see not only its usefulness but also its limitations and negative impacts.

Psychotherapy Research and Practice

The main ambition of most psychotherapy researchers is to have an impact on therapeutic practice. This ambition is, however, still not fully realized, though a positive trend of incorporating research studies into mainstream therapeutic practice has certainly been growing in recent years. Klaus Grawe (1997), a prominent psychotherapy researcher, predicted that *research-informed psychotherapy* will be the future of psychotherapy. Research-informed psychotherapy, according to him, should replace traditional therapeutic orientations: it should be based on the key mechanisms of psychological change regardless of the specific therapeutic approach (school) used in a work. Uncovering those 'basic therapeutic principles' should be one of the goals of psychotherapy research, and work based on these principles would be truly generic psychotherapy.

No matter how logical Grawe's (1997) proposition seems, the reality of the world of psychotherapy is that it exists quite independently from psychotherapy research. Training in psychotherapy and counselling still relies heavily on the accumulated clinical wisdom

Table 0.1   Critiques of psychotherapy research

Criticism	% agreeing
Research that treats all therapists or all responses by therapists as interchangeable obscures essential differences	75
Practical, relevant and scientifically sound measures of psychological change due to therapy are often unavailable	68
Studies designed to try to incorporate the complexities of psychotherapy are rarely done	67
In an effort to make studying psychotherapy more manageable, researchers often ignore important variables	66
Often researchers focus on specific therapeutic techniques while ignoring the importance of the relationship between therapist and client	66

Source: C. Morrow-Bradley and R. Elliott, 'Utilization of psychotheraphy research by practicing psychotherapists', *American Psychologist*, 41, 188–197, 1986. Published by American Psychological Association, adapted with permission.

and personal experience of trainers rather than on research findings. The roots of this detachment probably lie in how research has been taught on undergraduate pro-grammes. I suspect that the search for objectivity sometimes led to minimal validity.

Twenty years ago, Morrow-Bradley and Elliott (1986) investigated the use of psy-chotherapy research among members of the Division of Psychotherapy of American Psychological Association. They approached 10% (384 members) of this APA division and received answers from 73% of their sample. The results of their study showed that the average therapist had published in his or her entire career to date one research study, and read five psychotherapy research articles each month. Ten per cent of the sample stated that psychotherapy research articles or presentations informed their practice. Thirty-seven per cent read articles and 57% attended research conferences that they found meaningful, while 24 per cent of the respondents stated that a research article had helped them in work with a difficult client.

Respondents in Morrow-Bradley and Elliott's (1986) research were also offered a list containing 17 criticisms of psychotherapy research. The five key items that received the highest rating are presented in Table 0.1. Respondents were also asked to rate the use-fulness of seven different types of research: their order of usefulness is presented in Table 0.2. What can be seen from the tables is that practitioners see research as *reduc-tionistic*, not capable of gauging meaningful characteristics or simplifying them. The research methods are seen as insufficiently *sophisticated*. In regard to the areas that are worth study, process research dominated outcome research.

Goal of the Book

The goal of this book is to present the field of psychotherapy and counselling research to practising therapists and trainees. Hopefully, the book will also be valuable to

Table 0.2 Useful types of psychotherapy research

Research topic	% rating it as extremely or very useful
Research that emphasizes the description of how the therapy was done	84
Research that focuses on therapists and/or client behaviours leading to important moments of change during psychotherapy	83
Process–outcome research that links the process of therapy to differential outcomes	83
Research that focuses on the development and impact of the therapeutic or helping alliance	78
Process research that compares a treatment with a control group and/or other treatment approaches	62
Outcome research that compares a treatment with a control group and/or other treatment approaches	59
Research that emphasizes how research findings fit into a specific theoretical orientation	47

Source: C. Morrow-Bradley and R. Elliott, 'Utilization of psychotheraphy research by practicing psychotherapists', *American Psychologist*, 41, 188–197, 1986. Published by American Psychological Association, adapted with permission.

educators in psychotherapy and counselling. My goal is to present psychotherapy and counselling research in a way that will show the value of this kind of research for therapeutic practice. The book is also of potential interest to consumers of therapy and counselling, whether clients or those who pay for therapy. It should be helpful to novice psychotherapy and counselling researchers, and hopefully seasoned researchers will find something interesting in it too. I present what is being studied in therapy and how to give the reader a basic picture of the field, its achievements as well as problems. Throughout the book I use many examples of relevant studies so that the reader can gain an idea of what actual studies look like and what kind of results they can bring.

Organization of the Book

Psychotherapy and counselling research are traditionally divided into outcome research and process research. This division will be applied in this book. Outcome research usually attracts more interest because of its political influence, which stems from answering the question: what therapeutic approach works in which circumstances? Paradoxically, this kind of research does not contribute much to the development of new therapeutic approaches, but rather validates existing ones. Questions addressed by outcome research are numerous, including many on the assessment of outcome (e.g. how many clients got better, to what extent, how long changes lasted). Although it would seem more logical to start the presentation of psychotherapy research with psychotherapy process research and to look at change processes before looking at how to validate them, the emphasis in the current 'evidence-based' climate is on outcome research, so I will focus on that in the first part of the book.

We will look at different ways of measuring outcome in psychotherapy and counselling and will consider different designs that are employed in addressing whether a specific form of therapy works; however, we will spend more time on randomized controlled trials, as politically they dominate the field. We will also have a look at how findings are accumulated across several studies (meta-analysis, systematic reviews).

In regard to psychotherapy process research, we will focus on the different tools that are used in this type of research. We will also consider different types of studies, such as process–outcome studies, descriptive studies, significant events studies, studies testing theories of change, etc. In addition, the book will look at the context of psychotherapy, for example the development of therapists, supervision, psychotherapy training, etc. Finally, the last chapter is devoted to links between psychotherapy and counselling research and therapeutic practice. There we will examine some therapeutic approaches that were either developed empirically or were tested extensively.

The Presentation and Social Organization of Psychotherapy and Counselling Research

Psychotherapy and counselling research is an ever-developing scientific area. There are around 50 English-language international journals that regularly publish empirical studies on psychotherapy and counselling (see McLeod, 2003), the most important of which are presented in Table 0.3. These journals vary in their impact and in the types of studies they publish. The former is measured by scientific indicators such as impact factor (the frequency of citations of articles in the journal). Among the journals with the highest impact is *Archives of General Psychiatry*, published by the American Medical Association. The journal is devoted to psychiatry and related disciplines and in regard to psychotherapy studies usually publishes outcome studies that are high on validity and have high relevance. The *Journal of Consulting and Clinical Psychology* is a journal of the American Psychological Association and is devoted to clinical psychology. It contains mainly outcome studies, but also process–outcome studies and sometimes high-quality process studies. Process studies and studies conducted by counselling psychologists can be found in the American Psychological Association's *Journal of Counseling Psychology*. A special place among journals publishing empirical studies on psychotherapy is occupied by the journal of the International Society for Psychotherapy Research, *Psychotherapy Research*. This journal is on the edge of developments in psychotherapy and counselling research. It is open to innovative methodologies, to a variety of therapeutic orientations, as well as to various topics related to psychotherapy.

Table 0.3 Examples of relevant professional journals publishing psychotherapy studies and the type of psychotherapy and counselling research they publish

Journal	Brief characteristic
American Journal of Psychiatry	Journal of the American Psychiatric Association; publishes mostly outcome studies.
American Journal of Psychotherapy	Journal of the Association for Development of Psychotherapy; publishes mostly process–out come studies.
Archives of General Psychiatry	Journal of the American Medical Association; publishes mostly outcome studies.
Behavior Therapy	Journal of the Association for the Advancement of Behaviour Therapy; publishes mostly experimental investigations of behaviour therapy outcome (mostly smaller studies and experimental case studies).
British Journal of Clinical Psychology	Journal of the British Psychological Society; publishes different types of psychotherapy research.
British Journal of Guidance and Counselling	Journal published by Careers Research and Advisory Centre; mostly qualitative studies.
British Journal of Psychiatry	Journal of the Royal College of Psychiatrists; publishes mostly outcome studies with psychiatric patients.
Clinical Psychology: Science and Practice	Journal of the Division of Clinical Psychology of the American Psychological Association; publishes mostly overview studies and political issues of psychotherapy research.
Counselling and Psychotherapy Research	Journal of the British Association for Counselling and Psychotherapy; devoted solely to research in counselling and psychotherapy; publishes mostly qualitative process research.
International Journal of Group Psychotherapy	Journal of the American Association of Group Therapy; publishes different types of group therapy research.
Journal of Clinical Psychology	Journal of the International Society of Clinical Psychology; publishes different issues involved in psychotherapy research, and outcome studies that are not typically published.
Journal of Consulting and Clinical Psychology	Journal of the American Psychological Association; publishes mostly outcome studies and to lesser extent process–outcome studies.
Journal of Counseling Psychology	Journal of the American Psychological Association; publishes mostly process studies and qualitative studies.

(Continued)

Table 0.3 *(Continued)*

Journal	Brief characteristic
Journal of Counseling and Development	Journal of the American Counseling Association; publishes mostly process studies.
Journal of Marital and Family Therapy	Journal of the American Association for Marriage and Family Therapy; publishes research on couple and family therapy.
Psychology and Psychotherapy	Journal of the British Psychological Society that replaced the British Journal of Medical Psychology; publishes different types of research, including qualitative studies.
Psychotherapy	Journal of the Division of Psychotherapy of the American Psychological Association; publishes theoretical, practical and research articles, mostly process studies and overview studies.
Psychotherapy Research	Journal of the Society for Psychotherapy Research; entirely dedicated to psychotherapy research; publishes all types of research, often original and atypical methodology.

There are also many monographs as well as edited books dedicated to psychotherapy research. Some from the 1990s and the beginning of the twenty-first century are presented in Table 0.4. The leading edited book is the *Handbook of Psychotherapy and Behavior Change*, published for the first time in 1971. The editors of this book, Allen Bergin and Sol Garfield, are respected authorities in the area of psychotherapy research. Now in its fifth edition (Lambert, 2004), this book is published approximately every eight years and presents all psychotherapy research, with an emphasis on accumulated findings.

An important cornerstone in the development of psychotherapy research was the establishment of the International Society for Psychotherapy Research (SPR; see www.psychotherapyresearch.org). Every year this society organizes an annual conference which usually showcases the cutting edge developments in psychotherapy research. The society also has regional chapters (e.g. in the UK, Europe, North America) that organize regional conferences. Past presidents of the Society for Psychotherapy Research include distinguished researchers such as Ken Howard, David Orlinsky, Allen Bergin, Sol Garfield, Hans Strupp (a writer on time-limited psychodynamic therapy), Lester Luborsky (who writes on supportive-expressive psychoanalytic therapy), Aaron Beck (a founder of cognitive therapy), Irene Elkin (the first author of the first large randomized controlled trial of psychotherapy and pharmacotherapy for depression that will be mentioned several times in this book), Ed Bordin (originator of the best-known concept of therapeutic alliance), A. (John) Rush (co-founder of cognitive psychotherapy), Alan Gurman (a well-known representative of couples and family therapy), Larry Beutler (a founder of systematic eclectic therapeutic model), Les Greenberg (a founder of emotion-focused therapy), Horst Kächele (one of the most renowned German

Table 0.4 Some edited books on psychotherapy research from the 1990s and the beginning of the twenty-first century, with brief descriptions

Title and editors	Brief description
Aveline, M. (ed.) (1995). *Research Foundations for Psychotherapy.* Chichester, England: Wiley.	Chapters from different researchers on methodological issues in psychotherapy research.
Bergin, A. & Garfield, S. (eds) (1994). *Handbook of Psychotherapy and Behavior Change* (4th edn). New York: John Wiley.	Fourth edition of the book summarizing research findings of psychotherapy research.
Beutler, L. E. & Crago, M. (eds) (1991). *Psychotherapy Research: An International Review of Programmatic Research.* Washington, DC: American Psychological Association.	Presents international programmatic research projects from different research teams.
Cain, D. & Seeman, J. (eds) (2002). *Humanistic Psychotherapies: Handbook of Research and Practice.* Washington, DC: American Psychological Association.	Research-informed view of humanistic psychotherapies.
Castonguay, L. G. & Beutler, L. E. (eds) (2006). *Principles of Therapeutic Change.* New York: Oxford University Press.	Invited authors summarize evidence of client and therapist variables, therapeutic relationship variables, and treatment variables impacting the outcome of psychotherapy for four groups of disorders (mood disorders, anxiety disorders, substance abuse disorders, and personality disorders).
Fisher, J. E. & O'Donohue, W. T. (eds) (2006). *Practitioner's Guide to Evidence-based Psychotherapy.* New York: Springer.	An overview of empirically supported treatments and other research evidence for a broad range of psychological and psychiatric disorders.
Freeman, C. & Power, M. (eds) (2007). *Handbook of Evidence-based Psychotherapies: A Guide for Research and Practice.* Chichester: John Wiley.	Provides an overview of empirical findings on psychotherapy outcome across different theoretical orientations and client groups.
Fuhriman, A. & Burlimgame, G. M. (eds) (1994). *Handbook of Group Psychotherapy: An Empirical and Clinical Synthesis.* New York: John Wiley.	An overview of research on group therapy.
Goodhart, C. D., Kazdin, A. E. & Sternberg, R. J. (eds) (2006). *Evidence-based Psychotherapy: Where Practice and Research Meet.* Washington, DC: American Psychological Association.	Offers perspectives of practitioners as well as researchers on different positive and negative aspects of the evidence-based movement.
Gurman, A. S. & Jacobson, N. S. (eds) (2003). *Clinical Handbook of Couples Therapy* (3rd edn). New York: Guilford Press.	Research-informed view of couple therapies.

(Continued)

Table 0.4 *(Continued)*

Title and editors	Brief description
Horvath, A. O. & Greenberg, L. S. (eds) (1994). *The Working Alliance: Theory, Research, and Practice.* New York: John Wiley.	Theoretical formulations and research findings concerning the therapeutic relationship.
Miler, N. E., Luborsky, L., Barber, J. P. & Docherty, J. P. (eds) (1993) *Psychodynamic Treatment Research.* New York: Basic Books.	Overview of empirical research into psychodynamic therapies.
Nathan, P.E. & Gorman, J. M. (eds) (2007). *A Guide to Treatments that Work.* (3rd edn). New York: Oxford University Press.	An overview of empirically supported psychotherapeutic and psychopharmacological approaches to treatment of psychiatric disorders.
Norcross, J. (ed.) (2002). *Psychotherapy Relationships that Work: Therapist Contributions and Responsiveness to Patients.* New York: Oxford University Press.	An overview of findings regarding relational variables influencing the outcome of psychotherapy.
Norcross, J., Beutler, L. E. & Levant, R. F. (eds) (2006). *Evidence-based Practices in Mental Health.* Washington, DC: American Psychological Association.	Presents heated debates of researchers involved in psychotherapy research on what constitutes 'evidence' for evidence-based practice. Proponents of sometimes dramatically different views on what constitutes evidence and how to interpret existing evidence are matched and invited to comment on each other's contribution.
Russell, R. L. (ed.) (1994). *Reassessing Psychotherapy Research.* New York: Guilford Press.	An overview of methodological issues in psychotherapy research.
Sexton, T. L., Weeks, G. R. & Robbins, M. S. (eds) (2003). *Handbook of Family Therapy: The Science and Practice of Working with Families and Couples.* New York: Routledge.	Research-informed view of family therapies.
Sprenkle, D. & Piercy, F. (eds) (2005). *Research Methods in Family Therapy.* New York: Guildford Press.	An overview of methods and methodological issues in family therapy research.
Talley, P. F., Strupp, H. H. & Butler, S. F. (eds) (1994). *Psychotherapy Research and Practice: Bridging the Gap.* New York: Basic Books.	Psychotherapy researchers' views on using research for informing therapeutic practice.
Toukmanian, S. G. & Rennie, D. (eds) (1992). *Psychotherapy Process Research: Paradigmatic and Narrative Approaches.* Newbury Park, CA: Sage.	Prototypical quantitative and qualitative investigations of psychotherapeutic process.
Tryon, S. G. (ed.) (2002). *Counseling Based on Process Research: Applying What We Know.* Boston: Allyn and Bacon.	Chapters from prominent North American process researchers written from the perspective of the applicability of research findings to therapeutic practice.

psychoanalysts), Lorna Benjamin (an originator of interpersonal reconstructive therapy of personality disorders), Klaus Grawe (an author of a generic psychological model of psychotherapy), David Shapiro (who set up one of the most sophisticated RCTs conducted in Britain), Len Horowitz (an author of the Inventory of Interpersonal Problems, an instrument widely used for measuring psychotherapy outcomes), Clara Hill (whose cognitive-experiential model is used for working with dreams in psychotherapy), Michael Lambert (most recent editor of the above-mentioned *Handbook of Psychotherapy and Behavior Change*), Robert Elliott (a co-founder of emotion-focused therapy), William Stiles (whose assimilation theory will be mentioned later in the book) and many other well-known researchers.

The Historical Context of Psychotherapy and Counselling Research

Psychotherapy and counselling research has a long and rich history, which helps us to understand some of the current political issues in the field. The history of this research is a history not only of methodological approaches and significant findings, but also of a striving for the recognition of counselling and psychotherapy as interventions for the treatment of psychological and psychiatric problems and disorders.

Brief Historical Overview of Outcome Researching in Psychotherapy and Counselling

The first outcome studies of psychotherapy date back to the 1920s (Huddleson & Fenichel, cited in Bergin, 1971). The standards of the early psychoanalytic studies, however, cannot be compared by any means to the current experimental or even non-experimental studies. However, as early as the 1950s (see Bergin, 1971) experimental designs started to be used in psychotherapy research. At that time little was known about what symptoms or other characteristics of clients could be influenced by psychotherapy. Nor was much known about how the perspective adopted when evaluating change (e.g. client, therapist, external observer, significant other) influences the outcome. Few significant instruments had been developed to capture therapeutic change. Despite these problems, the level of methodological sophistication – for example the use of several measures to capture change or several perspectives when looking at the outcome – must be commended.

The 1950s saw several bigger projects at different American universities and the 1960s also brought the first comparative studies, where different psychotherapies were compared (see Strupp & Howard, 1992). An excellent example of the comparative studies of the time was a project carried out at Temple University, comparing brief behaviour therapy, brief dynamic therapy, and waiting list control (Sloane et al., 1975). From the perspective of current standards, the cornerstone for studying psychotherapy outcome was the Treatment of Depression Collaborative Research Program (TDCPR) project funded by the US National Institute of Mental Health (Elkin, 1994). This project was the first of its kind, an example of the randomized controlled trials that now dominate outcome research in counselling and psychotherapy. This study – which will be mentioned many times in this book – compared several interventions, psychotherapeutic as well as pharmacotherapeutic and a placebo. It used manualized therapies that were checked for adherence and quality of delivery, and also used well trained and supervised therapists. It had sufficient statistical power, a well-defined client group, and used multiple sensitive instruments to capture therapeutic change. It also assessed outcome in longer-term follow-up.

Psychotherapy outcome research also had some other cornerstones. One example was the researching of the dose-effect of psychotherapy, i.e. investigation of the relationship between length of therapy and therapeutic outcome (Howard, Kopta et al., 1986). The introduction of the use of therapeutic manuals (Beck, Shaw et al., 1979) can also be considered an important step in psychotherapy research.

Psychotherapy outcome research is connected with many controversies. These often have to do with evaluation of the body of research on the effectiveness of psychotherapy. The first controversy was started by Eysenck's (1952) overview of the effectiveness of psychotherapy, in which he reached the conclusion that psychotherapy other than behaviour therapy is no better than spontaneous recovery. He himself was a representative of behaviour therapy, which certainly led to a heated debate. Later overviews were more positive towards psychotherapy and certainly justified it as a valuable venture (Bergin, 1971; Luborsky, Singer & Luborsky, 1975).

One extremely important event in the history of psychotherapy research was a work by Smith, Glass and Miller (1980; see also Smith & Glass, 1977) who for the first time used the method of meta-analysis. These authors looked at the overall outcome of psychotherapy as well as at the many factors that influence the outcome. The overall conclusion was that psychotherapy as a whole works and that the average effect size (to be discussed in Chapter 2) in comparison to control group across different measures and client groups is 0.85. This means that an average patient who was in the 50th percentile of the experimental group before treatment, reached the 80th percentile after treatment, i.e. the average patient was better off than 80% of patients in the control group. Smith, Glass and Miller did not compare different therapies directly; however, they stated effect sizes separately for therapies from different theoretical orientations.

Since Smith et al.'s meta-analysis, meta-analyses literally flooded professional literature and we will devote sufficient space to them in this book. Meta-analytic investigations added to discussions on the effectiveness of psychotherapy and counselling. This method, though having its own methodological problems, also allowed for the assessment of outcomes of studies whose authors were of different theoretical orientations.

Psychotherapy and counselling outcome research is currently immensely rich. In it there are still traces of the influences mentioned in this short description of its history. We will note them in Chapter 2, where I will try to capture the diversity of methodological approaches to studying the effect of psychotherapy and counselling.

The History of Psychotherapy Process Research

A cornerstone of psychotherapy process research was the use of tape recordings of therapeutic sessions by Carl Rogers (1942) in the 1940s. Recording allowed scientific scrutiny of what was happening inside the therapeutic session. The 1950s and 1960s also brought the first instruments allowing the assessment of the therapeutic process. Most of them (see overview in Greenberg & Pinsof, 1986) were expert-rated scales, but some were participative methods using the perspectives of both participants in therapy (examples are Barrett-Lennard's Relationship Inventory or the Therapy Session Reports of Orlinsky and Howard; I present these and other methods in Chapter 8).

Most process research conducted from the 1940s to the 1960s came from the client-centred theoretical orientation. Most often, Rogers' facilitative conditions were studied, as well as the client's experiencing process. Psychoanalytic developments were represented by the Menninger Foundation's project, which started in the 1950s (Wallerstein, 1992). This project focused on the process and outcome of psychoanalytic therapy. One of the researchers involved in the project, Lester Luborsky, continued in Penn State University from the 1960s. He studied the effect of therapeutic alliance on therapy outcome and was also studying transference and developing a method to measure it (see Luborsky & Crits-Christoph, 1990, 1998; Luborsky & Luborsky, 2006).

The 1980s brought new types of research. For example, therapeutic events studies were developed by Laura Rice and Les Greenberg (1984). These studies looked at stages of the therapeutic process and processes leading to successful progress in those events. The 1980s also witnessed sophisticated studies by the Mount Zion Psychotherapeutic Group (Weiss & Sampson, 1986), which predicted therapeutic process in long-term psychoanalytic therapy. Technological development in video also allowed clients and therapists to comment on the session in 'Interpersonal Process Recall' immediately after therapeutic sessions (Elliott, 1986).

The 1980s also saw a huge growth in process-outcome studies (we will talk about them in Chapter 10). Though the first process-outcome studies could be dated to the 1950s, the real growth in the 1980s is documented by Orlinsky, Grawe and Parks (1994), who identified 192 studies between 1985 and 1992 that looked at the relationship of process variables and outcome. Together, these studies revealed 1,200 independent findings on the relationship of some aspect of therapeutic process to therapy outcome.

A contribution of the 1990s was the development of qualitative methodologies allowing a more flexible approach to the complexity of psychotherapeutic process. Clients and therapists were invited to comment on sessions in which they participated (e.g. Rennie, 1990). Studies focusing on the process of successful or unsuccessful cases also flourished in this decade (e.g. Honos-Webb, Stiles et al., 1998).

Institutional Cornerstones of Psychotherapy Research

Hans Strupp and Kenneth Howard (1992), in reflecting on the history of psychotherapy research until 1992, saw three main institutional cornerstones for psychotherapy research in the United States and internationally. The first was a series of conferences organized by the American Psychological Association in 1958, 1961 and 1966 dedicated to psychotherapy research. At these, leading researchers discussed contemporary developments of psychotherapy research. The second cornerstone, according to Strupp and Howard, was a research conference in 1970, at which the International Society for Psychotherapy Research was established. Ken Howard and David Orlinsky were elected as president and president-elect respectively. The third important cornerstone was the support of the National Institute of Mental Health in the United States, which facilitated collaborative research projects in different research centres. Another cornerstone that I would add to their list was the foundation of the scientific journal of the Society for Psychotherapy Research, *Psychotherapy Research*, which is entirely devoted to psychotherapy research. Because of its transtheoretical and pluralistic scope, it is a good platform for communication between researchers studying psychotherapy.

History and Presence

The history of psychotherapy research is implicitly present in current research. Many of the methodological approaches that shaped the history of psychotherapy research are now truly history; however, some are still well and alive. This is one reason why I will refer to some historical precedents of the current methodological approaches in the following chapters.

PART I

PSYCHOTHERAPY AND COUNSELLING OUTCOME RESEARCH

Despite the fact that psychotherapy and counselling are scientific methods of treating psychological and psychiatric problems and disorders, they are also considered as a sort of social care that is hardly recognised as a treatment. This is stressed, though less so in recent years, by some opponents of psychotherapy and counselling outcome research. The fact that what is happening in the therapeutic relationship cannot be captured in naturally reductive scientific inquiry leads to scepticism about the value of outcome and other research. Furthermore, studying therapeutic outcomes is potentially threatening for therapists, if it shows that their work is not that effective. So, why bother studying whether psychotherapy works?

There may be several reasons. In practice, psychotherapists often form their own creative ways of working with clients. Many psychotherapeutic theories were developed on the basis of clinical experience, reflection and cautious reasoning. Counselling and psychotherapy outcome research allows for the assesment of such theories. Similarly, outcome research assesses both approaches that exist and approaches that are developed as a variation on existing therapies due to the limitations of the original approaches with certain types of client. Outcome research may also assess approaches that are developed on the basis of process or other psychological research. Generally speaking, outcome research assesses therapeutic approaches that researchers consider to be potentially effective and therefore worth studying. It is a means of evaluating and validating the effectiveness and efficacy of psychotherapy and counselling. Outcome research often assesses the effectiveness and efficacy of a psychological treatment against alternative forms of treatment, such as pharmacotherapy or self-help groups. Costs are taken into consideration in these instances too.

Psychotherapy and counselling outcome research involves many stakeholders. Among them founders of different therapeutic approaches. They, as well as the therapists trained in their respective approaches, are substantially interested in having their approach empirically validated so that they can gain security in the therapy market. Other stakeholders are the training providers in the various therapeutic approaches. In many countries, the trend is to fund only the training that provides empirically based treatments. Outcome research is very relevant to another group of stakeholders – practising therapists – who may want to know what kind of approach could be promising in their work with a particular client.

Other potential stakeholders are politicians or insurance companies that decide what kind of treatment will be provided in state-funded or insurance-funded medical care. These stakeholders will naturally be cautious when assessing the effectiveness and efficacy of psychotherapy and counselling, as the funds for medical care are always tight and come under many competing pressures. Last but not least, an important group of stakeholders are clients, the consumers of psychotherapy and counselling. They are definitely entitled to know what kinds of effects they can expect from any psychological treatments they are about to undergo.

All these different expectations, interests and pressures influence how psychotherapy and counselling outcome research is conducted. There is a demand for high ethical standards so that findings are not consciously or unconsciously distorted.

1

Instruments Used in Psychotherapy and Counselling Outcome Research

What the goal of psychotherapy and counselling should be is often the subject of theoretical debate. For example, some approaches favour improvement in psychopathological symptoms, some changes in interpersonal functioning and biographical self-understanding, and some the pursuit of individuals' potential and personal development. The issue may be further complicated by a particular ethical perspective weighting the impact of different changes achieved in therapy (see Tjeltveit, 1999), e.g. the goals of treatment when working with real guilt.

This chapter will take a pluralistic approach, presenting targets for measuring therapy outcome regardless of their theoretical origin. The main guideline will be 'current' practice and currently used instruments. By this, however, I do not want to underestimate any particular context of how change is understood, which definitely influences how therapy is conducted and studied. I will not focus here on generic issues of measurement such as the reliability or validity of the instruments used (see Kaplan & Sacuzzo, 2005), but rather on issues more specific to therapy outcome.

Measuring therapy outcome is a complex matter not only because of problems with the delineation of areas we want to improve by therapy but also because of the complexity involved in quantitatively assessing whether enough change has occurred. This complexity arises from the fact that different methodological approaches to measuring differ in their sensitivity to the amount of change.

Furthermore, different therapeutic approaches may be differentially effective in different areas of therapeutic outcome. For example, two therapies for depression may be differentially effective, with one being more effective in reducing symptoms of depression and other more effective in the area of improved interpersonal functioning. Globally, we could say that the outcome measured may not only be the function of therapy, but also the function of the *construct* (*variable*) that is being assessed, its *sensitivity to change* (or the sensitivity of the instrument that was used), the *perspective* taken (client, therapist, expert, significant other, objective data, etc.), and the *time of assess-ment* (e.g. at the end of treatment vs. follow-up).

Before we move on to introducing different methods of measuring outcome, we will briefly focus on a quantitative expression of the magnitude of change, the so-called *effect size* (see Cohen, 1988) and criteria that tell us when we can talk about reliable and clinically meaningful change.

Effect Size and the Magnitude of Change

Effect size, in the context of measuring psychotherapy outcome, is a numerical expres-sion of the difference between the means of two or more compared groups as measured by an outcome measure. It includes comparisons of outcomes within the same group, before and after therapy, as well as comparisons of different groups after therapy, e.g. a group of patients receiving psychotherapy and a control group without therapy. Effect size allows us to be more specific about the magnitude of observed change (if it is pre-sent) than just simply stating whether the groups differ or not. In psychotherapy research, Glass (see e.g. Smith, Glass & Miller, 1980) adapted Cohen's *d* to allow the magnitude of difference between the experimental and control group to be measured. Mathematically speaking, we are using the following formula:

$$ES = \frac{\bar{x}_e - \bar{x}_c}{s}$$

where *ES* means effect size, $\bar{x}_e$ is the mean of the experimental group, $\bar{x}_c$ is the mean of the control group, and the standard deviation *s* is computed as the pooled standard deviation of both groups' distributions (sometimes the standard deviation of the control group is used).

I will illustrate the computation of effect size by using a simple example. Let us sup-pose that we have a group of depressed patients with the mean score before treatment of 25 on the Beck Depression Inventory (BDI) (the possible range of the score is from 0 to 63) and that the standard deviation of distribution of patients' score is 7. After treat-ment, the group's score is 10 on the BDI and the standard deviation would, let's suppose, remain the same.

To compare the difference measured by the BDI before and after treatment, we replace $\bar{x}_c$ in the formula above with the group mean before the treatment and $\bar{x}_e$ with the group mean after the treatment. Then we put the pooled mean of both standard deviations into the denominator (to make it easier, let's suppose it would be 7). The effect size is then 25 minus 10 divided by 7, which is 2.14. This is a large difference according to Cohen's categorization of effect sizes in social sciences, where an effect size greater than 0.80 is considered large, 0.50 as medium and less than 0.20 as small (Cohen, 1988). The example is graphically presented in Figure 1.1. As can be seen, the distributions of the score before and after treatment overlap minimally.

Figure 1.1 Distributions of BDI scores of our illustrative example with the pre-treatment mean score 25 (standard deviation 7) and post-treatment mean score 10 with the same standard deviation

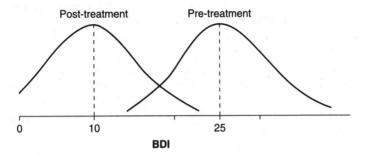

The above formula can also be used for comparing two different patient groups, e.g. an experimental and a control group, or two groups in two different active treatments (i.e. two experimental groups). In this case, $\bar{x}_e$ stands for the mean of one group and $\bar{x}_c$ for the mean of another group, with s computed as the pooled standard deviation of both groups. Use of the above formula assumes that both groups have almost identical parameters before treatment (means and standard deviations). A more conservative method computes pre-post ESs for both groups separately; the difference between the ESs for the first and second group is then considered the magnitude of difference between groups, hence the ES comparing these groups (see Elliott, 2002b).

Effect size has a broad use. Besides allowing for a more exact estimation of the difference between the groups compared, it also allows the magnitude of effect sizes across several studies to be measured. Thus it can be a basis for the meta-analysis of the cumulative results from several studies investigating outcome (I will address this issue in Chapter 4, which focuses on meta-analysis).

Reliable Change and Clinical Significance

Effect size expresses the magnitude of difference obtained using a particular instrument when comparing two groups, usually experimental and control. It does not, however, tell us whether the outcomes gained by individual patients are also significant in real life. The mean for a particular patient group can, statistically, significantly improve; however, this may not mean that the patients are no longer depressed. Statistically significant change can, for example, be an improvement in the group mean from a score of 25 on the BDI to a score of 20, which would mean that patients are on average still depressed. Therefore, if we want to assess change relevant to patients' real-life situation, we should be asking whether the patients in a particular treatment are no longer depressed after the treatment.

Whether change occurred, and how big this change is, is usually assessed against two criteria (Jacobson & Truax, 1991: (1) the score of a particular patient on a particular measure must move from the range of dysfunctional population to the functional range; and (2) this change must exceed the measurement error. For example, a patient who filled out the BDI repeatedly would not always achieve the same scores. The score is related to the reliability of the measure, i.e. the stability of measurement and how this measurement is affected by random errors. To say that an individual patient has really improved, his or her score after therapy has to differ from the score before therapy enough to exceed the estimated interval of measurement error. The index determining that the change is sufficiently reliable (i.e. it is not only the effect of random error) is called *Reliable Change Index* (RCI) (Jacobson & Truax, 1991) and is computed according to the following formula:

$$RC = \frac{x_2 - x_1}{S_{diff}}$$

where x_1 means pre-therapy score, x_2 means post-therapy score, and S_{diff} is the standard error of difference between two scores that can be computed using the standard error of measurement according to the formula:

$$S_{diff} = \sqrt{2(S_E)^2}$$

where S_E means standard error of measurement (we can compute it from the test–retest reliability of the measure and standard deviation of normative data). If the reliable change (RC) is greater then 1.96, then the probability that the post-therapy score expresses the real change is high (i.e. it exceeds the conventional interval of 95%).

As I mentioned above, the fact that change is real (not random) is usually not enough. We also need to know if the change is sufficient, i.e. that it is relevant in regard to the problem that was addressed by therapy. We can assess the relevance of change by the fact that the score after therapy not only really differs from the score before therapy, but that it is more likely to belong to the range of the healthy, non-clinical (e.g. not depressed) population than to the clinical (e.g. depressed) one. Jacobson and Truax (1991) suggest three ways of testing that the change which exceeds random error is clinically significant:

(1) The score after therapy should fall outside the range of dysfunctional population, i.e. to the range of two standard deviations beyond the mean for that population (i.e. in direction to the functionality).
(2) The score after therapy should fall within the range of two standard deviations of the mean of the functional non-clinical population.
(3) The score after therapy is closer to the functional population than it is to the dysfunctional population.

Which option we choose depends on what normative data are available and whether the normative data of both functional and dysfunctional populations overlap or not. If the norms of the functional population are not available, we should use option (1), i.e. the patient belongs to the 'healthy' population if the change is reliable (exceeds standard error of measurement) and is two standard deviations beyond the mean of the patients' group or other dysfunctional referential group. If the norms of the functional population are available, then we can use option (2), but if the norms of both functional and dysfunctional groups are available, and distributions of these groups overlap, then we should use option (3). For further details about computations of all three options, see Jacobson and Truax (1991).

Jacobson and Truax's (1991) approach to the calculation of clinically significant change is not the only one that can be seen in the literature. Different methods have been suggested (see Speer, 1992; Speer & Greenbaum, 1995; Tingey et al., 1996; Wise, 2004), leading to slightly different outcomes (see Bauer, Lambert & Nielsen, 2004), which, however, may be more similar given the increasing reliability of the measure (Atkins et al., 2005).

Instruments Used in Measuring Therapy Outcome – Source of Data, Constructs Assessed and Sensitivity to Change

The perspective taken when evaluating therapeutic change has a strong impact on the magnitude of observed change. In other words, whether the outcome is assessed by clients, significant others, therapists, expert raters, etc. influences the size of observed change if it is present. In following pages I focus on different evaluators of therapeutic outcome, the types of assessment they may adopt, and give examples of measures that are used.

Clients' Assessment of Outcome

The easiest and the most feasible way of evaluating therapeutic change is that of the clients' self-reports. These usually employ the format of self-report scales and questionnaires. We can categorize them according to the variables they are attempting to measure. We can distinguish personality questionnaires (measuring personality traits or dimensions), symptom scales, well-being and adaptability scales, instruments focused on the constructs related to mental health or instruments focusing on the quality of interpersonal relationships. There are also idiosyncratic measures, as well as instruments developed specifically for evaluating psychotherapeutic outcome. Recently, qualitative methods (mostly structured interviews; e.g. Elliott, 2002a) examining the impact of therapy have become more popular. Finally, we also encounter questionnaires evaluating clients' satisfaction with counselling or psychotherapy.

Personality Questionnaires

Common personality questionnaires that are routinely used in psychological assessment have also been employed in counselling and psychotherapy outcome research. For example, the *Minnesota Multiphasic Personality Inventory* (MMPI, see e.g. Hill, 1989) or the German *Freiburger Personality Inventory* (FPI, see e.g. Kächele et al., 2001) are often used. Although the MMPI was very often used in outcome research and some of its scales seem to be sensitive to therapeutic change, Lambert and Hill (1994), in their authoritative review of outcome instruments and their sensitivity to change, do not recommend this instrument for measuring therapy outcome (mostly because it is time consuming). Generally, it could be said that the personality questionnaires are not very sensitive to change, because they are focused on relatively stable personality traits (Lambert & Hill, 1994) and so are probably not sensitive to distress that the client is currently experiencing. Where a personality questionnaire is used as an outcome measure, it is probably better to use an instrument that also covers current pathology or distress.

Symptom Self-report Scales

These are the methods that focus on clients' psychopathological symptoms. They are usually very sensitive to change (Lambert & Hill, 1994). The most well-known multi-symptomatic tool is the Symptom Checklist-90 (SCL–90) (Derogatis, Lipman & Covi, 1973) and also its revised version, SCL–90–R (see e.g. Derogatis, 2000). SCL–90 is a 90-item self-report scale, also suitable for use as a psychopathological screening tool. It contains nine symptom scales: Somatization, Obsessive-Compulsive, Interpersonal Sensitivity, Depression, Anxiety, Hostility, Phobic Anxiety, Paranoid Ideation and Psychoticism, but for psychotherapy research the most often used is the Global Severity Index (GSI), which expresses the overall level of psychopathology. SCL–90 is very often used as an outcome tool and is recommended for heterogeneous patient groups (Lambert & Hill, 1994).

One of the most widely used monosymptomatic instruments is the *Beck Depression Inventory* mentioned earlier (BDI; Beck, Steer & Garbin, 1988). It is a 21-item self-report scale. The items cover cognitive, affective and behavioural symptoms of depression. There exist many other symptomatic scales focused on various psychopathological symptoms (anxiety, obsessive-compulsive, panic, etc.). An overview of many instruments can be found, for example, in Hersen (2004).

Questionnaires Assessing Constructs Related to Mental Health

One example of psychological constructs frequently employed as an indicator of psychotherapy outcome is self-esteem. Self-esteem is very often measured by the *Rosenberg*

Self-Esteem Scale (RSES) (Rosenberg, 1965). Focusing on self-esteem can be appropriate when measuring the outcome of therapy for depression (see, for example Greenberg & Watson, 1998).

Questionnaires Assessing the Quality of Social or Interpersonal Functioning

The quality of interpersonal relationships is strongly linked to the quality of mental health (this is most obvious in psychodynamic theories). One of the most widely used instruments focusing on relationships and social functioning is the *Inventory of Interpersonal Problems* (Horowitz et al., 1988). Broader social functioning is covered for example in the *Social Adjustment Scale* (Weisman & Brothwell, 1976). Questionnaires dealing with social functioning are probably less sensitive to change than instruments focusing on the psychopathological symptoms of depression or anxiety (see Greenberg & Watson, 1998).

Self-report Scales Assessing the Client's Idiosyncratic Problems

These instruments try to assess whether clients see any change in the issues they found troubling at the beginning of therapy. Generally, these tools are very sensitive to therapeutic change (e.g. Greenberg & Watson, 1998). In fact, they can probably overestimate therapy outcome. For example, problems that bothered the client at the beginning of therapy can become irrelevant due to change in the client's life situation. One of the best-known instruments is probably that of *Target Complaints* (Battle et al., 1966). This instrument can be used as a general basis for an interview about the client's most troublesome problems rather than just as a simple self-report scale. The client and the therapist may work together on the formulation of the client's target complaints and the extent to which they concern him or her (see a version of the instrument in Box 1.1).

Another similar tool is Shapiro's *Personal Questionnaire* (Philips, 1986; Elliott, Mack & Shapiro, 1999). This instrument, in comparison to the Target Complaints, allows not only formulation of the client's presenting issues at the start, but also the addition of problems that occur later in the course of psychotherapy. It also allows for an evaluation of how long these problems had lasted before therapy started. Like Target Complaints, this instrument may be used collaboratively with the client. The collaborative interview should then be conducted, in the research context, by a trained person other than the therapist to avoid the client's reactivity. The Personal Questionnaire may be used regularly before each session to evaluate the client's difficulties since the last session (see e.g. Elliott, 2002a).

Box 1.1   An example of a version of the Target Complaints

Instruction: Please list three target complaints (problems) that bothered you recently (if there are more, you can include them all). Mark the scale according to how much they distressed (bothered) you.

1 _____

| 0 | 1 | 2 | 3 | 4 | 5 | 6 | 7 | 8 | 9 | 10 | 11 | 12 |

not at all   very much   could not be worse

Note: Battle et al. (1966) recommend a vertical line with blank boxes without numbers.

Source: Battle et al., 1966.

Self-report Questionnaires Developed Specifically as Outcome Measures

For a long time psychotherapy researchers were trying to develop a standard battery of instruments that could be used to adequately and sensitively assess therapeutic change (see e.g. Waskow & Parloff, 1975; Strupp, Horowitz & Lambert, 1997). One product of such endeavours has been the development of questionnaires serving specifically to measure counselling and psychotherapy outcome. These questionnaires measure areas that proved to be sensitive to therapeutic change, such as well-being, psychopathological symptoms and life functioning (Howard, Lueger et al., 1993). One of the best-known instruments developed to measure therapy outcome is the *Outcome Questionnaire-45* (OQ–45) (Lambert, Morton et al., 2004); another is the *Clinical Outcomes in Routine Evaluation – Outcome Measure* (CORE–OM) (Barkham, Margison et al., 2001).

The OQ-45 contains 45 items that cover three specific domains: symptom distress, interpersonal relationships and social role performance. The instrument is currently widely used in so-called *patient-focused research* (e.g. Lambert, Hansen & Finch, 2001), which we will address further in Chapter 6. It comes with software enabling the therapist to benchmark the client's progress from session to session against successful as well as unsuccessful clients who filled out the questionnaire before.

The CORE–OM questionnaire developed by the British authors is becoming popular, as it is quite user friendly (e.g. the use of the questionnaire in hard copy is copyright free, which enables practitioners to easily photocopy the instrument). Thirty-four items of the CORE–OM cover four domains: subjective well-being, problems/symptoms, life functioning, and risk/harm. The first three domains, like the domains in the OQ–45, correspond to the phase model of change (Howard, Lueger et al., 1993) that we will discuss further in Chapter 6. The popularity of this questionnaire is also based on the possibility of benchmarking against a huge national database (Mellor-Clark et al., 2006). The instrument is part of a broader CORE package that consists of pre-therapy and after-therapy forms of collecting information on demographics, diagnosis, type of therapy provided, etc. An example of the items of the CORE-OM is in Box 1.2.

Box 1.2   An example of instructions and items of the CORE-OM

Instructions: This form has 34 statements about how you have been OVER THE LAST WEEK. Please read each statement and think how often you felt that way last week. Then tick the box which is closest to this.

not at all	only occasionally	sometimes	often	most or all the time
0	1	2	3	4

Example of items:
1. I have felt terribly alone and isolated
10. Talking to people has felt too much for me
12. I have been happy with the things I have done
14. I have felt like crying
28. Unwanted images or memories have been distressing me

Source: Barkham et al., 2001. Excerpt reproduced with premission of the authors.

Another similar tool, the *Outcome Rating Scale* (ORS), was recently developed by Miller and Duncan (see Miller, Duncan & Hubble, 2005). The ORS is a visual scale consisting of four items covering three areas (personal well-being, relationships, social functioning) as well as overall sense of well-being. The advantage of this tool is that it takes less than a minute to fill it in. A tracking system similar to the one used with the OQ-45 is being developed.

Qualitative Methods Investigating Changes Achieved by Therapy

An example of a qualitative method investigating changes brought by therapy is the *Client Change Interview* (CCI) (Elliott, 2002a). This is a structured interview that tries to assess what changes the client noticed since the beginning of therapy and to what extent therapy is responsible for them. The interview also considers hindering and helpful aspects of the treatment. The advantage of methods like CCI is their sensitivity to the wider impact of therapy, including its negative aspects (for this argument, see McLeod, 2001a).

Questionnaires Assessing Clients' Satisfaction with Therapy

Seligman's (1995) report of a survey carried out by the magazine *Consumer Reports*, which investigated clients' reported satisfaction with different aspects of therapy, is an example of the usefulness of the methods of looking at client satisfaction. Some examples of methods used in satisfaction studies are provided in McLeod (2003). In these questionnaires, clients are usually asked to answer questions on relevant aspects of therapy, e.g. how satisfied they were with therapy in general, to what extent therapy helped them to address problems that brought them to therapy, how they perceived the competence of the psychotherapist, whether they would recommend this psychotherapy to their relatives, and so on (see e.g. Larsen et al., 1979).

Experts' Evaluation

Experts' evaluation of change usually employs rating scales that are based on a structured interview. It is important that the expert who uses the rating scale is 'blind' to whether the person interviewed is in any kind of treatment. Otherwise the expert's judgement could potentially be biased. There exist several commonly used expert-rated instruments (see an overview in Hersen, 2004).

One frequently used instrument in the studies of depression is the *Hamilton Rating Scale for Depression* (HRSD) (Hamilton, 1960). The scale is used by the clinician for the evaluation of different aspects of depression (e.g. depressed mood, feelings of guilt, insomnia, psychomotor retardation, agitation, somatic anxiety). There are plenty of other rating scales for a variety of psychiatric diagnoses, for example the *Yale-Brown Obsessive-Compulsive Scale* (YBOCS) for obsessive-compulsive disorder (Goodman et al., 1989).

Another example of an expert-used instrument is the *Social and Occupational Functioning Assessment Scale* (SOFAS) that evaluates psychological, social and occupational functioning on a numerical continuum of mental health–illness (from 0 to 100). The SOFAS is based on Luborsky's *Health-Sickness Rating Scale* (Luborsky, 1962) that was revised by Spitzer et al. (Endicott, Spitzer et al., 1976; previously named the *Global Assessment Scale – GAS*). The SOFAS constitutes Axis V of *DSM–IV* (American Psychiatric Association, 2001).

For diagnostic as well as research purposes, especially in North America the *Structured Clinical Interview Diagnosis* (SCID) is widely used (First et al., 1996). It is a structured and standardized interview schedule aimed at improving reliability and validity in establishing *DSM–IV* diagnosis.

Therapist's Perspective on Outcome

One of the sources of the data on the evaluation of counselling and psychotherapy outcome can be the therapist. When thinking about the therapist as an evaluator of therapeutic change, we must not forget that he or she has a personal investment in the outcome of therapy. This can make the therapist's view somewhat unreliable. The therapist's bias may influence their perspective on therapy outcome in one of two ways: in the direction of inflating therapy outcome as well as in the direction of deflating its outcome, probably depending on whether the therapist has a tendency to be rather self-critical or self-promoting.

One example of the scales that can be used by the therapist is the therapist's version of the Target Complaints scale. The therapist using this instrument may judge the client's presenting problems and their intensity and then later in therapy repeat this evaluation.

Evaluation of Outcome by Significant Others

The evaluation of therapy outcome is sometimes performed by people close to clients in therapy, so-called significant others. Significant others are usually involved in rating the therapy outcome when the problem or the client population naturally calls for this kind of assessment. A good example, when it is definitely needed, is therapy with children, and to a certain extent therapy with adolescents. Typically, significant others in that case are parents and sometimes educators or teachers who are in contact with the client. In therapy for adolescents (and in family therapy), there are often-used instruments, where adolescents rate their relationship with their parents, and vice versa (see e.g. Brent et al., 1997 and their study of therapy for adolescents with depression). Examples of measures that can be used as outcome measures in psychotherapy with children and youth are Achenbach's *Child Behavior Checklist* (CBCL) (Achenbach, 1999) and the *Youth Outcome Questionnaire* (Burlingame et al., 2001).

Another type of research that uses the reports of significant others are studies evaluating outcome of treatment for substance abuse (e.g. Babor & Del Boca, 2003). The obvious reason for involving significant others is the presence of denial in clients with substance abuse problem as well as the important fact that the clients with this difficulty negatively impact on their closest environment.

Marital and couple therapy logically also uses reports from significant others. Typically, the perception of own satisfaction and own view of the partner and the mutual relationship is measured. An example of a measure focusing on the behaviour of the other is a version of the Barrett-Lennard's *Relationship Inventory* (to be discussed further in Chapter 8). In this inventory, the partners mutually rate different aspects of their relationship, such as perceived empathy, positive regard, congruency and unconditionality of the other partner as well as self-perceived conveyed empathy, positive regard, congruency and unconditionality. Probably the most commonly used method in couple therapy outcome research is the *Dyadic Adjustment Scale* of Spanier (1976) that asks both partners about their perception of agreement on things like handling family finances, religious matters, sex relations or household tasks. The instrument also has a briefer form (Prouty, Markowski & Barnes, 2000). This and other couple and family measures are briefly presented in Jay Lebow's book, *Research for the Psychotherapist* (2006).

Despite the above examples, the evaluation of outcome by significant others is not common in current psychotherapy outcome research (McLeod, 2003) and is not without problems. The problem of ratings by significant others is that evaluation may be confounded by their lack of motivation or, on the other hand, bias in their relationship with the client. For example, using the rating of family members or teachers can be questionable as it can be affected by their own interests in relation to the client. For example, when client changes result in negative consequences for the rater, e.g. the client becomes more assertive in school, the teacher may not always see it as progress.

Behavioural, Physiological and Other Objective Data

The nature of the problem being treated by counselling or psychotherapy sometimes requires its assessment by a behavioural, physiological or other objective measure. These may be somewhat conservative measures (see Lambert & Hill, 1994), for example monitoring physiological reaction (e.g. heart rate) to a fearful stimulus (e.g. spiders), in relation to specific phobias. In some cases behavioural data may be relevant, as in the case of agoraphobia (monitoring of the number of walks taken outside the house). Besides behavioural and physiological data, information on the length of hospitalization, frequency of absences from job, etc. can serve as objective data. An example of an objective measure is weight (Body Mass Index) in therapy for eating disorders (see e.g. Kächele et al., 2001). Similarly, in therapy for drug abuse urine check-ups are typical (Goldstein & Brown, 2003). Overall, this kind for measure is quite common for specific types of problem (those mentioned above) and more typical for behavioural therapy (see McLeod, 2003). More recently, the use of functional neuroimaging such as functional magnetic resonance imaging (fMRI), positron emission tomography (PET), or single photon emission computed tomography (SPECT) as tools for assessing the impact of psychotherapy is becoming more common (see Linden, 2006).

Evaluation of the Cost-effectiveness of Psychotherapy and Counselling

Recently, the monitoring of costs associated with counselling and psychotherapy has become more widespread. It enables a comparison of different therapeutic approaches and different types of treatment in regard to both costs and benefits – for example financial costs vs. improvement of symptoms or reduction of absence at work. For psychosomatic disorders, it may be a decrease in visits to the GP.

Estimating the cost-effectiveness and cost–benefits may sound a bit dehumanizing, but it is to a certain extent inevitable as the third-party payers responsible for public health seen to spend money available for mental health wisely and justly.

Choice of an Outcome Measure

The first condition for the selection of an outcome measure for a concrete study is its reliability and sufficient information on its validity. It is wise to use established measures as this enables a comparison of results from different studies. In regard to construct validity, it is sensible to use more measures (it is quite common to use at least four measures), to measure more variables simultaneously (e.g. self-esteem too in cases of depression), and to combine more perspectives (client, therapist, external rater, etc.). The most widely used outcome measures are the client-used self-report scales and expert-used rating scales. The researcher should also know what the magnitude of effect size he or she may expect with a particular measure, i.e. how sensitive the measure is. One should not forget that different measures may favour different therapeutic approaches. Some valuable information, though somewhat dated, may be found in Lambert and Hill (1994: 83–84; see also Box 1.3.). Finally, a good overview of available methods is provided in the edited volumes of Maruish (2004).

Box 1.3   Lambert and Hill's conclusions about the sensitivity of outcome measures based on their review of outcome measures used in outcome research up to 1994

1. Data from therapists and expert judges, in which judges are aware of the treatment status of clients produce larger effect sizes than data from clients (self-report data), data produced by significant others, data from relevant institutions (e.g. employer, educational) and physiological data.
2. Gross ratings of change (e.g. whether or not the client has improved) produce a greater estimation of change than ratings on specific dimensions or symptoms.
3. Change measures based on the specific targets of therapy (e.g. specific symptoms) produce larger effect sizes than measures more distal from psychotherapy (including the common personality questionnaires).
4. Life adjustment measures that focus on social functioning in natural settings produce smaller effect sizes than analogue and laboratory based measures.
5. Data collected soon after therapy show larger effect sizes than data collected later.
6. Physiological measures (e.g. heart rate) usually produce small effect sizes compared to other measures even when they are specifically targeted in psychotherapy.

Source: Lambert and Hill, 1994, pp. 83–84.

2

Randomized Control Trials

There are several methodological approaches to studying the outcome of psychotherapy and counselling. Research designs that are being applied are well known from general psychological and other research. We could easily talk about experimental designs, quasi-experimental designs, single-case experiments, descriptive studies, etc.; however, in the following chapters we will also encounter jargon typical of psychotherapy research or medical research, such as randomized clinical (control) trials. In the next two chapters I will focus on several research designs used in outcome research. The main emphasis will be on aspects of these research designs that are specific to studying outcome of psychotherapy and counselling. In each case we will look at sample studies using the design in question.

The gold standard in studying psychotherapy outcome, though often criticized, is the 'randomized control trial' sometimes called 'randomized clinical trial' (RCT, Bower & King, 2000; Haaga & Stiles, 2000). RCTs are experimental designs with high internal validity, achieved through the randomization of participants to therapeutic conditions as well as through extensive control of independent and potentially interfering variable(s). On the basis of randomization and experimental control, changes in the dependent variable (the client's state) are attributed to the independent variable (psychotherapy). Randomization should ensure that potential interfering variables are evenly distributed in the conditions compared, so that their influence is balanced.

Experimental control in randomization is secured in the first case by the use of a control or comparison group that can balance a lot of the interfering variables influencing the dependent variable (the client's state). Potential interfering variables are many, for example maturation (i.e. that the client undergoes change in a natural process such as grieving in the case of bereavement), factors having to do with the instruments used (e.g. statistical regression, repeated testing), reactivity of clients (awareness that they are being assessed), outside events contributing to the improvement or worsening of the client's state (life events such as career promotion or demotion).

The aim is to have no differences between the experimental condition and control condition other than the active treatment or its ingredient that is being provided. Every difference in outcome between the experimental and control group after therapy can then be attributed to the active ingredient that is provided in the experimental condition. To ensure experimental control, i.e. the fact that there is no difference other than treatment in the compared conditions, several measures are taken.

Control Group

One of the most important aspects of a RCT is the form of control group it uses. In addition to ethical challenges that the use of suboptimal treatment brings (placebo, waiting list, etc.) it presents a lot of methodological challenges. RCTs used in psychotherapy outcome research are inspired by those of pharmacological research. A typical control in pharmacological research is the placebo. This is a substance that has the same look and taste as the tested drug, but does not have an active therapeutic ingredient. The patient does not know whether he or she has been given a tablet containing the active substance. Similarly, the prescribing physicians, as they are not informed, do not know it either (double-blind placebo).

In contrast to pharmacological research, it is very difficult to utilize a *psychological placebo* in psychotherapy outcome research. It is hard to determine what psychological activity would be sufficiently similar to psychotherapy that did not contain an active therapeutic ingredient. The difficulty stems from the difference in theoretical conceptualizations of different therapeutic approaches. What is considered central to one approach in another may be considered incidental to other active ingredients. A good example of the difference in perspective on therapeutic ingredients is empathic exploration. While in client-centred therapy it is considered to be a central healing component, in cognitive-behavioural approaches it is viewed as a supportive component that has no decisive power in the therapeutic endeavour.

Furthermore, the therapist in counselling and psychotherapy always knows whether he or she is providing a placebo or an active treatment, so cannot be blind to this fact (the double-blind placebo used in pharmacological studies is questionable as side-effects of medication may inform both the patient and the physician that the patient is in an active condition; Even, Siobud-Dorocant & Dardennes, 2002). Therefore, the therapist knowing that he or she is not delivering the active treatment may undermine the client's trust that he or she is getting a potentially therapeutic treatment. Thus, the client's hope of getting better is undermined, which would certainly not contribute to the success of the treatment.

Wampold (2001) also emphasizes that if there was a psychological placebo that could be used as a control group, it would have to measure up to psychotherapy, for example in quality of therapeutic alliance, credibility, and in the therapist's belief that it is beneficial. Wampold (2001: 128) concludes his discussion of the usefulness of a psychological placebo by stating that it is 'logically and pragmatically impossible … to create psychotherapy placebos that contain, in terms of the quality and quantity, the same non-specific ingredients contained in the psychotherapeutic treatment'.

Another problematic control group is the *no-treatment* group or *waiting-list* control (see Haaga & Stiles, 2000). In these groups it is very hard to ensure that the clients would actually not seek alternative ways of treatment. Also, hope and expectancy, which are important interfering variables, can be expected to be higher in the active treatment group. It is difficult to imagine that clients placed on a waiting-list would be enthusiastic about their prognosis. Therefore, the control that uses no-treatment or waiting-list is not comparable to the active conditions as it does not contain important components that are part of the active treatment. Another problem is the ethical consideration that the clients in need of treatment are not getting it. This problem applies to all placebo controls.

Treatment as usual sometimes serves as a control group as well. For example, depressed patients who are in the care of their GP could be randomly assigned to an experimental condition containing psychotherapy, or they could just stay in the routine care of the GP. The routine GP care would then serve as a treatment-as-usual control for the experimental condition, i.e. psychotherapy. The main problem with the treatment-as-usual condition is a lack of control of what the treatment as usual consists of and the potential heterogeneity of such treatment across clinicians, sites and so on (Haaga & Stiles, 2000).

The most commonly used control group nowadays is *alternative treatment*. An alternative treatment usually means another psychological treatment or pharmacological treatment. In the case of the alternative treatment control group, it is important to consider whether the alternative should be delivered with the same parameters, such as length and frequency of therapy, or whether the parameters themselves represent an alternative. For example, (1) as the alternative can serve a different theoretical model, e.g. comparison of psychodynamic vs. cognitive-behavioural therapy; (2) the alternative can merely represent changed parameters of the same therapy, e.g. 16 sessions of cognitive-behavioural therapy vs. eight sessions of cognitive-behavioural therapy; or (3) the alternative can be a different modality of the same theoretical model (e.g. group therapy or adjacent couple or family therapy). If a therapy that differs in some parameters (e.g. length of treatment) is used as a control for the active treatment, then what is actually studied is not a specific therapeutic theory, but rather an optimal delivery of the therapy (see Haaga & Stiles, 2000).

If a different theoretical approach is used as an alternative it is important that this is a bona fide therapy (Wampold, 2001). Bona fide means that the treatment is conducted with the researchers and therapists believing that it will have therapeutic effects. In the current literature one can also find as an alternative treatments that are not intended to be therapeutic. For example, some CBT trials use non-directive therapy as an alternative control (e.g. Beck, Sokol et al., 1992); however, this non-directive therapy is delivered by therapists who do not believe in its potential and who are aware that it serves as a control to the 'active' treatment. Such alternatives should be considered as a form of psychological placebo (with all its problems) and not as an alternative therapy.

If as a control condition an equally administered alternative bona fide psychological therapy is used, we can talk about comparative research that tries to establish which therapy is more efficacious or effective. As many therapies are now already well established, Chambless and Hollon (1998) recommend comparing some new psychological therapy with an established therapy.

A specific form of alternative psychological therapy is used in so-called *component control* or *dismantled* and *combined treatment* designs (see Haaga & Stiles, 2000). The main feature of these designs is the use of variations of the same therapeutic approach. An example would be a comparison of cognitive therapy with and without the use of behavioural techniques. These types of design are usually found in cognitive-behavioural approaches (see, for example, the studies examining the effect of different components of CBT for generalized anxiety disorder of Borkovec and Costello, 1993). These designs try to achieve the optimal mixture of different treatment components to achieve the biggest effect. They also look at the contribution of different components by comparing conditions that systematically leave out different components of the treatment, so the weight of each component can be established. For example, a research question may be: is relaxation a beneficial component of treatment for panic disorder? Does the treatment that contains relaxation yield better results than treatment without relaxation? The fact that this kind of design endeavours to determine efficacious therapeutic factors makes it similar to process research that is trying to establish therapeutic factors responsible for the effect of therapy (we will talk more about this in Part II).

Research Sample

Another important aspect of randomized control trials is the research sample. The relevance of sample characteristics has to do with internal validity and the 'statistical conclusions validity' of the design. For example, RCTs try to use samples that have sufficient statistical power (statistical conclusion validity) as well as equal distribution of any variables that might interfere with psychotherapy (e.g. co-morbid personality disorder accompanying a primary diagnosis of depression – internal validity).

With regard to the validity of statistical conclusions, the required sample size must have sufficient statistical power to allow the detection of the differences between therapeutic conditions, if they exist. Statistical power expresses the probability with which the statistical test will detect any difference between the experimental and the control group if it exists. Statistical power equals $1 - \beta$, where β is the error type II, i.e. the probability that null hypothesis was wrongly accepted. Knowing the acceptable level of type I error α, statistical power $1 - \beta$, and effect size that the researcher expects between the compared groups (see Chapter 1), it is possible to calculate the sample size needed. In psychotherapy research, the medium effect size 0.47, type I error α 5% (statistical significance on 0.05 level), and statistical power 0.80 are often used (see Shapiro, 1995). Using these parameters the sample size is usually approximately 60 patients in each of the groups compared.

When thinking about the size of difference expected between the experimental and control group, it is important to be aware that the magnitude of difference between two bona fide therapies will be smaller, while a comparison of an active treatment and no-treatment control should produce much bigger differences. Therefore, in order to detect changes in two active treatments, we need a much bigger sample size than for detecting differences between an active treatment and no-treatment control.

Homogeneity of the sample, in relation to the main problem that is being targeted by psychological therapy, often plays an important role. For example, some dual diagnoses are excluded, so the researchers can control for factors potentially interacting with the treatment (e.g. personality disorder concurrent with the depression that is the main focus of therapy). Higher homogeneity contributes to greater internal validity of the study, because it can be argued that the therapy was affecting one specific problem (e.g. depression) and not other problems that might be confounded with the target of the treatment. The other side of this arrangement, however, is its lower external validity, as dual diagnoses are in reality very common and so homogeneous samples are not very typical of the general patient population.

Another important characteristic of the sample is control for interfering variables inherited in the sample. Some of the characteristics of patients in a study may interact with psychotherapy. For example, the level of perfectionism in depressed patients can influence the outcome of therapy (see Blatt, Quinlan et al., 1995), as can the fact of whether patients are in a happy romantic relationship (see Elkin, 1994). It may also be that a form of therapy is more suitable for a specific type of client. For example Beutler, Engle et al. (1991), in their study comparing three different therapies (cognitive, experiential and supportive), found that externalizing patients benefited more from cognitive therapy and internalizing patients benefited more from supportive therapy (we will discuss this further in Chapter 6). The main problem of interfering variables is that they may not be known prior to the study, and because the samples in psychotherapy and counselling research are small, randomization may not prevent uneven distribution of interfering variables.

Outcome Measures

An important question in RCTs is the selection of *outcome measures*. Different measures used in assessing the effectiveness of psychotherapy are presented in Chapter 1. As I mentioned there, the perspective taken (e.g. patient's, therapist's, that of significant others) and the construct assessed alongside the characteristics of a specific instrument are very relevant for how sensitive the instrument to therapeutic change can be. As I said before, to achieve good construct validity – which in the case of psychotherapy outcome research means to achieve an appropriate measurement of different aspects of therapeutic change – multiple instruments using multiple perspectives are generally used. For example, in psychotherapy for depression the Beck Depression Inventory (self-report) alongside the Hamilton Rating Scale of Depression (expert rating) can be used to assess the main depression symptoms, but a self-esteem measure could complement these (e.g. the Rosenberg Self-Esteem Scale, a self-report tool) as well as a measure of general functioning (e.g. Social and Occupational Functioning Assessment Scale, an expert-based tool).

One of the things that should not be forgotten when we think of assessing the outcome is the *acceptability* of a treatment, i.e. how many patients stay in therapy without premature termination, as well as the *cost-effectiveness* (whether the costs are worth the outcome) of the treatment or its *clinical significance* (the extent of change achieved; see Chapter 1). Nor must one forget measurement of outcome in the *follow-up*, which can bring differential results (e.g. in a comparative trial of two therapies one therapy may be more effective in short term and one in long term: see Tarrier et al., 2000).

Therapy Delivery

In regard to delivery of therapy, RCTs necessarily utilize manualized therapies. Manualization should minimize differences between therapists, so that the effectiveness of an approach rather than of a specific therapist is measured, thus contributing to the internal validity of the study. A *therapeutic manual* is a written procedure that is followed by the therapist delivering the therapy. Manuals can be quite prescriptive but also flexible, depending on the specific therapeutic orientation they represent. Whether a therapist in a RCT is following the manual is assessed by the measurement of *adherence* to the manual as well as by assessment of the quality of the therapist's work: so-called *competence* (Waltz et al., 1993). In comparison studies, the *discrimination* between the compared therapies is also assessed. Adherence, competence and discrimination when delivering therapies are assessed by independent raters using adherence and competence scales (e.g. Luborsky & Luborsky, 2006) or other therapy process scales for rating tapes and transcripts of therapeutic sessions. The manual of therapy studied should ensure that the therapy delivered is standard and very similar across therapists and clients. Nevertheless, significant differences among therapists' effectiveness in highly controlled studies using a manual are sometimes discovered (e.g. Kim, Wampold & Bolt, 2006).

Specifics of RCTs in Group Therapy, Couple and Family Therapy

From the methodological point of view, several issues arise when studying the effectiveness of group therapy. One is the co-dependence of clients' outcomes in the same group. For example, we cannot say that one group we study will give the same results as other potential groups: the results may be restricted just to this one group. Another group could have different results because of the processes attached to it. If a group develops well, the average of the whole group will be different from that of a group in which unsolvable conflicts emerge and the group therapy process stagnates. The problem of the dependence of outcomes in one group thus calls for an increased number of groups in the research plan. The area of outcomes dependence is still overlooked and not fully realized. For that reason, when interpreting results we have to keep in mind how many groups the clients belonged to and how stable the results of therapy were across individual groups. Similar issues are pertinent to couple and family therapy as they contain more than one client participant. In addition, a distinct feature of couple and family therapy is that the goal of therapy is not only change in an individual client but often mainly the change of the relationship between the clients participating in therapy.

An excellent example of RCTs relating to group therapy is the study of Wilfley et al. (2002) that compared the effectiveness of cognitive-behavioural therapy (CBT) and group interpersonal therapy (IPT) for binge-eating disorder. A good example of couple therapy RCT is the work of Goldman and Greenberg (1992), who compared the effectiveness of emotionally focused couple therapy and integrated systemic therapy. A well-conducted RCT on family therapy is the work of Henggeler, Melton, Brondino, Scherer and Hanley (1997), who investigated the effectiveness of multisystemic family therapy for violent and chronic juvenile offenders and their families.

Problems Associated with Randomized Therapeutic Trials

Randomized control trials are a controversial topic among psychotherapy researchers (see Elliott, 1998). Alongside their indisputable methodological superiority one can also hear strong criticism (Bohart, O'Hara & Leitner, 1998; Henry, 1998). Among the biggest problems of RCTs are *failure of experimental control, low external validity* and little focus on *explanation* of how therapeutic change comes about.

Failure of experimental control may be linked to differences in therapists' effectiveness, to differences in compared samples in interfering variables, and so on. The lack of focus on the explanation of therapeutic change in RCTs has to do with the fact that RCTs assume what should theoretically be responsible for change rather than monitoring it closely. Therefore, one cannot be completely sure whether the mechanisms that are responsible for change are the ones that are theoretically expected. For example one may assume that cognitive restructuring is a healing component of cognitive therapy, but in RCTs it is usually not tested. Therefore, dismantling studies or *post hoc* analysis of the data from a RCT can help to shed light on what variables are responsible for therapeutic change. The advantage of RCTs is in the richness of the data collected, which can be used for further analyses. The data, in the trials, are usually collected in the process of therapy and then linked with the outcomes.

Low external validity may be connected with factors such as not including certain types of client with dual diagnoses in the trials, under-representation of clients from certain socioeconomic backgrounds, unrepresentativeness of the therapists (usually these are highly trained and closely supervised), or rigidity of therapeutic work due to following the therapeutic manual. However, it is important to say that some RCTs, so called pragmatic randomized control trials (Hotopf, 2002), are attempting to address some of the problems of low external validity by including heterogeneous samples of clients and by having low exclusion criteria.

Examples of Randomized Clinical Trials

To illustrate the complexity of randomized clinical trials, we will now look closely at three examples of RCTs, one from the USA and two from Britain.

Treatment of Depression Collaborative Research Program

A perfect example of a randomized clinical trial is the National Institute of Mental Health Treatment of Depression Collaborative Research Program (Elkin, 1994; Elkin, Shea et al., 1989; Shea et al., 1992), which compared cognitive-behavioural therapy (CBT) (Beck, Shaw et al., 1979), interpersonal therapy (IPT) (the original treatment manual is from 1984 and the authors were G. Klerman, M. Weissman, B. Rounsaville and E. Chevron; a current description of IPT can be found in Weissman, Markowitz & Klerman, 2000), pharmacological treatment with imipramine hydrochloride plus clinical management (IMI–CM; imipramine-clinical management) and pill placebo plus clinical management (PLA–CM; placebo-clinical management – clinical management contained not only the management of medication and side-effects but also provision of encouragement and advice).

All treatments were planned for 16 weeks with the range of 16 to 20 sessions (in the case of pharmacotherapy and placebo, another 4–6 weeks were allowed for the gradual discontinuation of medication and one or two check-up sessions). The project was carried out at three different sites and the treatment was provided by highly trained therapists. In the case of psychotherapies, some of the founders of the respective treatments were involved in the training. The treatment was provided by 28 professionals (10 were psychologists and 18 psychiatrists), eight in CBT, 10 in IPT, and 10 providing drug treatment plus clinical management or placebo and clinical management (it was a double-blind control: neither psychiatrists nor clients knew whether they were using the placebo or the drug). Both therapies were also monitored for adherence to the respective manuals and in more than 95% of sessions were reliably discriminated.

A total of 239 patients diagnosed with major depressive disorder (MDD) started therapy. These patients were drawn from 560 patients originally screened and assessed for unacceptable co-morbidity or other excluding criteria. One of the criteria for inclusion was stability of depression, which led to the exclusion of 21 % patients who within two weeks of the original screening no longer met MDD criteria. The patients were randomly assigned to four conditions: 59 patients were in CBT, 61 patients in IPT, IMI–CM consisted of 57 patients and PLA-CM had 62 patients. The outcome was measured by four primary outcome instruments: the Hamilton Rating Scale of Depression (HRSD), which was used by independent interviewers, the Global Assessment Scale (GAS) again used by independent interviewers, and two self-reports: the Beck Depression Inventory (BDI) and Symptom Checklist 90 (SCL–90). The outcome was assessed at the end of therapy as well as in a two-year follow-up. As many patients did not finish the treatment, the outcome was measured separately for three different groups. The first group consisted of all 239 patients who started treatment (intent-to-treat group), the second group consisted of patients who stayed in treatment at least 3.5 weeks, i.e. were exposed at least to a 'minimal therapeutic dose', and the third consisted of patients who stayed in treatment for at least 15 weeks and 12 sessions and were considered completers. All in all, the biggest number of patients stayed in interpersonal therapy (47 out of 61). Thirty-seven out of 59 stayed in CBT, 37 out of 57 in IMI–CM and 34 out of 62 in PLA–CM.

The outcomes for all four conditions on all four measures at the end of treatment did not differ dramatically. This included the results for placebo. The three active treatments

Table 2.1 Patients who reached the recovery cut-off score criterion (≤9 in raw score) on BDI (≤9 raw score) and HRSD (≤6) after 16 weeks in treatment. Results are in percentages

Outcome measure	CBT	IPT	IMI–CM	PLA–CM
		Completers		
BDI	65%	70%	69%	51%
HRSD	51%	55%*	57%*	29%
		Patients with at least 3.5 weeks of treatment		
BDI	58%	60%	61%	50%
HRSD	40%	47%*	49%*	26%
		Intent-to-treat sample		
BDI	49%	56%	53%	40%
HRSD	36%	43%*	42%*	21%

Note: Percentage marked * were statistically different from PLA–CM.

Source: Elkin, 1994: 121. Copyright © 1994 I. Elkin, reprinted with permission of John Wiley & Sons, Inc.

showed no statistically different results from each other. The CBT group did not differ even from the PLA–CM group on any of the measures or in any of the groups (intent-to-treat group, at least 3.5 weeks of treatment, and completers). Interpersonal therapy had statistically better results than placebo on the Hamilton Rating Scale of Depression (HRSD) on the intent-to-treat group. Interpersonal therapy had significantly better results than PLA-CM when the cut-off score on HRSD was used as a criterion in all three groups. Imipramine plus clinical management had significantly better results than PLA–CM on SCL–90 in the completers sample, on Global Assessment Scale (GAS) in the sample that had at least 3.5 weeks of treatment and on GAS and BDI in the intent-to-treat sample. Imipramine and clinical management, like interpersonal therapy, was better than PLA–CM when the cut-off score on Hamilton Rating Scale of Depression was used as the criterion. The results achieved at the end of therapy are shown in Table 2.1.

What can be seen from Table 2.1. is that interpersonal therapy and imipramine with clinical management appeared to be slightly more effective than a placebo with clinical management. This trend was even stronger, mostly for imipramine, if more severe depression was considered (HRSD ≥ 20; see Elkin, 1994).

Outcome in the follow-up in this project was assessed by the LIFE–II method (Longitudinal Interval Follow-up Evaluation II; Keller et al., 1987). LIFE–II is a semi-structured interview focused on a retrospective evaluation of psychopathology in a period of six months. The method was used to assess whether a relapse into depression appeared among patients in the study. The method was used at 6, 12 and 18 months after the end of treatment. In these assessments no differences were found between the conditions, though the trend was in favour of both psychotherapies in comparison to drug treatment and placebo with clinical management. Two different criteria were assessed: how many patients achieved recovery, and how many retained it without relapse. Shea et al. (1992) concluded that overall a low percentage of patients recovered, especially those who did not relapse (see Table 2.2). In psychotherapy, only around 24%

Table 2.2 Percentage of recovered patients without relapse 18 months after the end of treatment

CBT	IPT	IMI–CM	PLA–CM
		Intent-to-treat patients	
24%	23%	16%	16%
		Patients from whom follow-up data were available	
30%	26%	19%	20%

Note: Both groups are identical in absolute numbers. The difference exists because not all of the patients provided follow-up data. A realistic estimate is somewhere between the intent-to-treat group results (a conservative estimate) and the group that provided follow-up data.

Source: Elkin, 1994: 127. Copyright © 1994 I. Elkin, reprinted with permission of John Wiley & Sons, Inc.

of those who started the treatment had recovered and had not relapsed (the percentage was 26–30% among the patients for whom follow-up data were available). In the group with imipramine and clinical management it was even worse: only 16% had recovered without relapse in the intent-to-treat group (the percentage was 19% among patients for whom follow-up data were available). Shea et al. concluded that four months of treatment, which effectively became a routine 'dosage' of treatment, is not sufficient in cases of depression.

The Sheffield Study

Another representative example of a randomized clinical trial is the Sheffield study by Shapiro, Barkham et al. (1994) which examined the effect of cognitive-behavioural (CBT) and psychodynamic-interpersonal therapy (PI; using Hobson's, 1985 conversational model utilizing psychodynamic, interpersonal and experiential concepts) for depression. The authors, after screening 540 clients, selected 138 clients and analysed data for 117 of them (data for others were missing for various reasons; e.g. 15 clients did not finish treatment). Patients who, apart from depression, showed signs of psychosis, mania, obsessive-compulsive disorder or organic impairment were excluded from the study. The clients were divided into three groups according to the severity of depression: high severity BDI score 27 and above, medium severity BDI 21–26, and low severity with the score 16–20. The therapists were five clinical psychologists originally trained in CBT, but later trained in PI as well. The therapists had equal allegiance to both treatments. Two hundred and twenty sessions were rated for the adherence to the respective manuals and 97% of sessions were correctly classified as delivering the therapy that was intended. The clients also evaluated the credibility of therapies, i.e. as to the relevance of the therapy for the problems that brought them to therapy as well as the potential effectiveness of the therapy. No difference was found in clients' perception of the credibility of the two treatments.

The experimental design consisted of four experimental conditions to which the clients were randomly assigned. The four conditions were: eight sessions of CBT, eight sessions of psychodynamic-interpersonal therapy (PI), 16 sessions of CBT, and 16 sessions of psychodynamic-interpersonal therapy. Shapiro et al. (1994) formulated the

Figure 2.1   The design of the Sheffield project

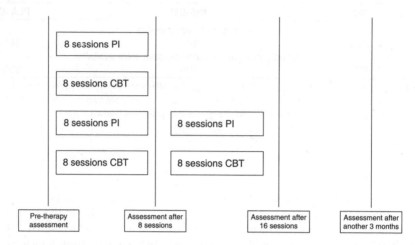

Source: D. A. Shapiro et al., 'Effects of treatment duration and severity of depression on the effectiveness of cognitive-behavioral and psychodynamic-interpersonal psychotherapy', *Journal of Consulting and Clinical Psychology*, 62(3), 522–534, 1994. Published by American Psychological Association, reprinted with permission.

following research questions: Is CBT more effective than psychodynamic-interpersonal therapy in the hands of investigators without allegiance to CBT? Is CBT quicker in its effects than PI? Are there any differential effects of CBT and PI in regard to severity of depression?

The clients' symptom status was measured before therapy, after eight sessions of therapy (in the case of the therapies with eight sessions, it was the measurement of therapy outcome at the end of treatment), after 16 sessions (the end of treatment of 16 sessions of therapy and three-month follow-up of eight sessions of therapy) and the groups having 16 sessions of therapy also had another assessment after three months (see Figure 2.1).

The outcome was assessed by six outcome measures: BDI (Beck Depression Inventory), SCL–90 (Symptom Checklist 90; Global Severity Index and Depression sub-scale), IIP (Inventory of Interpersonal Problems), SAS–SOC (Social Adjustment Scale self-report – Social subscale), SE (Self-esteem measure) and PSE (Present State Examination). Except for PSE, which is a structured interview schedule conducted by the clinician, all methods were self-report methods.

In regard to the first research question – whether CBT is more effective than PI – there were practically no differences between CBT and PI. The exception was the score on BDI that favoured CBT. A similar trend was visible on PSE, while the opposite trend was visible in the high severity condition, which favoured PI. In regard to the length of treatment, there were practically no differences between eight sessions and 16 sessions, with the exception of a trend on BDI favouring longer treatment. Interestingly, in the middle of the 16 sessions-therapy (that is, at eight sessions) the outcome for this condition was worse than in eight-sessions therapy. This would suggest that in longer therapy the therapeutic work is spaced out across more sessions.

If the severity of depression was taken into account, the 16-sessions therapy showed better results in the group with high severity of depression on several measures (depression, social adjustment, self-esteem). In contrast, the low severity group achieved better results in the eight-sessions condition (SCL–90 Depression subscale, self-esteem). With regard to the speed of change, there was no major difference between CBT and PI (some instruments favoured one condition, some favoured the other).

This study had several methodological problems. An interesting thing was that randomization failed and the groups differed in initial severity of depression even though the clients were already stratified by severity of depression. All analyses then had to adjust for that problem. Another major problem was the statistical power in some of the analyses, because the number of clients in groups according to severity and length of treatment was around ten.

Shapiro, Rees, Barkham et al. (1995) continued in this project by assessing the outcome in the follow-up. Out of 117 clients, 104 filled out self-report measures (not PSE) one year after the treatment (the 13 who did not fill out the form had an average score at the end of therapy worse than that of the 104 clients who underwent assessment at follow-up). Several measures (BDI, SCL–90 and Inventory of Interpersonal Problems) showed worse results for PI therapy of eight sessions, when compared with the other three conditions. The authors' interpretation was that eight sessions did not allow sufficient time for PI therapy. The authors used a BDI score of 8 or less as the criterion for considering a client not to be depressed. At the end of therapy, 54 clients met this criterion, 54 clients met it three months after the end of treatment and 69 one year after the end of therapy. If, however, they considered as recovered only those whose score was equal to or lower than 8 at the end of treatment as well as at three-month and one-year follow-up, only 30 clients met this criterion. The criterion was met by six out of 28 clients who completed self-report measures at all assessment points in PI therapy lasting eight sessions (PI–8), six out of 26 clients in CBT–8, seven out of 24 in PI–16 and 11 out of 25 in CBT–16. The authors, like Shea et al. (1992), concluded that treatment outcomes are not very great. This conclusion is again very interesting in light of the current perception in the field of psychotherapy and counselling, where brief treatments (usually CBT and interpersonal therapy) for depression are seen as the gold standard.

British Pragmatic Clinical Trial in Primary Care

The last example of a randomized control trial that we will look at is the RCT that was conducted in primary care in the UK and was led by King et al. (2000; see also Bower et al., 2000; Ward et al., 2000). It was a pragmatic controlled clinical trial as it was carried out in real conditions of primary care. The study compared non-directive counselling provided by counsellors who followed a manual based on Carl Rogers' (1951) work, cognitive-behavioural therapy (CBT, provided by trained clinical psychologists), and normal GP care (discussion of patients' problems and prescription of anti-depressants and anxiolytics). The patients in the trial had depression and/or mixed anxiety and depression with a score of at least 14 on the BDI.[1] Exclusion criteria included serious suicidal intentions, organic brain impairment and being on medication prior to treatment. The patients were recruited through their GPs. Introductory diagnostic assessment consisted of BDI; a demographic questionnaire; Clinical Interview Schedule-Revised, a method of classifying psychiatric symptoms allowing diagnosis according to ICD–10; Brief Symptom Inventory (BSI), a briefer version of SCL–90; modified Social Adjustment Scale (SAS), a method originally used in the interview format, but in this study modified into a self-report scale measuring functioning in social activities and relationships; and EuroQol, a method measuring general quality of life. The patients were also asked to describe their common problems and express how hopeful they were about their treatment as well as to state what kind of treatment they would hope to receive.

The patients were divided into three trials. In the first one, the patients were randomly assigned into three conditions: non-directive counselling, CBT, and GP practice as usual. In the second, the patients were randomly assigned into two groups: non-directive counselling and CBT. The third trial was a so-called preferential trial. It did not use randomization. The patients could choose whether they wanted CBT, non-directive counselling, or standard GP care. Each patient chose treatment on the basis of a short description of the treatments. An overall outline of the study is presented in Figure 2.2.

Fourteen counsellors provided non-directive counselling (they were accredited by the British Association for Counselling and Psychotherapy), and 12 psychologists provided CBT (they were accredited by the British Association for Behavioural and Cognitive Therapies). Adherence to the respective treatments was assessed by the Cognitive Therapy rating scale of Young and Beck (1980). The four primary outcome measures were: BDI, BSI, SAS, and EuroQol. The assessment was conducted before the start of therapy, after four months and after 12 months. The therapy was limited to 12 sessions with a recommendation to end treatment at around the sixth session.

Comparison of CBT and non-directive counselling did not yield any difference in any of the trials, including the preferential treatment trial. CBT and non-directive counselling brought better results than standard GP care at four-month assessment on BDI; however, at 12 months this advantage disappeared. BSI showed a similar trend. SAS showed a trend favouring CBT and GPs, if the change between the fourth and the twelfth month was taken into consideration.

The authors also looked at the patients' satisfaction with their treatment. For that, they used a modified version of the Session Impact Scale of Robert Elliott (Elliott & Shapiro, 1988). In the preferential trial, the patients in non-directive therapy scored higher (reporting more helpful impacts) on this scale. In the randomized trial of three treatments, non-directive counselling was rated higher than GP care at 12 months.

One of the analyses looked at the costs related to each of the treatments. Both direct (e.g. session costs, drugs costs, travel expenses, child care) and indirect (lost productivity) costs were taken into consideration. No differences were found between the treatments.

1 This was a relatively low threshold because the authors wanted to compare their study with a previous study and also wanted to capture clients with anxiety symptoms.

Figure 2.2 The presentation of experimental conditions in the study comparing GP care, CBT and non-directive counselling in the treatment of depression and/or depression and anxiety.

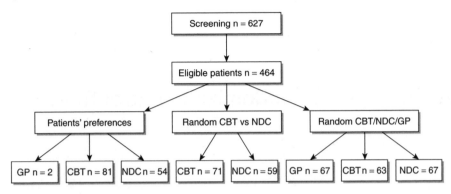

Note: GP – general practitioners, NDC – non-directive counselling, CBT – cognitive-behavioural therapy

Source: adapted from King et al., 2000: 11.

The three examples of randomized clinical trials presented here are examples of well-conducted experimental trials. As the reader may have noticed, they showed no dramatic differences between the treatments examined. This finding is quite representative, as the majority of RCTs examining equally credible treatments yield similar results (Wampold, 2001). Well-conducted trials with a good balance of researchers' allegiance to different therapeutic approaches often find no differences between active treatments. The three examples also point to the complexity and expensiveness of such trials. They involve a huge number of therapists, clients, researchers and other collaborators. RCT is a very expensive venture that requires a lot of experience on the researchers' part so that all tasks can be properly managed. The advantage is that the results of well-conducted trials often influence policy-making for many years, although often, as was the case with the NIMH Treatment of Depression Collaborative Research Program, in a distorted manner (in this particular case forgetting to indicate the limited effectiveness of treatment in the longer-term follow-up).

Although I have picked examples that compare CBT and non-CBT treatment, it is noticeable that CBT was examined in all three trials. In reality, CBT trials totally dominate the field and it is very hard to find examples of studies that do not include CBT. The three studies I have cited here are also examples of quite sophisticated designs, as they compare three or four conditions and in two cases include some form of control (placebo or treatment as usual). One study (the Sheffield study) also controlled for parameters of therapy such as length and its interaction with the theoretical approach to therapy, which brings another extra layer of sophistication. In reality, many RCTs contain just two conditions (experimental and some form of control).

3

Alternatives to Randomized Control Trials

Randomized control trials (RCTs) are considered the most highly valued types of research design by many reviewers of evidence in psychotherapy (e.g. Chambless & Hollon, 1998). This is because their experimental nature allows quite strong causal inferences about the efficacy of psychological therapies and counselling. However, psychotherapy outcome is assessed in other ways as well. We will now focus on other designs used in outcome research.

Experimental Case Studies and Quantitative Descriptive Studies

Experimental case studies are, like RCTs, focused on capturing the causal links in therapy. They have a long tradition, especially in behavioural therapy (Chambless & Hollon, 1998). They are most valuable when developing a new treatment or when an existing treatment is being delivered to a new type of problem or population. Many different experimental case designs exist (see Kazdin, 2003). A typical example is the ABAB design. This type of design requires that the client is first assessed for a certain period of time (baseline), then exposed to treatment and assessed; the client then remains without treatment for a certain period of time, is assessed and then finally exposed to treatment and assessed (ABAB – no intervention – intervention – no intervention – intervention). Causal inference is then made on the basis of covariance of positive change in the immediate outcome and exposure to the active therapeutic intervention.

This basic design may have many other forms (e.g. ABAC or ABACAD), which then examine how variations in the treatment influence immediate outcome. The experimental nature of these case studies lies in the fact that the experimenter actively controls and adjusts the treatment, so that it can be established what parameters of the treatment elicit what forms of outcomes.

Alan Kazdin (2003), one of the methodologists of experimental case study, recommends for this kind of design that the status of a patient is monitored before the treatment in order to determine the stability of the patient's problems. The status of problems should then be monitored during and following the treatment as well as in long-term follow-up. Kazdin (2003) also recommends using multiple sources of data, heterogeneous patients in a series of case studies, and a focus on changes of sufficient magnitude to correspond with therapeutic procedures specifically targeting them that would not be explicable otherwise. Kazdin (2003), as well as others (e.g. Kerlinger & Lee, 2000), points out the advantages of *multiple-baseline design*, which either sequentially administers different aspects of treatment to one patient or sequentially administers the same treatment to different patients.

Quantitative descriptive case studies differ from experimental case studies in that they do not use an experimental control of the therapeutic condition. They follow the case in its natural environment and, like experimental case studies, look for covariance of different aspects of treatment and outcome. The covariance is, however, studied as it naturally occurs without the possibility of controlling and adjusting therapeutic conditions.

An exemplary experimental case study using multiple-baseline is the work of Matthew Nock (2002), who investigated the effectiveness of behavioural treatment for food phobia in a four-year-old boy. The use of an experimental case study was indicated since the diagnosis is quite rare and, according to Nock, there were no outcome studies examining treatment of this problem in children. Nock decided to explore the use of a therapeutic procedure that was successful in the treatment of adolescent clients with this problem.

The participant in the study was a four-year-old boy who had been choking on solid food since the age of seven months and since then had been refusing to eat all solid food. He ate only soft baby food. The boy's food phobia was contributing to tension in the family as well as in his peer relationships. The boy's problems were diagnosed with the help of K-SADS-PL, a semi-structured interview method for children and their parents used for the assessment of affective disorders and schizophrenia in children. This method was used for the pre-treatment assessment, post-treatment assessment and the six-month follow-up. Apart from this method, the client was also asked to fulfil a behavioural test asking him to consume three feared foods: rice, beans and small pieces of chicken. The test consisted of several tasks: sitting next to the food, holding a spoon, placing the spoon in the food, lifting the spoon with the food, touching the food with the lips, putting it in the mouth, chewing it and swallowing. All of these tasks were evaluated by independent raters for level of avoidance and present anxiety. Another indicator of therapy effectiveness was the parents' monitoring of the boy's food intake.

The treatment consisted of 21 sessions over 27 weeks in which the therapist instructed the parents in the presence of the boy in the use of modelling and contingency management. The therapist and parents reinforced the desired food consumption behaviour and ignored any behaviour that interfered with the desired food consumption. If the boy vomited, they ignored it and reintroduced food consumption.

The study used multiple-baseline design demonstrating a causal link between the treatment and the desired behaviour. The targeted food was divided into four categories:

(a) fluids; (b) soft foods; (c) hard, crunchy foods and (d) tough, chewy foods. In the third week of treatment, the therapist and parents started, by selectively reinforcing and selectively ignoring, to introduce fluids: from that time on the boy consumed fluids. In the fifth week, they started to target soft foods, and the boy ate soft food from that time on In the eighth week, when soft food was introduced, the boy started vomiting; however, this was not reinforced by providing attention, and the food was reintroduced anyway. The vomiting ceased in week 12 and did not reappear. In week 14, the treatment focused on hard food, again followed by its consumption by the boy. In week 20 the treatment focused on chewy food, which led to an increase in its consumption as it was already starting to be eaten by the boy without the researchers deliberately focusing on it.

Apart from this procedure, which unquestionably shows a causal connection between the intervention and outcome (see also Figure 3.1), the boy's behaviour also changed in the behavioural test of consumption of rice, beans and chicken. Before the treatment he was afraid even to lift a spoon containing the food, while after the treatment he consumed all kinds of food with minimal anxiety. The change was also visible in the K-SADS-PL semi-structured interview.

Nock's study nicely illustrates the processes and benefits of experimental case study. Nock applied well-controlled procedures to a problem that is rare and had been insufficiently studied in larger outcome studies. He adapted a procedure that seemed to work with a different age cohort and tested it in a way that allowed for causal inferences. The alterations in the treatment procedure were followed by directly observable changes in the client's behaviour in a way that the principles of treatment had predicted. The multiple-baseline design as well as any other experimental case study may be applied across several clients. A good example of this can be found in the older study of Chadwick and Lowe (1990), who looked at the effect of two interventions (verbal challenge and reality testing) targeting delusions in six schizophrenic patients. All six clients were observed for five weeks and then the first client was exposed to the intervention. A week later the second client was exposed to it, another week later another client, and so on. The impact of these sequentially administered interventions on clients' delusions was then assessed.

Systematic Case Studies

Intensive systematic case studies differ from experimental case studies and quantitative descriptive studies in their depth of inquiry, which usually contains elements of qualitative methodology. Apart from strategies mentioned in experimental case studies and quantitative descriptive studies, clients' and therapists' perspectives on therapy are often collected (e.g. Hill, 1989).

An example of intensive case study methodology is a design proposed by Robert Elliott (2002a), the Hermeneutic Single-Case Efficacy Design (HSCED). HSCED collects quantitative data on pre-post outcome; however it also looks at quantitative and qualitative evaluation of every single session. In-depth interviews are conducted to look at the process and follow-up of a psychological therapy. Elliott tries to establish not only whether the therapy worked, but also why and how it worked.

Figure 3.1 An outline of the design and results of Nock's multiple-baseline design study

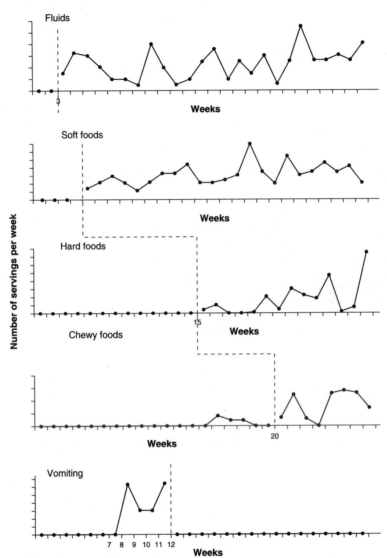

Source: reprinted from *Journal of Behavior Therapy and Experimental Psychiatry*, 33, M. K. Nock, 'A multiple-baseline evaluation of the treatment of food phobia in a young boy', pp. 217–225 © 2002, with permission from Elsevier.

Generalizability of findings can then be established by replication, but knowledge can also be enhanced by establishing a precedent of what kind of therapy worked and how in a particular case.

This systematic case study design (Elliott, 2002a) uses: (a) basic facts about the client and therapist (e.g. diagnosis, demographic information, presenting problems, therapist approach); (b) quantitative outcome measures (e.g. SCL–90, Inventory of Interpersonal Problems) that were periodically administered throughout the therapy and in follow-up; (c) qualitative evaluation of therapeutic process and outcome that was assessed by the repeated Client Change Interview (Elliott, Slatick & Urman, 2001; see Box 3.1.); (d) weekly outcome measure (e.g. Personal Questionnaire, see Chapter 1); (e) Helpful Aspects of Therapy form (Llewelyn, 1988), a questionnaire exploring helpful events immediately after the session and; (f) therapy session transcripts (these can be used for clarification of other data).

Box 3.1   Excerpts from the Client Change Interview schedule

General questions:
What medication are you currently on? (researcher records on form, including dose, how long, last adjustment, herbal remedies)
What has therapy been like for you so far? How has it felt to be in therapy?
How are you doing now in general?

Self-description:
How would you describe yourself?
How would others who know you well describe you?
If you could change something about yourself, what would it be?

Changes:
What *changes*, if any, have you noticed in yourself since therapy started?
Has anything changed for the *worse* for you since therapy started?
Is there anything that you *wanted* to change that hasn't since therapy started?

Change ratings:
For each change, the client rates how much s/he *expected* it vs. were *surprised* by it. (Using this rating scale:)

(1) Very much expected it
(2) Somewhat expected it
(3) Neither expected nor surprised by the change
(4) Somewhat surprised by it
(5) Very much surprised by it

For each change, the client rates how *likely* s/he thinks it would have been if s/he *hadn't* been in therapy. (Using this rating scale:)

(1) *Very unlikely* without therapy (clearly would *not* have happened)
(2) *Somewhat unlikely* without therapy (probably would *not* have happened)
(3) Neither likely nor unlikely (no way of telling)
(4) *Somewhat likely* without therapy (probably would have happened)
(5) *Very likely* without therapy (clearly would have happened anyway)

For each change, the client rates how *important* or *significant* to him/her personally s/he considers this change to be. (Using this rating scale:)

(1) *Not at all important*
(2) *Slightly important*
(3) *Moderately important*
(4) *Very important*
(5) *Extremely important*

Attributions:
In general, what do you think has *caused* these various changes? In other words, what do you think might have brought them about? (Include things both *outside* therapy and *in* therapy)

Helpful aspects:
Can you sum up what has been *helpful* about your therapy so far?

Problematic aspects:
What kinds of things about the therapy have been *hindering*, unhelpful, negative or disappointing for you?
Were there things in the therapy which were *difficult* or *painful* but still OK or perhaps helpful? What were they?
Has anything been *missing* from your treatment?

Review Personal Questionnaire (PQ):
Comparison of pre-therapy (screening) and post-therapy PQ ratings.

Review Pre-therapy Self-description:
Comparison of pre-therapy (screening) and post-therapy self-description.

Source: Elliott et al., 2001, adapted with permission.

The effectiveness of the case is established through the interpretation of the whole variety of data. Retrospective evaluation obtained in the Client Change Interview and pre-post outcome data are complemented by process–outcome data, data on helpful aspects of therapy and changes on outcome measures between the sessions. The researcher can, for example, establish whether reported changes in life outside the therapy sessions match developments in the therapy sessions. When tracking potential changes the likelihood of change happening without therapy is also assessed. Negative changes are also inspected and explanations other than those favouring the therapy are assessed (e.g. statistical or relational artefacts, psychobiological explanations, helpful factors outside the therapy, etc).

Elliott (2002a) illustrated HSCED on a running case example of emotion-focused therapy for a 49-year-old depressed client. The client in this case study considered it important for therapy that the therapists helped him to start the process of mourning (the client lost three members of his family). Elliott showed that the client achieved stable changes on the Personal Questionnaire measure and attributed these changes to therapy. The client also identified 12 highly helpful therapeutic events. Indirect evidence ruled out any explanation for the changes achieved other than the therapy effect. The case is a nice example of multiple evidence providing an explanation for the successful outcome.

Intensive case studies have the advantage of combining practice and research. They are relatively easy to conduct by practitioner-researchers. They can quite quickly inform theory and practice as they can be accomplished within a relatively short time. These advantages of systematic case studies led to the creation of the international online journal *Pragmatic Case Studies in Psychotherapy* (http://pcsp.libraries.rutgers.edu/index.php) edited by Daniel B. Fishman. One of the journal's goals is 'to generate a growing database of systematic, rigorous, and peer-reviewed therapy case studies across a variety of theoretical approaches'. The guidelines for authors submitting for this journal are presented in Box 3.2.

Box 3.2   The guidelines for authors for *Pragmatic Case Studies in Psychotherapy* (journal)

1. Case Context and Method
2. The Client
3. Guiding Conception with Research and Clinical Experience Support
4. Assessment of the Client's Problems, Goals, Strengths and History
5. Formulation and Treatment Plan
6. Course of Therapy
7. Therapy Monitoring and Use of Feedback Information
8. Concluding Evaluation of the Therapy's Process and Outcome

---

Preferential Trials

A specific form of clinical trial is the 'preferential trial'. These trials are more representative of real-life therapy as clients can actively seek the treatment they prefer. An example of preferential trial was one arm of King et al.'s (2000) study comparing CBT and non-directive counselling that we looked at in the chapter devoted to randomized control trials. The fact that the preferential trials do not use randomization limits inferences about differential benefits of different treatments. On the other hand, however, these trials allow for a comparison of interaction of the client's choice and a specific treatment against a different choice and some alternative treatment. Despite the fact that we do not know whether it is the specific characteristics of the clients who choose one form of treatment over another, or the interaction of clients' characteristics that determine the choice with the treatment, or the treatment itself, or all of these variables combined that make therapy work, what we know is the general effectiveness of such a treatment in comparison to some other therapy.

For example, in King et al.'s (2000) study, no differences were found between self-selected CBT and non-directive therapy. If changes were found, we would not know whether it was the clients' characteristics that determined the choice, or the choice itself, or the treatment itself, or the interaction of all of these factors that were responsible for changes. However, the results would in any case be very important as we would know that one self-selected treatment does better than the other. Furthermore, in the context of King's et al. study, which also ran RCT of the two conditions, we could infer whether the possibility of choice produced better results than simple randomization. (In that particular study the possibility of choice did not bring better results.)

Another thing that preferential trials allow us to establish is what type of treatment clients prefer. For example in King et al.'s (2000) study, clients preferred CBT over non-directive counselling, though NDC also elicited significant interest.

Naturalistic Studies

At the opposite end of the spectrum from RCTs, from the perspective of external validity, are *naturalistic studies*, which assess outcomes of a specific form of therapy in the routine practice. While the main benefit of naturalistic studies is their high external validity, the main weakness is low internal validity. Naturalistic studies, for example, do not control for homogeneity and the quality of therapy that is provided. They do not use randomization if several therapies are being compared, so do not control for clients' characteristics when these are involved in the selection of different therapies that potentially may be relevant to treatment outcome.

Despite the lack of experimental control, naturalistic studies can contribute to psychotherapy and counselling knowledge. For example, they can serve as a way of assessing therapies, previously tested in RCTs, in everyday practice. They may allow testing of the *effectiveness* of a specific therapy in comparison to testing the *efficacy* of a specific treatment tested in a RCT. Naturalistic studies can serve as benchmarks for individual practitioners who may compare their own effectiveness with the effectiveness found in studies examining large samples of clients with similar kinds of problem. Also, the practitioner may use information from naturalistic studies as a proxy for expectancies about the outcome of his or her own patients. Large naturalistic studies also allow for comparison of the effectiveness of different sites delivering treatment as well as of specific therapists.

A good example of naturalistic study is the work of Kächele et al. (2001) that examined inpatient psychodynamic therapy for anorexia (anorexia nervosa, AN) and bulimia (bulimia nervosa, BN) in 43 specialized hospitals and psychosomatic and psychotherapeutic units in Germany. Altogether 1,171 patients participated in the research (355 with anorexia, 647 with bulimia and 169 with anorexia and bulimia). Around 97% were female.

A battery of outcome measures was used that contained SCL–90–R, Eating Disorder Inventory (EDI), the Freiburg Personality Inventory (FPI), the Narcistic Personality Inventory (NPI), and the Parental Care Index. Patients were assessed before the treatment, one year after the start of the treatment and again 2.5 years since the after the start

Table 3.1 Percentage of recovered patients in inpatient psychodynamic therapy for eating disorders in Germany

Perspective	After treatment			At 2.5 year follow-up		
	Treatment weeks ≤ 11	Treatment weeks ≥ 11	Overall	Treatment weeks ≤ 11	Treatment weeks ≥ 11	Overall
	Anorexia nervosa					
Patients	8%	13%	11%	35%	31%	33%
Therapists	10%	15%	12%	37%	34%	36%
	Bulimia nervosa					
Patients	33%	29%	31%	21%	24%	22%
Therapists	48%	43%	45%	35%	37%	36%
	Anorexia and bulimia nervosa					
Patients	14%	16%	15%	27%	17%	22%
Therapists	14%	19%	17%	32%	22%	26%

Source: Kächele et al., 2001, adapted with permission © Society for Psychotherapy Research.

of treatment. The Longitudinal Interval Follow-up Evaluation (LIFE) method was used at the 2.5 year follow-up assessment. Apart from the outcome assessment, several variables were inspected as possible predictors of successful treatment (e.g. motivation for treatment, age, impairments caused by eating disorder, low weight, diagnosis, length of illness, type of clinic where patients were hospitalized). Therapy was considered successful when at least two of the three criteria for each therapy were fulfilled. In the case of anorexia, one of these criteria had to be weight gain as measured by Body Mass Index (BMI) and in the case of bulimia less than two episodes of binge eating weekly. Other criteria for anorexia were fear of weight gain as measured by EDI and Body Image Distortion (measured as the relation of patient-estimated BMI and real BMI as well as by the therapist's assessment). Other criteria for bulimia were abstinence from weight-reducing methods as well as from weight and shape concerns.

The researchers were trying to answer the following questions: What is the effectiveness of treatment? What factors determine the length of treatment? What are the predictors of successful treatment? How does treatment duration influence the outcome?

With regard to the overall effectiveness, the results did not differ significantly from previous findings in the field (Kächele et al., 2001) and were quite moderate. Especially low were the results for anorexia immediately after the end of treatment (8–15% success rate). In follow-up, the success rate increase to 31–37%. For bulimia the effect showed the opposite pattern: 33–43% after the treatment and 21–37% in follow-up. More detailed results are presented in Table 3.1. Interestingly, the therapists rated results more positively than the patients.

With regard to some other results, for example, the study found that intensity of treatment did not influence the results; however, patients with problematic interpersonal patterns benefited more from the longer treatment. Furthermore, findings suggested that the predictors of low effect in cases of anorexia were low weight and older age. In the case of bulimia, it was multi-impulsivity (e.g. substance abuse, agressivity, etc.), and additive anorectic symptoms.

Table 3.2 Pre-post effect sizes of different treatment groups in Stiles et al.'s study comparing CBT, person-centred therapy and psychodynamic/psychoanalytic therapy and their integrative derivates in routine practice

Treatment group	Pre-post effect size
CBT	1.27
PCT	1.32
PDT	1.23
CBT+1	1.59
PCT+1	1.48
PDT+1	1.38

Source: Stiles et al., 2006. Reproduced with permission of Cambridge University Press.

The study, like that of Kächele et al., though having very little internal control, can offer quite a substantial picture of service effectiveness in a country. It shows that, regardless of the mechanisms involved, we know how many clients are clinically meaningfully helped by the treatment. It also allows us to make a prognosis for prospective patients who would use similar services. The findings from routine practice can also be compared to those of clinical trials (see Franklin et al., 2000). If in the future new interventions are used in the health services, these findings can be used as a benchmark for them.

Another good example of naturalistic study is the comparative study of Stiles, Barkham, Twigg, Mellor-Clark and Cooper (2006), who used data collected in the routine care treatment evaluation. Fifty-eight National Health Service sites in the UK used CORE–OM and CORE Assessment as evaluation tools for the therapy they provided. The authors studied pre-post data of 1,309 patients on the CORE–OM. Patients were pooled out from a larger sample of 10,351. The criteria for selecting the sample were: availability of pre-post data and subscription to one of the six different types of therapy as indicated on the CORE End of Therapy form. The six types of therapy were classified according to orientation claimed by the therapists, which could consist of one major approach or two main approaches: CBT, person-centred therapy (PCT), psychodynamic/psychoanalytic therapy (PDT), CBT + one treatment other than PCT or PDT, PCT + one treatment other than CBT or PDT, and PDT + one treatment other than CBT or PCT.

The results showed no difference in the effects of therapy (counted as pre-post mean difference) between CBT, PCT and PDT. The CBT+1, PCT+1, and PDT +1 did slightly better than the single theoretical orientation therapy (results expressed in effect sizes are in Table 3.2.). There were similar findings when the outcome was assessed through the percentage of reliable recovered or improved patients (Stiles et al., 2006). A comparison of the number of presenting problems in different types of therapy and the number of sessions that therapy lasted showed that the patients in psychodynamic therapy were judged as reporting slightly more issues and had slightly longer therapy.

Stiles et al.'s (2006) study had quite a few methodological problems. There was no specification and control of the treatments (the therapists simply stated what they did). There was no random assignment and just one outcome measure was used. Also there was no attempt to look at the intent-to-treat samples analysis, to establish for example, whether attrition across treatments differed. Therefore, we do not know whether there was a differential dropout, which may be important information as more than 5,000 patients lacked post-treatment results on CORE–OM.

Nevertheless, regardless of the problems inherent in both naturalistic studies I have presented here, one can also see their advantages. Knowledge of the effectiveness of treatment in the national context may be very important information that can shape expectations about therapy offered to new clients and it can also serve as a benchmark against which practitioners can compare their own results. Barkham and Mellor-Clark (2000) as well as other authors coined the term 'practice-based evidence' to capture the essence of naturalistic studies. Barkham and Mellor-Clark emphasize that the important part of practice-based evidence is the creation of practice research networks that use the same set of instruments to assess their outcomes.

One successful example of practice-based evidence that serves as an audit tool for the monitoring and development of services is the use of Clinical Outcomes in Routine Evaluation system (see Chapter 1) in collecting evidence on the effectiveness of counselling services in the UK (Evans et al., 2003; Mullin et al., 2006).

Satisfaction Studies

Naturalistic studies are well complemented by satisfaction studies. The latter look at the effectiveness of psychological therapies and counselling from the consumers' perspective. The client's own perceived satisfaction with what therapy offers is central to this type of study. Satisfaction studies usually see the effectiveness of therapy more broadly than just its efficacy. The questions they try to answer may look at aspects of therapy such as availability, the helpfulness of its different aspects, etc. Such studies are often used in practitioner research as they may answer local questions that are important to a specific agency so that it can improve its services.

Probably the largest satisfaction study ever conducted was the study commissioned by the American journal *Consumer Reports* that focuses on consumers' satisfaction with services and products in a variety of contexts. The professional public was exposed to the findings of this study by M. Seligman (1995), who presented its methodology and findings in the *American Psychologist. Consumer Reports* has around 180,000 readers who respond to surveys. In 1995, the journal focused on mental health issues: 7,000 responders answered questions in reference to psychiatric and psychological problems. Of these people, 2,900 had sought the help of a mental health professional: 37% saw a psychologist, 22% a psychiatrist, 14% a social worker, 9% a marriage counsellor and 18% another professional. The questionnaire contained 26 questions asking: Who was the therapist? What brought the client to therapy? How did the client feel before therapy and how the client feels now? What kind of therapy was delivered (theoretical approach, frequency, length)? How much did the therapy cost? How much of it was covered by insurance? How much did the therapy help (in different areas such as the problem that led to therapy, interpersonal relationships, coping with stress, insight, enjoyment of life, etc.), How competent was the therapist? How satisfied was the client with the therapy?

The study produced several interesting findings. Of clients who rated themselves in the 'very poor' category of pre-treatment self-report questionnaires, before therapy, 87% reported improvement; 92% of those who reported feeling 'fairly poor' before therapy improved. Clients in long-term therapy reported more improvement than those in shorter treatment. No difference between psychotherapy alone and psychotherapy plus medication was reported. Psychologists, psychiatrists and social workers were similarly effective, and more effective than marriage counsellors. Family doctors were as effective as mental health professionals in the short term but less effective in the long term. Those clients who actively sought treatment and chose their therapist did better than passive recipients of therapy. Different therapeutic orientations did not produce different effects. Those clients whose therapy was limited because of limited insurance coverage did worse than those with unlimited coverage.

Despite the fact that the study was retrospective and contained several methodological caveats (Seligman, 1995), Seligman, otherwise a proponent of RCTs, acknowledges the value of the report. He especially points to the fact that the research was not conducted by researchers with vested interests and therefore the study appears to him as independent and realistic.

The *Consumer Reports* study represents an exemplary case of a satisfaction study. The main strength of such studies is that that they look at the outcome of psychotherapy and counselling more broadly and acknowledge other relevant aspects of care than just pre-post outcomes compared to an alternative treatment. Their major strength is high external validity and the fact that they answer questions important to consumers and stakeholders of psychotherapy that other studies do not assess, such as the accessibility of therapy.

Qualitative Outcome Studies

Outcome research in psychotherapy and counselling is significantly influenced by the traditional positivistic thinking so dominant in psychology. However, recent years have witnessed a huge development in qualitative research in social sciences and this development has not bypassed psychotherapy research. Empirical phenomenology, hermeneutics as well as developments in ethnography and linguistics has influenced empirical investigations in psychotherapy and counselling (see McLeod, 2001a).

The roots of qualitative outcome research in psychotherapy and counselling can be traced mainly to phenomenology and biographic studies. Qualitative outcome research, like the previously mentioned 'satisfaction' research, to a great extent uses clients' view of psychotherapy and its impacts. Qualitative methodology enables clients to talk about different relevant aspects of their psychotherapy experience without prior restriction to the concepts that are defined by an instrument. The qualitative approach, with its exploratory framework and empowering emphasis, also allows the clients to refer to those aspects of their experience in psychotherapy that had not previously been conceptualized by the researcher. In some studies, such as the outcome of family therapy, multiple perspectives can be employed (see Howe, 1996).

Qualitative research that uses mostly in-depth interviewing can uncover clients' cognitive representations of psychotherapeutic influence in its full complexity. Qualitative research creates a space for mapping helpful and unhelpful experiences in psychotherapy and their impact on the client's life outside therapy. It also provides an opportunity to look at the client's life in the context of the broader life experience (McKenna & Boyd, 1997). McLeod (2001a), who offers a summary of qualitative research in counselling and psychotherapy, sees the main advantage of qualitative outcome research in the fact that this type of research is more sensitive to negative aspects of therapy outcome.

A nice example of a qualitative study is the work of Irene Kuhnlein (1999), who studied post-therapeutic autobiographic narratives of 49 neurotic patients. Kuhnlein and her colleagues interviewed patients who underwent inpatient cognitive-behavioural treatment. The interview was carried out two years after the end of therapy and focused not only on the psychotherapeutic experience and its impact, but also had an autobiographic character focusing on the personal history that had led to psychological problems. Patients were also asked to integrate the experience during treatment with the period after the treatment.

One of the findings of the study was that the effect of psychotherapy was judged on the basis of how coherently it fitted with 'biographical continuity'. Another main finding was the discovery that patients conceptualize their experience in psychotherapy differently, on the basis of their previous personal schemas. These influence patients' view of psychological problems, psychological treatment, and its effects. As Kuhnlein puts it, patients do not reinterpret their personal history, but include psychotherapy in their personal history. First, the author and her team analysed the biography of each patient and then employed ideal type analysis, which tries to find similarities across different cases. The research team analysed 17 interviews and identified four different types of patients' experiences of therapy and its outcomes. The four types were grouped according to similarities in autobiographical construction, understanding of emotional disorder, understanding of therapy in the context of the patient's life and in future life after therapy.

The first type of patient was the *overburden* type. These patients saw the roots of their difficulties in a negative life event 'that would have an overwhelming effect on everybody'. Psychotherapy was seen as potentially threatening their stability, especially if they were asked to explore their functioning. On the positive side, they considered that therapy was linking negative life events and their psychosomatic symptoms, thus helping them to accept their problems. The effect of psychotherapy was judged by these patients on the basis of whether it was preparing them to recognize when 'the burden' they face is too heavy to bear.

The second type of patient was a *deviation* type. These patients evaluated their life externally on the basis of what is considered normal or not. The psychological problems were considered to be inexplicable malfunctions independent of life events. These patients saw psychotherapy as an expert-provided medical treatment and were trying to transform therapist interventions into advice that they should follow. The goal of treatment was to recover without the need for future contact with the therapist, as this would be interpreted as a continuation of the disorder. The basic benchmark of the therapy effect was to be the norm.

The third type of patient was a *deficit* type. These patients focused on life conditions that resulted in personal shortcomings. Therefore, psychological problems were seen as consequences of latent deficits acquired during personal history. The goal of therapy, for these patients, was to understand their problems and to increase their own competency. The effect of psychotherapy was seen as the patients continuing to work on identifying and overcoming their own deficits. The reappearance of problems would not be considered tragic, and therapy would be considered an appropriate form of help.

The last type of patient was a *developmental disturbance* type. These patients were closest to professional views on their difficulties and their treatment. They saw their life journey as a complex interconnection of personal characteristics, life events, and family and social conditions. The psychological problems were seen as the natural consequence of a complex interplay of many factors. Psychotherapy was seen, by these patients, as a tool for psychological growth. These patients were introspective and were actively trying to interpret and cope with their difficulties. They saw potential recurrence of the problems as a natural part of life and were prepared to develop further. They were interested in future therapy and other means of personal growth.

This example illustrates the freshness of the qualitative perspective, which can lead to new conceptualizations of therapy impacts. It also points to the complexity and contextual embedding of the psychotherapy experience and its impact. Qualitative outcome studies seem to be an area of potential growth (see McLeod, 2001a). New studies are being done (e.g. Lilliengren & Werbat, 2005; Levitt, Butler & Travis, 2006) though the rigour and methodology do not yet seem to be established. Potential benefit can also arise from the combination of perspectives, and from looking at qualitative outcomes of quantitatively successful and unsuccessful clients (e.g. Nilsson et al., 2007).

Alternatives to RCTs – Concluding Comments

The alternatives to RCTs that we explored above are quite well represented in the research literature. Despite the fact that they are producing a lot of interesting information about the effects of psychotherapy, their impact on the lists of empirically supported treatments is almost non-existent. The main methodological disadvantage of this type of design is its non-experimental character (with the exception of experimental case studies whose main problem is generalizability of findings), which in 'traditional' scientific thinking is an insurmountable deficiency. However, as can be seen, some of these alternatives show even more causality than RCTs (e.g. intensive case studies). Some are more representative of everyday practice (preferential trials, naturalistic studies) and some contextually decipher the differential effectiveness of psychotherapy with different types of people (qualitative outcome studies). My personal prediction would be that alternatives to RCTs will grow in their influence on the field of psychotherapy and counselling. The RCTs themselves do not capture the entirety and contexts of therapeutic effects. Therefore, it might be prudent for therapists in practice to be interested in the findings and methods of such alternatives.

4

Meta-analyses and Systematic Reviews

One empirical study, regardless of how well conducted, cannot answer the question of psychotherapy's effectiveness (or the effectiveness of a specific therapy for a specific problem). Every study has some problems and limits to its external or internal validity. Therefore, to reach more definite conclusions about the effectiveness of psychotherapy and counselling, it is necessary to look at a series of studies.

The efforts to accumulate findings from different outcome studies dates back to Eysenck's 1952 overview (see Introduction). Until 1977, outcome overviews used quite arbitrary and rough criteria for the evaluation of therapy outcome. In 1977 a new tool for evaluating a series of studies was presented (Smith & Glass, 1977): meta-analysis. In 1980, Smith, Glass & Miller published a book meta-analysing 475 therapy outcome studies. Since then a number of meta-analyses evaluating the outcome of therapy have been published. A lot of work has also been devoted to improving the rigour of meta-analysis (see Hunter & Schmidt, 2004).

Meta-analyses

Meta-analysis is 'the quantitative representation of key research findings in the studies reviewed and the statistical analysis of the distribution of findings across studies and the relationship of study features to those findings' (Durlak & Lipsey, 1991: 293). Meta-analysis uses effect sizes of single studies or their equivalents (e.g. correlation coefficients) as data for further quantitative analysis (Cohen's d, see Chapter 1).

For example, we can investigate all studies examining outcome of cognitive therapy for depression. Effect sizes capturing differences between the treated group and control from the single studies then create a sample of effect sizes of potential outcome studies measuring the effectiveness of cognitive therapy for depression. The effect sizes from single studies are considered to represent a sample of effect sizes from the potential population of effect sizes. The average effect size then indicates a more precise estimate of the 'real' effect size. The average effect size of cognitive therapy for depression versus control group should then be a more precise estimate of the effectiveness of that therapy than an effect size from a single study. Furthermore, through regression and correlation analysis we can investigate the relationship of the effect size magnitude to relevant aspects of the examined studies. For example, we can examine whether the effect sizes of cognitive therapy for depression are greater in more recent studies, thus hopefully pointing at further refinement of that therapy.

Meta-analysis can be divided into *treatment effectiveness meta-analysis* and *covariation meta-analysis* (see Durlak & Lipsey, 1991). Covariation meta-analysis in the context of psychotherapy research usually captures the correlation of some aspect of therapy with the therapeutic outcome (we will also cover this partially in Part II, which is devoted to process research). Meta-analysis allows us to answer different questions. For example, in therapy for depression it could be: Which therapies show the greatest effect? Which outcome measures show the greatest effect? What type of control group is responsible for a smaller effect? The questions can be answered either by comparison of the effect sizes' means or through regression analysis predicting the size of the effect on the basis of the variable studied (e.g. therapy or outcome measure). Meta-analysis can equally be used to test hypotheses – e.g. cognitive therapy is more effective than client-centred therapy for depression – as well as to explore the magnitude of the examined relationship, e.g. what is an average correlation of therapeutic alliance and treatment outcome?

Meta-analysis is a popular research tool, though it is still an evolving procedure (Hunter & Schmidt, 2004). The basic feature of meta-analytic processing is inclusion of all relevant studies. This protects against the potential bias of the author. It also means that meta-analysis includes studies with a different methodological quality, therefore the quality of studies is usually assessed (coded) and then controlled for (e.g. through regression analysis looking at whether the quality predicts the effect size). Similarly, other relevant aspects of primary studies are assessed, for example the type of therapy, type of outcome measures, client diagnoses, theoretical orientation of researchers, type of clients recruited for the study, length of therapy, dropout rate, type of publication (e.g. book, peer reviewed journal), and different therapist characteristics (see Smith, Glass & Miller, 1980). These aspects of particular studies are then related to the variation in effect size. Regression models then allow the prediction of effect size on the basis of study characteristics.

Statistical analysis used in meta-analyses must, for example, also adjust for different numbers of patients in different studies. Effect sizes must be weighted, so the sample size from a particular study is taken into consideration when using the effect size from this particular study. Statistical analysis also has to adjust for different numbers and different types of instrument in primary studies. Usually instruments are clustered to similar types of instruments and effects sizes are averaged across similar instruments used in one study (see Durlak & Lipsey, 1991 and Box 4.1).

Box 4.1   Specific aspects of meta-analysis

Formulating the research problem
- explicit hypotheses and research questions
- definition of criteria for the inclusion of studies to be meta-analysed

Literature search
- e.g. use of several modes of searching literature
- e.g. inclusion of non-published studies

Coding
- explicit criteria for coding (should be accessible to other researchers) and train-ing in their utilization
- use of several raters and assessment of their agreement

Index of effect size
- methods of calculating effect sizes
- contextual information about effect sizes
- testing for homogeneity of effect sizes (whether they represent the same popu-lation of effect sizes)

Statistical analysis
- weighting of effect sizes in regard to the sample size in the study
- identification of outliers (effect sizes that significantly differ from other effect sizes)
- precautions against an inflation of dependent effect sizes from the same study (one effect per construct per study)
- use of statistical tests corresponding with the nature of data and research ques-tions (e.g. search for effect size moderators (ANOVA or regression analysis)

Interpretation
- adequate conclusions restricted to the reviewed literature and its database

---

Source: abbreviated and adapted from Durlak and Lipsey, 1991, with kind permission from Springer Science and Business Media.

When interpreting meta-analytic studies one must be cautious and aware of meta-analytic procedures. For example, if we wanted to compare meta-analytically two different types of therapy, it would be important to include in the meta-analysis only studies that directly compare the two therapies. If we did not include only the studies that contained the direct comparison, we would have a problem, as every study uses a different design, differ-ent outcome measure, different therapists, different clients, etc. If, however, we include only the direct comparison studies, many of these variables would be controlled for within the study. It is very likely that the same study would use similar therapists and clients, and would definitely have the same outcome measures. Therefore, despite the fact that studies would differ in many aspects, the test of whether the two therapies differ across studies would not be influenced by these as they would be matched in every study.

Meta-analysis has become a standard tool of assessing outcome of psychotherapy and counselling. The main criticism levelled at meta-analysis is that no matter how good and sophisticated the control of characteristics influencing the outcome, it cannot match the control involved in randomized control trials (Chambless & Hollon, 1998). However, one can counterbalance this criticism by examining the studies included in meta-analysis properly and by accounting for deficiencies in the original studies either through statistical procedures or through the use of inclusion criteria.

Examples of Meta-analyses

Meta-analyses often try to provide a more definite answer to the questions that are examined in a number of studies. That is why they often arouse controversial reactions, this was the case with the two studies we will look at now.

Wampold, Mondin et al. (1997) attempted to answer the question of whether a difference exists between different therapeutic approaches if they are compared directly in the same studies and the therapies are delivered in a bona fide manner, i.e. the therapist believes in the effectiveness of the therapy that he or she is delivering. Wampold et al. wanted to test whether the average effect size from studies comparing two or more bona fide therapies is larger than zero. They wanted to perform a fair test of the so-called Dodo bird verdict (originally presented by Rosenzweig in the 1930s and then by many others), stating that there are no differences between the effectiveness of different therapies. If the verdict was true, it would mean that the average effect size of compared studies is zero.

To answer this question they included in their analysis all comparison studies that appeared between 1970 and 1995 in the main journals publishing psychotherapy outcome studies. They calculated the average effect size for each study (one study generally used up to 4–5 outcome instruments, some of which measured similar constructs). Two main analyses that Wampold et al. (1997) conducted were: (1) testing whether effect sizes across studies are normally distributed with the peak close to zero; and (2) testing whether the absolute value of the average effect size is significantly different from zero.

The second question stemmed from the fact that it was not possible to establish whether a comparison of similar therapies would not show an advantage of one therapy at one time and the other therapy at another time. That is why Wampold et al. (1997) took into consideration the absolute value of differences between the compared therapies and tested whether overall they differed more than zero in effect size in whichever direction. This way of testing was therefore more conservative as it could potentially inflate any differences found. If in one study therapy A was more effective than therapy B by, let us say, effect size 0.3 and in another study therapy B was more effective than therapy A by 0.4, the overall outcome would not be a difference of 0.1 (0.4–0.3), but the absolute value, that is 0.35 (0.4 + 0.3/2).

Figure 4.1 Two possible distributions of differential effect sizes of compared therapies

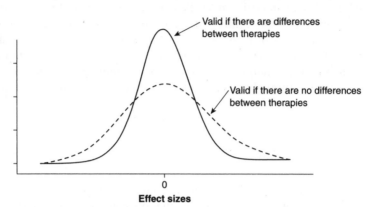

Source: B. E. Wampold et al., 'A meta-analysis of outcome studies comparing bona fide psychotherapies: empirically "All must have prizes"', *Psychological Bulletin*, 122, 203–215, 1997. Published by American Psychological Association, reprinted with permission.

Wampold et al. (1997) gathered 277 comparisons that were homogeneously distributed. The conservatively measured average difference among them was around 0.2[1], which statistically did not differ from zero (it was less than two standard errors of measurement). The authors also performed regression analysis, which tried to answer whether the year of publication is relevant to the amount of differential effect size or whether similar therapies bring similar differential effect sizes. The regression analysis questions arose from the theoretical thinking that newer therapies could be more effective (hence the year of publication) and comparisons of similar therapies should yield similar results. Neither of these hypotheses was confirmed. The authors concluded their findings with the statement: 'Empirically, "All must have prizes"' (again a parallel to the Dodo bird verdict) – there are no differences among psychotherapeutic approaches. Graphically, the hypothesis and findings of Wampold et al. are presented in Figure 4.1.

Another example of meta-analysis is the work of Westen and Morrison (2001). They decided to critically evaluate 'high quality' randomized control trials (RCTs) published in highly prestigious journals during the period 1990–99. Their goal was not only to meta-analyse outcome results, but also to assess the external validity of these studies, i.e. the representativness of the samples used in studies of the everyday clinical population. The authors focused on the three most commonly studied disorders: depression, generalized anxiety disorder (GAD), and panic disorder. Their review of ten prestigious journals, including *Archives of General Psychiatry, Journal of Consulting and Clinical Psychology, British Journal of Psychiatry, Psychotherapy Research*, found 34 RCTs (12 studies of depression, 17 of GAD, and five of panic disorder). For each study, they recorded the number of

1 The differential effect size slightly varied around the value of 0.2, depending on whether every measurement of outcome or just the last measurement, e.g. in following-up, was taken into consideration.

patients who were screened for treatment, who started treatment, who finished it, the number of improved patients, effect size on the main outcome measure (for depression it was either the Hamilton Rating Scale for Depression or BDI; for GAD it was the Hamilton Anxiety Rating Scale or STAI–T (State–Trait Anxiety Inventory-Trait Version); and for panic disorder different measures of the frequency of panic attacks were used).

Westen and Morrison (2001) found that studies measuring outcome of psychotherapy for depression included 32% of those patients originally screened for depression (the rest met some of the criteria for exclusion), 36% patients with GAD and 35% patients with panic disorder. The percentage of patients who finished treatment was: 74% for depression, 86% for panic disorder and 84% for GAD. The effect size at the end of treatment in comparison with the control group, which was usually some form of placebo, was 0.3 for depression, 0.8 for panic disorder and 0.9 for GAD. The percentage of improved patients for depression was 54% of those who finished the treatment (37% of those who started the treatment), for panic disorder 63% (54%) and for GAD 52% (44%).

As to the follow-up, only nine studies looked at 12–18-month follow-up, while only five of them looked at patients continuously over the follow-up period, i.e. not just at certain points in time. Twenty-four-month follow-up was assessed in just four studies. As to the percentage of patients who remained improved over the two years for depression, the figures were 37% of those who finished the treatment (27% of those who started therapy) and for panic disorder 54% (46%). Data for GAD over this period of time were not included in any of the studies.

Westen and Morrison (2001) also ran correlations relating criteria for exclusion and outcome. They found that when more criteria of exclusion were used the outcome of therapy was better and fewer patients sought further treatment during follow-up. This result undermined trust in the representativeness of RCTs for the real clientele. Overall, Westen and Morrison concluded that outcomes of RCTs for depression and GAD cannot be considered as satisfactory and they recommend putting more emphasis on naturalistic studies monitoring the most effective therapists, whose effectiveness should then be explored for efficacious interventions.

The two examples of meta-analysis I have presented offer a good illustration of its use. The first example (Wampold et al.'s study) answers the question that cannot be resolved by one single study: whether bona fide therapies are in general equally effective. The second example evaluates external validity and overall effectiveness of psychological treatment for the disorders most often studied. With regard to the first example, the comparison of the effectiveness of different therapies is a commonly studied problem. In some cases the outcome of such comparisons yields a different picture, that of differences among treatments (e.g. Grawe, Donati & Bernauer, 1994). However, these differences can sometimes be explained by other factors, for example the theoretical allegiance of researchers (see Elliott, 2002b). In every case a high-quality meta-analysis may go beyond the remit of single studies and answer the questions more globally. Though as I mentioned above, meta-analytical procedures also have their opponents (Chambless & Hollon, 1998).

Alternatives to Meta-analyses – Reviews and Systematic Reviews

Reviews are a classical alternative to meta-analyses. Despite the fact that they were replaced in the literature by meta-analyses, one can still find review studies. They remain important as they often represent a creative theoretical evaluation of findings as well as the methodology used in those studies and other relevant factors in the field. Examples of high-quality reviews are contained in the edited book of Bergin and Garfield (Bergin & Garfield, 1994; Lambert, 2004). For example, the chapter from 1994 on the effectiveness of psychotherapy by Lambert and Bergin and its update by Lambert and Ogles in 2004 present a narrative overview of findings from meta-analyses of outcome studies as well as studies comparing psychotherapy and placebo, follow-up outcomes, etc. They also review evidence on common and specific factors influencing the effectiveness of psychotherapy as well as evidence accounting for the deterioration of some patients in therapy. Lambert and Ogles (2004), in the updated version of this chapter, add, for example, the evaluation of the effect of manualization on psychotherapy outcome.

Reviews attempt to answer questions raised by authors by covering and analysing all available literature. The quality of a review study depends on how well and inclusively the literature search is done as well as how well the studies are assessed and interpreted. An important step forward in overview studies are *systematic reviews* (Gilbody & Sowden, 2001). If we consider meta-analysis as quantitative analysis of outcome findings, we can consider systematic reviews as their qualitative equivalent. Like meta-analyses, they pose research questions, and have criteria for identifying reviewed studies and criteria for assessing the methodological quality of reviewed studies (e.g. design, sample, outcome instrument used). Systematic reviews may also use independent raters. Sometimes they may use not only narrative accounts but also meta-analytical analyses. The final product is then a synthesis of current knowledge in the area on the basis of systematic, rigorous and repeatable steps.

Systematic reviews are published in general scientific journals or in specialized databases mapping outcomes of interventions in mental or generic health. One such database is the Cochrane Database of Systematic Reviews. This is a part of the Cochrane Library and is the product of an international Cochrane collaboration which aims at preparing and promoting reviews of the effectiveness of medical interventions. The Cochrane Database of Systematic Reviews therefore contains systematic reviews of medical interventions (evidence-based medicine). The structure of reviews that is used in this database is presented in Box 4.2. The Cochrane Database of Systematic Reviews is an online database that is regularly updated (there is also a printed version). It contains reviews of the effectiveness of psychotherapy and other psychological interventions. One very interesting feature of this database is that the reader can actually see the raw data on which the authors based their analysis and can comment on the study.

Box 4.2   The structure of systematic reviews used in the Cochrane Library

Date of most recent substantive amendment
Abstract
Plain language summary
Background
Objectives
Criteria for considering studies
Search methods for identifying studies
Methods of the review
Description of studies
Methodological quality
Results
Discussion
Conclusions
Conflicts of interest
References
Analyses

Another database from the Cochrane Library is the Database of Abstracts of Reviews of Effectiveness (DARE) maintained by the NHS Centre for Reviews and Dissemination at the University of York in Britain. This database represents *critical reviews of systematic reviews or meta-analyses* of outcome of interventions used in medicine. The reviews are presented in the form of larger abstracts. The DARE database is freely accessible via the internet and is updated more often than the Cochrane Database of Systematic Reviews. Every review has a firm structure, an example of which is presented in Box 4.3.

Box 4.3   Example of the review structure from DARE

Objective
Type of intervention
Specific interventions included in the review
Outcomes assessed in the interview
Study designs included in the review
Methods of literature search
Validity of original studies
Relevance of reviewed studies
Number of reviewed studies
Results of the review
Cost analysis
Conclusions
Reviewers' commentary

An example of the systematic review is the work of Bower and Rowland (2006), who reviewed studies assessing the effectiveness of counselling in primary care in the UK. The authors identified eight trials comparing counselling to standard GP practice (five trials), or alternative treatment (one CBT, one anti-depressants) or a mixture (one trial counselling vs. GP and CBT). Counselling was usually provided by counsellors accredited by the British Association for Counselling and Psychotherapy. The authors concluded that counselling was more effective than standard GP care in a short-term perspective; however, there were no differences when a long-term perspective was taken into consideration other than higher satisfaction of clients with counselling. The study comparing counselling and anti-depressants did not show any difference. Two comparisons with CBT showed no difference in one study of depressed clients and a difference in favour of CBT in the study using clients with anxiety disorders.

The goal of systematic reviews, as in the case of meta-analysis, is to offer an overview of broader knowledge in the reviewed area. The systematic reviews, through their emphasis on communicativeness and dissemination of the best available knowledge, can serve as an important source of material in informing one's practice. Though this information will be very abstract and general, it can allow the practioner to benchmark his or her own work and put it into a broader perspective of interventions available to clients.

5

Empirically Supported Treatments

Researching the outcome of psychotherapy and counselling has a direct impact on the politics of providing therapy. Since the 1990s, there has been a growing emphasis on the use of the most efficacious and effective psychological treatments inside professional organizations as well as in the broader societal context of health care organizations. Where this trend comes from within professional organizations, it may be motivated by the ethical imperative of providing treatment that can best alleviate human suffering. For stakeholders purchasing psychological therapy, motivation can also be led by limited financial resources, forcing the stakeholders to prioritize competing needs within general health care or, in the case of clients, to prioritize potential options that might address their suffering and needs best. Both of these pressures are characteristic not only of the area of mental health, but indeed of health care as a whole. Hence, we are confronted with evidence-based medicine, evidence-based mental health and, specifically in the case of counselling and psychotherapy, evidence-based psychological treatment.

The above-mentioned reasons mean that the importance of psychotherapy outcome research is significant for the provision of therapeutic care. Ethical reasons as well as practical reasons relating to limited resources are legitimate concerns that lead the trend towards establishing empirically supported psychological treatments. However, as providers of psychological treatments are many, and all of them have their own interests too, it is important to pay close attention to understanding how the evidence in conclusions about 'evidence-based psychological treatments' is established.

Empirically Validated Therapies

One of the first proponents of empirically supported psychotherapy was the Society of Clinical Psychology of the American Psychological Association. This division, responding to pressure from biological psychiatry, formed the Task Force on the Promotion and Dissemination of Psychological Procedures (APA, Division 12, 1995). The goal of this

Task Force was to contribute to the training of clinical psychologists and also to inform stakeholders benefiting from psychological treatments. For that purpose, the Task Force (APA, Division 12; Chambless et al., 1995, 1998) formulated criteria for the identification of empirically validated treatments (EVT), later also called empirically supported treatments (EST). The main emphasis in the criteria was placed on the methodology of randomized control trials and clearly defined client populations (see Box 5.1).

The Task Force (Chambless et al., 1998) published a list of 'well-established treatments' as well as 'probably efficacious treatments' (see Box 5.2). All other therapies were considered to be 'experimental'. Well-established treatments as well as probably efficacious treatments were intended to become recommended for the training of clinical psychologists as well as for their continuous professional development. However, the Task Force stated that the fact that a treatment is not on the list does not mean that it is not empirically based, as the science of psychotherapy is continually evolving. Similarly, the Task Force emphasized the role of the clinical judgement of the individual psychologist. It also stressed that the list should not be used by insurance companies in deciding on whether to cover specific therapeutic approaches. It pointed to limitations in generalizations from RCTs to minority populations. Similarly, it noted the importance of studying the interactions of personality characteristics of clients with a specific treatment (aptitude treatment interactions: for more see Chapter 7).

Box 5.1 *Task Force on the Promotion and Dissemination of Psychological Procedures* **Division 12 criteria for empirically validated therapies**

Criteria for Empirically Validated Treatments
Well-Established Treatments

I. At least two good between-group design experiments demonstrating efficacy in one or more of the following ways:
    A. Superior to pill or psychological placebo or to another treatment.
    B. Equivalent to an already established treatment in experiments with adequate statistical power (about 30 per group).

OR

II. A large series of single-case design experiments (n ≥9) demonstrating efficacy. These experiments must have:
    A. Used good experimental designs and
    B. Compared the intervention to another treatment as in IA.

FURTHER CRITERIA FOR BOTH I AND II:

III. Experiments must be conducted with treatment manuals.
IV. Characteristics of the client samples must be clearly specified.
V. Effects must have been demonstrated by at least two different investigators or investigatory teams.

Probably Efficacious Treatments

I. Two experiments showing the treatment is more effective than a waiting-list control group.

OR

II. One or more experiments meeting the Well-established Treatment Criteria I, III and IV, but not V.

OR

III. A small series of single-case design experiments (n ≥3) otherwise meeting Well-Established Treatment Criteria II, III and IV.

Source: D. L. Chambless et al., 'Update on empirically validated therapies, II', *The Clinical Psychologist*, 51, 3–16, 1998. Published by American Psychological Association, reprinted with permission.

Box 5.2   Examples of therapies on the list of empirically validated therapies (EVTs) from 1998

Well-Established Treatments Citation for Efficacy Evidence

ANXIETY AND STRESS:

Cognitive-behavior therapy for panic disorder with and without agoraphobia
Cognitive-behavior therapy for generalized anxiety disorder
Group cognitive behavioral therapy for social phobia
Exposure treatment for agoraphobia
Exposure treatment for social phobia
Exposure and response prevention for obsessive-compulsive disorder
Stress Inoculation Training for Coping with Stressors
Systematic desensitization for simple phobia

DEPRESSION:

Cognitive therapy for depression
Interpersonal therapy for depression

HEALTH PROBLEMS:

Behavior therapy for headache
Cognitive-behavior therapy for irritable bowel syndrome
Cognitive-behavior therapy for chronic pain
Cognitive-behavior therapy for bulimia
Interpersonal therapy for bulimia

(Continued)

(Continued)

PROBLEMS OF CHILDHOOD:

Behavior modification for enuresis
Parent training programs for children with oppositional behavior

MARITAL DISCORD:

Behavioral marital therapy

SEXUAL DYSFUNCTION:

Behavior therapy for female orgasmic dysfunction and male erectile dysfunction

OTHER:

Family education programs for schizophrenia
Behavior modification for developmentally disabled individuals
Token economy programs

Probably Efficacious Treatments Citation for Efficacy Evidence

ANXIETY:

Applied relaxation for panic disorder
Applied relaxation for generalized anxiety disorder
Exposure treatment for PTSD
Exposure treatment for simple phobia
Stress Inoculation Training for PTSD
Group exposure and response prevention for obsessive-compulsive disorder
Relapse prevention program for obsessive-compulsive disorder

CHEMICAL ABUSE AND DEPENDENCE:

Behavior therapy for cocaine abuse
Brief dynamic therapy for opiate dependence
Cognitive therapy for opiate dependence
Cognitive-behavior therapy for benzodiazepine withdrawal in panic disorder patients

DEPRESSION:

Brief dynamic therapy
Cognitive therapy for geriatric patients
Psychoeducational treatment
Reminiscence therapy for geriatric patients
Self-control therapy

HEALTH PROBLEMS:

Behavior therapy for childhood obesity
Group cognitive-behavior therapy for bulimia

MARITAL DISCORD:

Emotionally focused couples therapy
Insight-oriented marital therapy

PROBLEMS OF CHILDHOOD:

Behavior modification of encopresis
Family anxiety management training for anxiety disorders

OTHER:

Behavior modification for sex offenders
Dialectical behavior therapy for borderline personality disorder
Habit reversal and control techniques

Source: D. L. Chambless et al., 'Update on empirically validated therapies, II', *The Clinical Psychologist*, 51, 3–16, 1998. Published by American Psychological Association, adapted with permission.

The work and conclusions of the Task Force on the Promotion and Dissemination of Psychological Procedures provoked significant controversy and critique. The controversy was apparent in special issues of several journals devoted to presenting the work of the Task Force and/or commenting on it (see e.g. *Clinical Psychology: Science and Practice*, 3, 1996; the *Journal of Consulting and Clinical Psychology*, 1, 1998; and *Psychotherapy Research*, 2, 1998). Garfield (1996), for example, criticizes the criteria for identifying empirically validated therapies. According to him, such an important endeavour needs to have a broader consensus. As an example he singles out the fact that all research conducted before 1981 is ignored as it, a priori, cannot meet the criteria (e.g. manualization of therapies). He further comments that some of the treatments included were tested on a very small number of patients. Nor is he enthusiastic about the fact that *DSM-IV* diagnosis is emphasized even though it has disputable validity. Garfield also points out the great variability between therapists and clients, as well as the large number of variables other than treatment that influence the outcome of therapy.

Henry (1998: 127), in his criticism of the Task Force, goes even further. He states that the EVT approach:

a) fundamentally sacrifices a traditional *psychological* approach in favour of a medical model of dubious utility to the phenomenon under study; b) has the potential to *decrease* the quality of psychotherapy training; c) may give even greater power to third-party payers as *de facto* untrained 'supervisors'; d) actually discourages empirical research in some areas (such as personality disorders); e) disseminates 'findings' of little true value that may ultimately work against consumers' best interest; and f) entrenches an outdated research paradigm that militates against the discovery of new knowledge.

Henry comments that the EVT Task Force, for example, ignores therapeutic alliance as a variable that influences the outcome of therapy. He is ironic, saying that 'almost anything remotely plausible would technically make the EVT list if a manual was written and two different investigators took the trouble to engage in the required trials' (Henry, 1998: 132). In line with this argument he points to the fact that the two therapies that are considered to be well established in the treatment of depression – cognitive therapy and interpersonal therapy – were developed clinically and not empirically, which in the Task Force's understanding would mean that they would have problems in gaining funding nowadays. Henry, like other critics (see Bohart, O'Hara & Leitner, 1998; Wampold, 1997) offers alternatives to the Task Force focus on EVTs (Chambless et al., 1998). One of the alternatives would be studying 'central therapeutic processes for core pathologies' (based of case formulation broader than diagnosis); another studying 'the effectiveness of treatment formulations'; yet another studying 'a phase of treatment-specific therapy goals'.

Elliott (1998), in his editorial for the special issue of *Psychotherapy Research* dedicated to EVTs, summarizes arguments for and against EVTs. As arguments in favour of EVTs (he uses the term Empirically Supported Treatments, EST) he argues that:

1. A lot is known about the effectiveness of psychotherapy.
2. ESTs can improve patient care.
3. ESTs can influence health care policy.
4. ESTs can improve training in psychotherapy.
5. ESTs may encourage psychotherapy research.
6. The EST project is a collaborative effort.
7. The EST project can lead to further development of guidelines for practice.

Elliott (1998) also summarizes criticisms against ESTs. He divides these into two groups, one stating that the dissemination of ESTs is premature, and the second claiming that the criteria outlined for identification of ESTs are invalid and unhelpful. As to the premature dissemination, Elliott puts forward the following arguments:

1. Effectiveness data on listed treatments are inadequate.
2. Therapies presented on the list have limited effectiveness (e.g. relapse rates in the treatment of depression).
3. The EST list shows systematic discrimination of certain types of research, therapies and patients.
4. The EST list seems to be influenced politically (e.g. some therapies included have a problem in fulfilling the criteria and some therapies fulfilling them are missing).
5. The EST list may inhibit clinical innovation.

As to the problem of validity of the EST project criteria, Elliott (1998) makes the following arguments:

1. EST criteria are too restrictive (ignoring a large area of relevant research).
2. On the other hand, the criteria are too lenient (e.g. do not place enough emphasis on the statistical power of the samples researched and do not evaluate clinical significance such as cut-off score).
3. EST criteria distract from important research.

4. EST may stifle psychotherapy research by placing too much emphasis on RCTs.
5. The design of RCTs has its flaws.
6. The assumption of diagnostic specificity is problematic and dehumanizes clients.
7. Manualization of treatments may have negative effects (may hinder therapist flexibility) and may make therapists into technicians.

Elliott (1998) calls proponents of EVT in its original form as well as their critics representatives of extreme positions. He calls for the development of psychotherapy research as a whole, for a higher quality of methodology (e.g. allegiance control) and its use in the development of recommendations for practice. He emphasizes UK developments that will be presented later in this chapter.

Elliott's commentary nicely summarizes the heated debates that started with the launch of the Task Force on empirically supported psychotherapies. Now several years later, the debate is probably less heated and ESTs have a firm place in policy-making on the provision of psychotherapy and counselling, still the battles continue.

Response to the Clinical Psychology Task Force

Two other APA divisions that cover psychologists providing psychotherapy, the Society of Counseling Psychology and the Division of Psychotherapy, formulated their response to the empirically supported treatments movement. The Society of Counseling Psychology defined Principles of Empirically Supported Interventions in Counseling Psychology. The Division of Psychotherapy summarised elements of the therapy relationships that delineate Empirically Supported Therapy Relationships (Division of Psychotherapy) (APA, Division 29, 2002). Similarly, another division, that of Humanistic Psychology, published guidelines for the provision of 'humanistic psychosocial services' (APA, Division 32, 1997).

The Society of Counseling Psychology formed a Special Task Group on empirically supported interventions in counselling psychology (Wampold, Lichtenberg & Whaeler, 2002), which delineated seven principles that should be used in reviewing the effectiveness of different interventions addressing different types of problem. The first principle emphasizes that the *level of specificity should be considered when evaluating outcomes*. This would, for example, mean that on one level the effectiveness of psychotherapy in general would be assessed, on another level the effectiveness specifically of cognitive-behavioural therapies could be assessed, on a third level the effectiveness of CBT for depression, and on a fourth level the effectiveness of cognitive restructuring for a specific type of client suffering from depression.

The second principle outlined by the Special Task Group (Wampold, Lichtenberg & Whaeler, 2002) emphasized that the *level of specificity should not be restricted to diagnosis*, meaning that other characteristics (gender, values, motivation for treatment, etc.) should also be included. The third principle focused on the fact that the *scientific evidence needs to be examined in its entirety and aggregated appropriately*, which was a direct reaction to the fact that ESTs take into consideration only randomized control trials. The fourth principle expressed the need that the *evidence for absolute and relative efficacy* should be assessed. What is meant by this is that not only one type of efficacy (e.g. reduction in symptoms) should be considered, but that global evidence should take into account a broader area of impact (e.g. treatment acceptability, cost-effectiveness).

The fifth principle emphasized by Wampold, Lichtenberg & Whaeler (2002) was that the *causal attribution for specific ingredients should be made only if the evidence is persuasive*. This principle responds to the problem that the effectiveness of 'treatment package' is often presented as evidence for efficacy of the ingredients that make up the package. As research using dismantled design shows, this does not have to be true (Ahn & Wampold, 2001; see also Chapter 2). The sixth principle states that *outcomes should be assessed appropriately and broadly*, taking into account general life functioning. Finally, the last principle reminds us that *outcomes should be assessed locally and psychologists/clients' choice should be recognized*.

As can be seen, the principles presented by the Special Task Group of the Society of Counseling Psychology are in many cases an antidote to the activity set up by the Task Force of the Society of Clinical Psychology. The Counseling Division stresses the *holistic understanding of psychological problems* that clients bring to therapy and the *complexity of evidence for the effectiveness of psychological interventions*. These two aspects differentiate between the two movements aiming at evidence-based psychological care.

Another response to the Task Force of the Clinical Psychology Division was the creation of Task Force on Empirically Supported Relationships by the APA Division of Psychotherapy. This Task Force aimed at the creation of a list not of 'relationships' responsible for therapeutic change but of relational variables influencing the therapy outcome.[1] The basic assumption beyond this endeavour was the empirically established fact that relationship variables are, after client variables, the second most important group of variables affecting outcome of therapy (Lambert & Barley, 2002).

The Task Force on Empirically Supported Relationships set itself two goals: (1) *to identify elements of effective therapy relationships;* and (2) *to determine efficacious methods of tailoring therapy to the individual patient* (Norcross, 2002: 6). The results of the Task Force effort were published in a special issue of *Psychotherapy* (4, 2002), published by APA Division of Psychotherapy and in the book edited by Norcross (2002) *Psychotherapy Relationships That Work*. Box 5.3. shows the effective elements of therapy relationships and the methods of tailoring therapy relationships to the individual patients. Box 5.3 also presents promising variables worth further research.

Box 5.3 Effective and probably effective variables in therapy relationships and in customizing the therapy relationship to the individual patient – conclusions of APA Division of Psychotherapy *Task Force on Empirically Supported Therapy Relationships*

General Elements of the Therapy Relationship primarily provided by the psychotherapist.

Demonstrably Effective
Therapeutic Alliance
Cohesion in Group Therapy

---

1 When assessing evidence, Task Force members mostly used process–outcome research that will be presented in Chapter 10.

Empathy
Goal Consensus and Collaboration

Promising and Probably Effective
Positive Regard
Congruence/Genuineness
Feedback
Repair of Alliance Ruptures
Self-disclosure
Management of Countertransference
Quality of Relational Interpretations

Customizing the Therapy Relationship to Individual Patients on the basis of patient behaviors or qualities.

Demonstrably Effective as a Means of Customizing Therapy
Resistance
Functional Impairment

Promising and Probably Effective as a Means of Customizing Therapy
Coping Style
Stages of Change
Anaclitic/Sociotropic and Introjective/Autonomous Styles
Expectations
Assimilation of Problematic Experiences

Source: adapted from APA, Division 29, 2002.

The Task Force of Division 29 (APA, Division 29, 2002) recommended not only the dissemination of its conclusions, but also their combination with the conclusions of the Task Force on Empirically Supported Treatments. Similar to the EST Task Force, it called for its conclusions to be used in the training of future therapists. It also called for plurality in the use of methods for studying such a complex phenomenon as the therapy relationship. It emphasized the role of intensive investigations of the formation of the therapy relationship and its influence on therapy outcome.

After the work of the Division of Psychotherapy on therapeutic relationships, the Society of Clinical Psychology, Division 12 of APA and the Northern American Chapter of the Society for Psychotherapy Research sponsored another Task Force, this one focused on Empirically Based Principles of Therapeutic Change. The work of this Task Force resulted in the publication of the edited book *Principles of Therapeutic Change That Work* (Castonguay & Beutler, 2005). This Task Force explicitly focused on the combination of findings from the Society of Clinical Psychology *Task Force on the Promotion and Dissemination of Psychological Procedures*, and the Division of Psychotherapy *Task*

Force on Empirically Supported Therapy Relationships complementing it with some extra evidence.

The Task Force looked at: (1) *participant (client and therapist) factors contributing to the therapy outcome*; (2) *relationship factors contributing to the therapy outcome*; and (3) *technique factors contributing to the therapy outcome*. The factors were reported on the level of principle, 'the conditions under which a concept (participant, relationship quality, or intervention) will be effective' (Beutler & Castonguay, 2005: 6). An integration of three types of factors (stated above) was also provided. The whole process was done for four broad diagnostic groups: dysphoric disorders, anxiety disorders, personality disorders, and substance abuse disorders. Examples of common and specific participant, relationship and intervention factors for dysphoric disorders are presented in Box 5.4.

Box 5.4 Examples of common and specific participant, relationship and intervention factors for dysphoric disorders

Examples of common principles of therapeutic change applied to participant factors:
- Severity: the more severe the problem the fewer benefits in time-limited treatment (long-term unknown).
- Therapist characteristics: when working with depression and personality disorders, therapist flexibility, adapting, tolerance and creativity are related to improvement.
- Patient demographics: perceived levels of social support are predictors of treatment benefits.

Examples of common principles related to the therapeutic relationship:
- Therapists should be careful not to use relational interpretations excessively.
- Therapists are likely to resolve alliance ruptures by addressing them empathically and flexibly.

Examples of common principles of selecting techniques and interventions:
- An ongoing assessment of how treatment goals are addressed may maximize treatment gains.
- Helpful treatments educate clients about the nature of the problem and rationale for treatment.

Unique principles for treating depression and dysphoria:
An example of participant factors:
- Benefits may be enhanced when the interventions selected are responsive to the patient's level of problem assimilation.

An example of relationship factors:
- Therapist's self-disclosure may be helpful when working with depressed clients.

There were no techniques unique to dysphoric disorders.

Source: adapted from Beutler, Castonguay and Follette, 2005: 112–115.

The debate around empirically supported treatments still contines in the USA (e.g. Westen, Novotny & Thompson-Brenner, 2004). For example, the APA's position on different treatment guidelines – those published by APA bodies, but also others outside the APA – was formed in the mid-1990s and revised in 2002 (American Psychological Association, 2002). Most recently, the APA Presidential Task Force on Evidence-Base Practice addressed this issue in 2006. The policy statement stemming from this Task Force states that 'evidence-based practice in psychology (EBPP) is the integration of the best available research with clinical expertise in the context of patient characteristics, culture, and preferences' (APA, 2006: 284). The question, 'What is the best research evidence?' was addressed in a lively manner in the edited book *Evidence-Based Practices in Mental Health* (Norcross, Beutler & Levant, 2006). The book was launched at about the same time as the publication of the report of the APA's Presidential Task Force on Evidence-Base Practice. In the book, expert researchers engage in dialogue (often defending opposing positions) about what constitutes the best research evidence. Nine questions that the editors posed to invited contributors are presented in Box 5.5.

Box 5.5   Questions addressed in *Evidence-based Practices in Mental Health*

- What qualifies as evidence of effective practice?
- What qualifies as research on which to judge effective practice?
- Does manualization improve therapy outcome?
- Are research patients and clinical trials representative of clinical practice?
- What should be validated? (Treatment method, therapist, therapy relationship, active client, principles of change?)
- What else materially influences what is represented and published as evidence?
- Do therapies designated as empirically supported treatments for specific disorders produce outcomes superior to non-empirically supported treatment therapies?
- How well do both evidence-based practices and treatment as usual satisfactorily address the various dimensions of diversity?
- Are efficacious laboratory-validated treatments readily transportable to clinical practice?

Source: Norcross, Beutler and Levant, 2006.

The Situation in Europe – the United Kingdom and Germany

Empirically supported therapies became relevant in Europe as well as America. Different countries applied different approaches to evidence-based psychological therapies. We will briefly introduce two substantially different models, the British and the German.

In 2001, the UK Department of Health published the evidence-based clinical practice document *Treatment Choice in Psychological Therapies and Counselling* (Department of Health, 2001). The document was developed by the British Psychological Society Centre for Outcomes Research and Effectiveness with the support and participation of the British Association for Counselling and Psychotherapy, the British Confederation of Psychotherapists, the Royal College of Psychiatrists, the UK Advocacy Network and the UK Council for Psychotherapy. A team of experts from relevant professional organizations reviewed research evidence gathered by commissioned reviewers and, using consensus and the Delphi technique, drew up recommendations.[2] The approach was sophisticated and used several steps. The experts assessed the weight of the evidence and on its basis also the strength of recommendations (see Box 5.6).

Box 5.6   Categories of evidence and strength of recommendations

Categories of Evidence
Ia   Evidence from meta-analysis of randomized controlled trials
Ib   Evidence from at least one randomized controlled trial
IIa   Evidence from at least one controlled study without randomization
IIb   Evidence from at least one other type of quasi-experimental study
III   Evidence from descriptive studies, such as comparative studies, correlation studies and case-control studies
IV   Evidence from expert committee reports or opinions, or clinical experience of respected authority or both

Strength of recommendations
A.   Directly based on category I evidence
B.   Directly based on category II evidence or extrapolated from category I evidence
C.   Directly based on category III evidence or extrapolated from category II evidence
D.   Directly based on category IV evidence or extrapolated from category III evidence

---

Source: Department of Health, 2001. Reproduced under the terms of the Click-Use Licence.

The expert team then prepared a draft document that was further audited by external scientific reviewers as well as nominees of consumer services. The results are presented in abbreviated form in Box 5.7. The recommendations did not cover all problems for which psychological therapy is usually proscribed.

---

2 Despite the rigorousness of the guidelines' methodology, the influence of theoretical allegiance that was assessed for control was significant. For example, experts with CBT allegiance considered other treatments inappropriate (Department of Health, 2001: 17).

Box 5.7 Recommendation from Treatment Choice in *Psychological Therapies and Counselling*

Initial assessment

Psychological therapy should be routinely considered as a treatment option when assessing mental health problems (strength of recommendation B).

In considering psychological therapies, more severe or complex mental health problems should receive secondary, specialist assessment (D).

Therapeutic relationship

Effectiveness of all types of therapy depends on the patient and the therapist forming a good working relationship (B).

Treatment length

Therapies of fewer than eight sessions are unlikely to be optimally effective for most moderate to severe mental health problems (B).

Often 16 sessions or more are required for symptomatic relief, and longer therapies may be required to achieve lasting change in social and personality functioning (C).

Specific phobias and uncomplicated panic disorder (without agoraphobic symptoms) can respond to brief interventions (B).

Age, sex, social class and ethnic group

The patient's age, sex, social class or ethnic group are generally not important factors in choice of therapy and should not determine access to therapies (C).

Ethnic and cultural identity should be respected by referral to culturally-sensitive therapists (C).

Patient preference

Patient preference should inform treatment choice, particularly where the research evidence does not indicate a clear choice of therapy (D).

Skill level of therapist

The skill and experience of the therapist should also be taken into account. More complex problems, and those where patients are poorly motivated, require a more skilful therapist (D).

Patient characteristics

Interest in self-exploration and capacity to tolerate frustration in relationships may be particularly important for success in interpretative (psychoanalytic and psychodynamic) therapies, compared with supportive therapy (C).

Adjustment to life events

Patients who are having difficulty adjusting to life events, illnesses, disabilities or losses (including childbirth and bereavement) may benefit from brief therapies, such as counselling (B).

(Continued)

(Continued)

Post-traumatic stress

Where post-traumatic stress disorder (PTSD) is present, psychological therapy is indicated, with best evidence for cognitive-behavioural methods (A).

Depressive disorders

Depressive disorders may be treated effectively with psychological therapy, with best evidence for cognitive-behaviour therapy and interpersonal therapy, and some evidence for a number* of other structured therapies, including short-term psychodynamic therapy (A).
Number of therapies includes behavioural therapy, problem-solving therapy, group therapy, systemic therapy, non-directive counselling in primary care and psychodynamic interpersonal therapy.

Anxiety disorders

Anxiety disorders with marked symptomatic anxiety (panic disorder, agoraphobia, social phobia, obsessive compulsive disorders, simple phobias and generalized anxiety disorders) are likely to benefit from cognitive-behaviour therapy (A).
The lack of evidence on other therapies does not mean they are ineffective.

Eating disorders

Bulimia nervosa can be treated with psychological therapy; best evidence is for interpersonal therapy and cognitive-behaviour therapy (A).
Individual psychological therapy for anorexia nervosa may be of benefit; there is little strong evidence on therapy type (B).

Personality disorders

A co-existing diagnosis of personality disorder may make treatment of the presenting mental health problem more difficult and possibly less effective; indications of personality disorder include forensic history, severe relationship difficulties and recurrent complex problems (D).
Structured psychological therapies delivered by skilled practitioners can contribute to the longer-term treatment of personality disorders (C).

Somatic complaints

Cognitive-behaviour therapy should be considered as a psychological treatment for chronic fatigue and chronic pain (B).
Psychological intervention should be considered for other somatic complaints with a psychological component, such as irritable bowel syndrome and gynaecological complaints (pre-menstrual syndrome, pelvic pain) (C).

Contraindications

Routine debriefing shortly after a traumatic event is unlikely to help prevent post-traumatic stress disorder and is not recommended (A).
Generic counselling is not recommended as the main intervention for severe and complex mental health problems or personality disorders (D).
For some patients counselling could be helpful in a supportive or adjunctive capacity, as part of a care programme, and this view was supported by service users.

Source: abbreviated from Department of Health, 2001. Reproduced under the terms of the Click-Use Licence.

The recommendations presented in *Treatment Choice in Psychological Therapies and Counselling* (Department of Health, 2001) are based on all available evidence, though experimental methodology (RCTs) has a bigger weight. This approach appears to be quite balanced and was accepted by all stakeholders in the UK. Another important contribution is the multi-step analytical approach used in reviewing the research evidence. An original aspect is the involvement of representatives of users' groups.

Since 1999 the National Health Service in the United Kingdom has used the services of the National Institute for Health and Clinical Excellence (NICE) for the development of guidelines on best clinical practice and best health care in general. NICE is an independent organization responsible for providing national guidance on the promotion of good health and on prevention and treatment of ill health. From the perspective of psychotherapy and counselling what is most important is NICE's involvement in the development of the best clinical practices based on the best available evidence. For that purpose NICE has established several National Collaborating Centres (NCCs) that are responsible for the development of clinical guidelines. One of the NCCs focuses on mental health and one on primary care. Both have now produced clinical guidelines on several mental health disorders (e.g. depression, anxiety).

The situation with regard to 'empirically informed psychotherapy' is somewhat different in Germany. Dietmar Schulte and Kurt Hahlweg (2000) presented in an American journal the German legislation on psychotherapy in the health system. Since the start of 2000, a new law on psychotherapy has been effective. This law introduced the professions of medical psychotherapist, psychological psychotherapist, and child and adolescent psychotherapist. The law also recognized certain forms of psychotherapy as scientifically valid, namely psychoanalysis, psychodynamic therapy and behavioural therapy. Schulte and Hahlweg state that it is not clear how these therapies were picked. Their explanation is that it was the result of the influence of medical psychotherapists, who are predominantly psychodynamically oriented and who used their influence when the law was being prepared.

The therapies that were not automatically recognized by the law could be recognized as scientifically valid if the newly formed Scientific Advisory Board (Wissenschaftlicher Beirat für Psychotherapie) recognized them as such. The Board assesses 12 psychopathological disorders in areas where psychotherapy is applicable: mood disorders, anxiety disorders, PTSD and acute stress disorders, somatoform and dissociative disorders, eating disorders, sexual dysfunction and sleep disorders, psychological symptoms affecting medical conditions, personality disorders, substance-related disorders, schizophrenia and delusional disorders, mental retardation, and neuropsychological disorders. The criterion for recognition of a therapy as scientifically valid for a specific disorder is the existence of three independent studies showing the efficacy of the therapy for the specific psychopathological area. For a therapeutic approach to be recognized as scientific in general, the approach must be efficacious in at least five of above-mentioned 12 types of disorders, or in at least four of the first eight listed. This criterion was fulfilled in September 2002 by person-centred therapy (which is indicated for mood disorders, anxiety disorders, PTSD, and psychological symptoms affecting medical conditions). Person-centred therapy, though recognized as scientific, still struggles to be recognized and covered by insurance companies and will not be considered a suitable method for the training of future psychotherapists until at least one more area of disorders proves to be treatable by this therapy. All other approaches are not considered scientifically validated.

6

Dose–Effect Research

A specific area of outcome research is research that looks at the relationship between length of therapy and therapy outcome. This type of research follows the pattern of pharmaceutical trials searching for an optimal dosage of treatment. In the context of psychological therapy, it means studying the relationship between the number of therapy sessions and the achieved outcome. We will have a look at the state of this type of research by considering the cornerstone studies.

'Dose–effect' research was started by Howard, Kopta, Krause and Orlinsky (1986). These authors contributed to a special issue of the journal *American Psychologist* devoted to the future of psychotherapy research with a study in which they explored what number of patients improved in relation to the number of therapy sessions they underwent. Howard and colleagues used various procedures for establishing the relationship between the number of sessions and symptomatic improvement of these patients. For example, they used the Therapy Session Report method for assessing the session-to-session emotional well-being of around 148 patients over 2,400 sessions. Similarly, they used the data from other research, where the researchers rated the improvement of observed patients in different lengths of therapy. Using probit analysis, they estimated the course of patients' improvement in relation to number of therapy sessions. Furthermore, Howard et al. (1986) separately examined the numbers of sessions needed for *improvement* of depressed, anxious and borderline-psychotic patients, and showed that borderline patients were less responsive to treatment. Howard and colleagues (1986) also analysed findings from another 15 studies, in which psychotherapy was used for a different number of sessions. Again they found that the length of therapy impacts its outcome.

Howard et al.'s study was the first of a series of similar studies. One of the first of these was a work by Howard, Lueger, Maling and Martinovich (1993), who focused on the verification of the phase model of psychotherapy. This model suggested that there were three phases in patients' improvement over the course of psychotherapy (Howard et al., 1993). The model was based on the observation from the previous study (Howard et al.,

1986) that different clusters of symptoms responded within a different timeframe. The model suggested that in the first phase of therapy, called *remoralization*, the patient's improvement is observable in his or her subjective well-being. In the second phase, called *remediation*, a reduction in symptoms and life problems appears. The third phase is a phase of *rehabilitation* characterized by an improvement in longstanding problematic patterns. In the rehabilitation phase the patient's personality may be addressed, as well as the maintenance of therapeutic gains and the prevention of relapse.

To assess this model Howard et al. (1993) used three instruments measuring outcome of therapy in the areas of subjective well-being, symptomatic distress, and life functioning (each measuring the construct corresponding to the different phase of therapy). The instruments were used after the second, fourth and seventeenth session of therapy of more than 400 patients in psychodynamic therapy. The authors found that the phase model of psychotherapy they postulated corresponded with their findings. The greatest change after the second session was achieved in patients' well-being, and this degree of change was approximated after the seventeenth session by the change in severity of symptoms, whereas the change in global life functioning was smaller after the seventeenth session. Howard and his colleagues also brought evidence that in general the improvement in well-being preceded a reduction in symptoms, and the reduction in symptoms preceded changes in global functioning.

An important contribution to the dose–effect research, and a good example of it, is the study of Kopta, Howard, Lowry and Beutler (1994) that looked at patterns of symptomatic recovery in psychotherapy. The authors investigated patients' (n = 854; mostly anxiety and mood disorders) responsiveness to predominantly psychodynamic therapies. The responsiveness was assessed by looking at changes in 64 symptoms from the SCL–90 in relation to the number of sessions the patients underwent.

Based on the difference in patients' responsiveness to treatment of different symptoms, Kopta et al. (1994) differentiated acute distress symptoms (e.g. feeling fearful, crying easily, hopelessness about the future, etc.), chronic distress symptoms (e.g. lonely around people, feelings easily hurt, etc.) and characterological symptoms (e.g. people can't be trusted, feeling watched, etc.). The authors examined how many sessions were needed for 50% of patients to achieve clinically significant change (they had to pass the cut-off score) for each group of symptoms. Findings showed that for acute symptoms it was five sessions, for chronic it was 14 and for characterological symptoms it was more than 104 sessions on average. The authors also made an estimate of the temporal course of clinically significant recovery during therapy (see Figure 6.1).

Furthermore, Kopta et al. (1994) selected the symptoms that were the most prevalent in their patient sample. These symptoms had to be present in at least 50% of patients and had to be acute or chronic, because, according to the authors, patients with these symptoms are the most representative of people seeking therapy and are also the group most likely to be amenable to psychotherapy. Kopta and colleagues (1994) then examined how many sessions were necessary for clinically significant recovery of 50% and 75% of patients. For clinically significant recovery of 50% of patients with the most common symptoms, 11 sessions were needed; for recovery of 75% of patients, 58 sessions were necessary.

Figure 6.1 Estimate of clinically significant improvement (recovery) for individual groups of symptoms (patients mostly with affective and anxiety disorders)

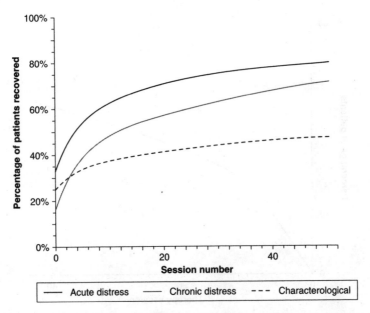

Source: S.M. Kopta et al., 'Patterns of symptomatic recovery in psychotherapy', *Journal of Consulting and Clinical Psychology*, 62(5), 1009–1016, 1994. Published by American Psychological Association, reprinted with permisson.

Another important step in the dose–effect research was the study of Howard, Moras, Brill, Martinovich and Lutz (1996) that represented *patient-focused research*. In this study Howard and his colleagues continued research on the phase model of psychotherapy. They used the Mental Health Index (MHI), consisting of three scales (Subjective Well-Being, Current Symptoms, Current Life Functioning) corresponding with domains differentially sensitive to change as it occurs in time, as the criterion of an overall outcome. On the basis of data taken from more than 6,500 patients, taking into account 18 patients' clinical characteristics at the start of therapy (e.g. severity of problems, chronicity of problems, attitudes towards treatment), they created, through the use of hierarchical linear modelling, a *profile of successful or unsuccessful session-by-session progress for the clients with particular clinical characteristics*. The profile that was prepared in this way offered an outline of the optimally expected course of improvement for a particular patient with a clear indication of when progress is not sufficient or not occurring at all.

Patient-focused research was further developed by Michael Lambert and his collaborators (Lambert, Hansen & Finch, 2001). For measuring the dose–effect relationship, Lambert and his colleagues used the Outcome Questionnaire–45 (OQ–45; see Chapter 1), which measures three domains sensitive to change: symptom distress, interpersonal problems and social role performance. The advantage of Lambert Hansen and Finch's

Figure 6.2 Clinically significant recovery in time based on a sample of approximately 6,000 patients, who completed psychotherapy (results regardless of diagnosis; mostly patients with affective, adjustment and anxiety disorders)

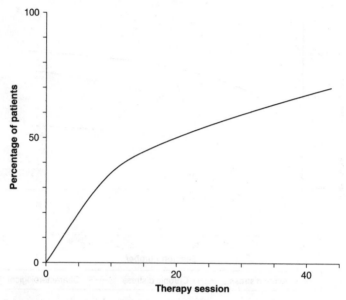

Source: M. J. Lambert et al., 'Patient-focused research: using patient outcome data to enhance treatment effects', *Journal of Consulting and Clinical Psychology*, 69(2), 159–172, 2001. Published by American Psychological Association, reprinted with permission.

method, in comparison to the work of Howard et al. (1996) was the fact that they administered the data from the OQ–45 *in every session*. The dose–effect estimate in their study was, therefore, based on more comprehensive and precise data on how patients progress in the course of psychotherapy.

Lambert, Hansen and Finch (2001) used survival analysis that is based on the events of clinically significant improvement or recovery in therapy. They collected data from more than 6,000 patients (mostly from patients with anxiety and affective disorders, and adjustment disorders as well) in the United States (the therapy provided was mostly eclectic, with a slight trend towards CBT methods). Two indexes were monitored: Reliable Change Index and clinical significance measured as recommended by Jacobson and Truax (1991; see Chapter 1). One of the findings was that in order to have 50% of patients reaching the range of the normal population (i.e. meeting the criterion of clinically significant change), 21 sessions were needed. To increase that to 75% of patients, 45 sessions were needed. To achieve a reliable change (i.e. clinically meaningful improvement, but not recovery) by 50% of patients, seven sessions were needed, and 14 sessions were needed for 75% to improve. The expected curves of improvement for clinically significant change and reliable change are presented in Figures 6.2 and 6.3. It is important to note, however, that the study excluded dropouts and unsuccessfully finished cases.

Figure 6.3 Reliable change (improvement) in time based on a sample of approximately 6,000 patients, who completed psychotherapy (results regardless of diagnosis; mostly patients with affective, adjustment and anxiety disorders)

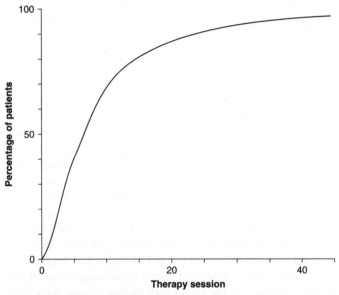

Source: M. J. Lambert et al., 'Patient-focused research: using patient outcome data to enhance treatment effects', *Journal of Consulting and Clinical Psychology*, 69(2), 159–172, 2001. Published by American Psychological Association, reprinted with permission.

After adding another 6,000 patients, Lambert, Hansen and Finch (2001) conducted a further part of their research, in which they used hierarchical linear modelling to create the expected recovery curves of patients in relation to the number of completed sessions. The hierarchical linear modelling took into account two criteria: initial level of distress on intake and early response to treatment (early response means that the patient improves very quickly, i.e. within the first three sessions). They used the intake score of the OQ–45 as a measure of level of distress and the score after a few initial sessions as a measure of early response to treatment. On the basis of these data, Lambert and his colleagues created 50 expected recovery curves for different cohorts of patients, with a cohort defined by similarity in intake score. For each curve, they also outlined the borders of when the therapy could be considered as unsuccessful or progressing slowly (for that they used cases from the 68th and 80th percentiles of their data set).

Outlining the course of successful treatment was followed by research examining the impact of feedback about an individual client's progress provided to the therapist (i.e. feedback with information on whether the session-by-session improvement of an individual client represents more successful or unsuccessful cases) (Lambert, Hansen & Finch, 2001; Lambert, Whipple et al., 2001). The feedback to therapists was provided in messages in the form of colour codes. There were four different colour coded messages: white – client is functioning in the normal range; green – client is progressing in the adequate range; yellow – the rate of change the client is making is less than adequate; red – client is not progressing at the expected level. For all coloured codes there were corresponding feedback messages: white meant that the therapist should have considered termination as treatment was progressing extremely well; yellow meant that the therapist should have considered altering the treatment plan, e.g. by intensifying the treatment; red meant that the therapist should have considered carefully reviewing the case and changing the treatment.

Six hundred and seven patients were randomly assigned to two groups: one group where feedback was provided to the therapist (experimental group) and another group without feedback (control group); 34 patients in the experimental and 31 patients in the control group were considered 'signal' cases (red- and yellow-coded patients, who did not make the expected progress and so were 'not on track'). In the experimental group with feedback, 26% of the 'signal' patients achieved clinically significant or reliable change in comparison to 16% of the 'signal' in the control group. Additionally, in the experimental group with feedback only 6% of the 'signal' patients deteriorated, whereas in the control group the number was 23%. The therapists in the experimental group provided a significantly higher number of sessions to clients who were not 'on track' and a significantly lower number of sessions to 'white' feedback clients, i.e. clients already in the functional state.

Whipple, and colleagues (2003) continued and extended the research of Lambert, Hansen and Finch (2001). In their study, 981 clients from a large university counselling centre were randomly assigned to the group with feedback about their progress (n = 499) and to the group without feedback (n = 482). The therapists were 48 counselling centre staff with various theoretical orientations. Feedback was provided in the same manner as in the study of Lambert, Hansen and Finch (2001). Clients were assigned to therapists so that each therapist had the same number of clients with and without feedback. Additionally, therapists could decide if they wanted to use clinical support tools that could help them address problems in therapy and that were based on empirical findings. The clinical support tools consisted of several steps focusing on assessment of domains such as social support therapeutic alliance, readiness to change and corresponding interventions. The findings showed that the patients who did not progress at the expected level (patients 'not on track') achieved better outcome if their therapists received feedback. Additionally, the best outcome was achieved by the patients of the therapists who utilizied the clinical support tools (see Table 6.1).

The authors also compared the success rate of the therapists who used the clinical support tools at least once with that of the other therapists, showing that the former were no more successful on average. Thus Whipple et al. (2003) excluded the explanation that the therapists using clinical support tools would also be more effective if they did not use them. The authors also found that the therapists who used the clinical support tools had more sessions with the 'not on track' patients. This may also explain their higher effectiveness.

'Dose–effect' research is attempting to answer the extremely important question asked by practitioners and relevant stakeholders of how much therapy is enough therapy. The studies by Lambert, Hansen and Finch presented here, and similar studies that are

Table 6.1 Outcomes of 'not on track' clients from Whipple et al.'s study

Outcome classification	Clients not on track whose therapists received feedback and used the clinical support tools	Clients not on track whose therapists received feedback and did not use the clinical support tools	Clients not on track whose therapists did not receive feedback
Deteriorated	8.5%	13.6%	19.1%
No change	42.4%	53.4%	55.7%
Reliable or clinically significant change	49.1%	33.0%	25.2%

Source: J. L. Whipple et al., 'Improving the effects of psychotherapy: the use of early identification of treatment failure and problem-solving strategies in routine practice', *Journal of Counseling Psychology*, 50, 59–68, 2003. Published by American Psychological Association, adapted with permission.

present in the current literature (Harmon et al., 2007), seem to be very relevant to improving outcomes in routine practice. 'Dose–effect' research and especially its 'feedback' stream will probably impact the field in the near future. Studies like those of Lambert and his colleagues can also be readily applied in the therapeutic practice of an individual therapist, as was shown by Asay, Lambert, Gregerson and Goatess (2002). In their study, the authors created expected recovery curves based on the outcome of patients treated by one therapist in one year. These then formed a basis for tracking new clients coming to see the same therapist, so that the therapist could assess whether a particular new client was on track, taking his or her previous patients as a reference point.

Dose–effect research provides valuable information about the length therapy should be to achieve the desired outcome. In the context of previously mentioned cost-effectiveness issues of psychological therapies, and also in connection with the 'empirically supported therapies' movement, this kind of research offers a different perspective in addressing empirically informed delivery of therapy. It may be an important source of information when planning the length of psychotherapy services that should be provided to potential clients so that the chances of the therapy 'dosage' being meaningful are increased.

However, one must not forget that a specific population of clients and the specific instrument used for assessing the dose–effect may influence the results significantly. Also, in practice 'a good enough level' approach may be applied, meaning that the clients leave the service (therapy) when they achieve a sufficient change (see Barkham, Connell et al., 2006). As Barkham, Connell et al. (2006) showed, if the outcome is assessed *only at the planned end of the treatment*, the dose–effect curve does not apply (the percentage of recovered clients may be the same regardless of the number of sessions they had). They observed that when therapy in routine practice was ended as planned by the therapist and the client, the likelihood that the client would be considered as recovered was approximately the same regardless of length of treatment. This can be explained by the fact that the therapist and the client adjust the needed dose to the state of the client.

7

Client and Therapist Characteristics and the Effect of Psychotherapy

The outcome of psychotherapy is often studied in the context of variables, predictors, moderators, or mediators, affecting it. The most obvious variables to study are client and therapist characteristics and their relationship to the outcome of therapy. This type of research is often done through *post hoc* analysis of the data from RCTs. However, some studies, mostly correlational, specifically look at client and therapist variables influencing the outcome of therapy.

Client and therapist variables studied for their influence on the outcome of psychotherapy are relatively stable characteristics present in the client and therapist prior to entering therapy. It is important to clarify this definition as characteristics that manifest themselves during the process of psychotherapy (e.g. the client's level of self-exploration) are measured on the basis of client or therapist behaviour, and will be addressed in the chapters dedicated to psychotherapy process research. This chapter will focus on research concerning predictors of psychotherapy outcome that are visible (measurable) independently of behaviour during the psychotherapy process. This classification is mainly didactic since behaviour during psychotherapy to a large extent correlates with the participant's characteristics prior to therapy. Despite this, such a classification is useful since it often requires an alternative research strategy.

Client Variables and Therapy Outcome

Client characteristics measured prior to therapy show little and often contradictory relationships to therapy outcome (Garfield, 1994). This is often caused by many confounding variables that influence therapy outcome. For example, if we want to study the influence of the client's socioeconomic characteristics on the success of therapy, it is very difficult to control for other variables, such as personality or the severity of psychological problems.

As already mentioned, confounding variables are particularly problematic because studies looking at the relationship of client characteristics and therapy outcome often use data from major projects which primarily look at the effect of psychotherapy, while the question of which patient groups benefited more comes later. Therefore, specific client characteristics that need to be assessed are not experimentally controlled for prior to the therapy.

Despite these methodological difficulties, research on the relationship between client characteristics and the outcome of therapy has a rich tradition. Sol Garfield (1994) provides an excellent overview of findings on this subject until 1994. For example, he demonstrates that age and gender do not have a significant influence on the outcome of therapy. When it comes to personality traits, the available literature points to the advantages of characteristics such as higher IQ, low rigidity, and a wide spectrum of interests. As Garfield suggests, despite interesting exceptions, the severity and range of initial problems (most often co-morbidly present personality disorder; see also Clarkin & Levy, 2004) in most cases predict a smaller effect of psychotherapy. Another predictor according to Garfield appears to be the psychodynamic concept of ego strength, as well as whether the therapist finds the patient likeable, etc. In a review linked to Garfield's work, Clarkin and Levy (2004) also highlight predictors such as the level of readiness for change, the psychological mindedness and so on.

Another important area of research establishing links between client characteristics and outcome are studies looking at rates of clients who drop out from therapy. Reis and Brown (1999) report a range of 30% to 60% of patients dropping out. This field of research, just like the broader field of research related to client and therapist characteristics and the effects of psychotherapy, suggests that meaningful predictors can be found in process characteristics, i.e. those that manifest themselves during the therapy, rather than in static characteristics that can be identified prior to the beginning of therapy. As far as variables measured prior to the initiation of therapy are concerned, consistent predictors of premature termination appear to be the client's socioeconomic status and ethnicity (studies were conducted mainly in the USA; Reis & Brown, 1999).

Also related to the outcome of therapy and therapy dropout rates are the client's preferences and expectations in relation to psychotherapy. The relationship between the client's expectations regarding the effectiveness of the therapy he or she is about to undergo and the actual outcome has some predictive power (Arnkoff, Glass & Shapiro, 2002). Similar levels of predictive power can be associated with role expectations, i.e. whether clients correctly anticipate what is expected of them during therapy. Somewhat less explored are preferences for specific types of psychotherapy, which do not appear to be powerful predictors (for more on the client's expectations and preferences and the effect of therapy, see Arnkoff, Glass & Shapiro, 2002).

A good example of research on client variables influencing the outcome of therapy is a work by Blatt, Quinlan, Pilkonis and Shea (1995), which tested the differential prognosis of two different types of depression: one based on the need for approval by others (anaclitic/dependent), the other related to self-criticism (introjective/self-critical). Blatt et al. analysed data from the National Institute of Mental Health Treatment of Depression Collaborative Research Program (NIMH TDCRP), which we discussed in detail in Chapter 2, which studied the effectiveness of drugs combined with clinical management (imipramine, IMI–CM), CBT, interpersonal therapy (IPT), and a drug placebo combined with clinical management (PLA–CM) in the treatment of depression. The tool used for evaluation of types of depression was the Dysfunctional Attitudes Scale (DAS). Factor analysis of this scale repeatedly found that it contained two dimensions: 'need for approval' and 'perfectionism'. The scale was used not only during the initial examination but also for monthly patient evaluations (during treatment).

The authors studied the relationship between DAS scores and the effect of therapy as measured by the Beck Depression Inventory (BDI), Hamilton Rating Scale for Depression (HRSD), Global Assessment Scale (GAS), SCL–90 and the Social Adjustment Scale (SAS) (see Chapter 1). The authors used data from between 143 and 154 patients (the data for individual methods were collected from different numbers of patients, due to missing data). Blatt et al. (1995) carried out several analyses. The first was an analysis of covariance of DAS and the results of individual outcome scales administered at the end of therapy. 'Perfectionism' proved to have a negative relationship with the treatment outcome on all of the outcome instruments. Furthermore, the homogeneity of covariance of the DAS scores and the therapy outcome in all four treatment conditions showed that this effect held across all treatment groups (imipramine, placebo, CBT and interpersonal psychotherapy).

The dimension 'need for approval' showed a null or opposite (positive), although statistically insignificant, correlation with the therapy outcome. Blatt, Quinlan, Pilkonis and Shea (1995) thus convincingly demonstrated that the prognosis of patients with high levels of perfectionism being treated for depression is far from optimistic. As will be shown in Chapter 10, such findings can initiate further research into how perfectionism impacts on the process of psychotherapy; in other words, why highly perfectionist patients do not benefit from psychotherapy.

Blatt et al.'s (1995) study represents an example of studying how a client's pre-treatment characteristics relate to the therapy outcome. This type of study is not a typical example of a client variable-outcome study as it examines psychological theory (perfectionism and its persistence) rather than sociodemographic characteristics, which is more typical of this kind of research. In any case, it does represent an example that can interestingly inform therapeutic practice.

Therapist Variables and Therapy Outcome

Beutler, Machado and Allstetter-Neufeldt (1994) emphasize the importance of therapist variables and their influence on therapy outcome. According to the authors, the reasons why studying therapist variables is of great importance are because research had consistently proven that:

(1) The nature of the therapy outcome correlates more with the therapist than with the type of psychotherapy she or he adheres to.
(2) Some therapists consistently produce stronger effects regardless of the therapeutic approach employed.
(3) Some therapists consistently produce negative outcomes.

Beutler, Machado and Allstetter- Neufeldt (1994) and Beutler, Malik et al. (2004) offer exhaustive overviews of cumulative findings on the effectiveness of psychotherapy in relation to variables on the side of the therapist (again, I am referring to characteristics observed prior to therapy). For example, Beutler, Malik et al. (2004) found the therapist's professional experience (how long he or she has been practising therapy) to be a more promising predictor than specific training, or in other words training in a specific procedure. Similarly, they claim that less controlling and less dominant therapists appear to be more effective, and that the therapist's emotional stability proves a relevant variable. Again, however, the therapist's behaviour during the psychotherapy process is a stronger predictor of its effect than therapist characteristics measured prior to therapy.

An important argument for studying therapist variables comes from the fact that therapists differ in their effectiveness (see above Beutler, Machado & Allstetter-Neufeldt, 1994). Several studies looked specifically at this problem. Of particular interest are early studies carried out by Lester Luborsky and his colleagues. Luborsky, McLellan, Woody et al. (1985) studied the effectiveness of different therapists using data from a study comparing the effectiveness of different therapies in the treatment of methadone patients. The study analysed data from previous research (Woody, et al., 1983), which found that adding six months of supportive-expressive psychotherapy (SE) and cognitive-behavioural therapy (CBT) to standard drug counselling (DC) resulted in an improvement when compared with using drug counselling on its own (measurement tools included: Addiction Severity Index: BDI, SCL–90, Maudsley Personality Inventory).

For each form of therapy, Luborsky, McLellan, Woody, et al. (1985) chose the three therapists with the most patients (from 7 to 11). As expected, they found differences in the success rates of therapists, which could not be explained by the differences in patients' problems. The differences were measured both individually for each measurement tool, as well as on the basis of the average effect size (post-therapy vs. pre-therapy condition) across all the measurement tools. For example, the most successful psychoanalytic therapist (see Table 7.1) had an average effect size of 0.74, while the least successful had an effect size of 0.19 (for these two therapists, for example, the sum of BDI scores for the most successful therapist would drop by 58%, while there would only be an 8% decrease for the least successful therapist).

Luborsky, McLellan, Woody et al. (1985) used several approaches to establish how differences between therapists might be explained. For example, they looked at the evaluation of the therapists' characteristics by their colleagues. They found that three of the chosen characteristics – interest in helping the patient, psychological health and psychological skills – were moderate predictors of the therapist's success. Process aspects (therapeutic alliance and compliance with the therapeutic manual), which we will introduce in Chapter 8, turned out to be stronger predictors.

Luborsky, Crits-Christoph et al. (1986) then conducted three more studies examining differences in the effectiveness of therapists. In all three studies, they found differences in the effectiveness of different therapists, which in general were greater than between different therapies; and all the therapists also observed large differences in the results of their own patients. Similarly, Luborsky, McLellan, Diguer et al. (1997) studied the success rates of 22 therapists from seven different research projects looking at the treatment of depression and

Table 7.1 Differences among the average effect sizes of individual therapists treating patients on methadone using either supportive-expressive therapy (SE), cognitive-behavioural therapy (CBT), or drug counselling (DC). The measure is averaged across all the measurement tools: Addiction Severity Index, BDI, SCL–90, Maudsley Personality Inventory

Therapists	Average effect size
A (SE)	0.74
B (SE)	0.59
C (SE)	0.19
D (CBT)	0.53
E (CBT)	0.44
F (CBT)	0.44
G (DC)	0.20
H (DC)	0.13
I (DC)	0.27

Source: adapted with permission from Luborsky, McLellan, Woody et al., 1985.

addictions, and again confirmed that the effectiveness of these therapists varied greatly. Furthermore, three of the 22 therapists participated in two or three of the seven projects, being similarly effective in each one of them. Two of the therapists were particularly effective in all of the projects in which they were involved. Luborsky, McLellan, Diguer et al. (1997) concluded that the therapist's personality is important; that the therapist's effectiveness plays an important role in research on the effectiveness of psychotherapy; and that it is important to identify the factors behind the therapist's success.

Another example of research looking at the differential effect of therapists is a study by Blatt, Sanislow, Zuroff and Pilkonis (1996), who analysed the effectiveness of individual therapists involved in the National Institute of Mental Health Treatment of Depression Collaborative Research Program (NIMH TDCRP) mentioned earlier. This project studied the effectiveness of cognitive-behavioural therapy, interpersonal therapy (IPT) and pharmacotherapy involving imipramine combined with clinical management (IMI–CM), and involved 28 carefully trained and selected psychiatrists or psychologists with an average of 11 years' experience. Of these, 10 provided interpersonal psychotherapy, 10 pharmacotherapy, and eight CBT. The original project collected a number of data related to the 28 therapists, including demographic indicators, level of experience in treating depression, the proportion of psychotherapy, medication and their combination used in the therapist's everyday practice, and the types of treatment the therapists had used in the past when treating depression. The therapists used a seven-point scale to rate the probable aetiology of depression (biological, environmental, interpersonal or psychological). They also had to estimate the proportion of severely depressed patients from their practice who showed at least moderate improvement. They were also asked how many seriously depressed patients they expected to show at least moderate improvement with and without treatment. They were also asked at what stage in the treatment one could expect change and what length of time was needed for the treatment of a severely depressed patient.

Using factor analysis of five outcome measures used for the assessment of the effectiveness of treatment, Blatt et al. (1996) first demonstrated that the results from each of the instruments were closely related (they related to the same factor). They then used an aggregate of residualized therapeutic change score of the five outcome measures to divide the therapists into three groups according to the effectiveness of their treatment. All three treatment groups (CBT, interpersonal therapy and pharmacotherapy) contained successful, moderately successful and less successful therapists. Though successful therapists' outcomes did not differ statistically from moderately effective therapists and moderately effective therapists did not differ from less effective therapists, the therapists at the extreme ends (successful vs. less successful) differed statistically.

The three groups were different in several ways. Less successful therapists had fewer patients who completed their treatment. More successful therapists had less variance in their patients' results. The group with the most successful therapists had more psychologists than psychiatrists. The more successful therapists claimed to have rarely used pharmacotherapy in their practice, preferring a psychological treatment. The successful therapists also expected change to come at a later stage and the treatment of depression to require longer time periods.

The same data were later analysed by Elkin, Falconnier, Martinovich and Mahoney (2006a) who, using hierarchical linear modelling, looked not only at the effects of therapists in the TDCRP study, but also at differential effects of therapists depending on initial patient severity (across the main outcome measures) and difficulty (measured by Personality Assessment Form, Interpersonal Style Inventory, perfectionism factor of Dysfunctional Attitudes Scale and patient expectations about therapy). Elkin did not find differential effects of therapists either on their own or when severity or difficulty of patient was taken into consideration. Elkin et al., however, state that there were a few outliers: one therapist performed exceptionally poorly (one in four of his patients stayed in treatment and no patient recovered) and two exceptionally well (more than 80% of their patients stayed in treatment and more than 60% recovered).

In contrast to Elkin et al.'s (2006a) study, Kim, Wampold and Bolt (2006), who analysed the same data set, again using hierarchical linear modelling, came to a different conclusion, finding differential effects among therapists. The extent of difference they found depended on the analysis they performed, but on average about 8% of variance in the outcome could be explained by therapist, and therapists were found to be differentially effective when treating more severe patients. It must be noted that the models used in the analyses of Kim, Wampold and Bolt and Elkin et al. differed, and not all outcome measures were included in both studies. The differences provoked quite a controversy and were discussed by authors as well as other researchers (e.g. Crits-Christoph & Gallop, 2006; Elkin, Falconnier et al., 2006b; Wampold & Bolt, 2006).

Studies of therapists' effectiveness can also be carried out in routine practice. For example Wampold and Brown (2005) studied outcome variance attributable to differential effects of therapists in a sample of 6,146 patients treated by 581 therapists. A version of the Outcome Questionnaire–45 served as an outcome tool. Wampold and Brown found that around 5% of variance in the outcome could be explained solely by the therapists' effects.

An interesting study in routine practice using elements of dose–effect research was conducted by Okiishi, Lambert, Nielsen and Ogles (2003). The authors investigated differential effects of 56 therapists who saw 1,779 clients in a university counselling

Figure 7.1   Differential effects of the three most effective and three least effective therapists in Okiishi et al.'s study

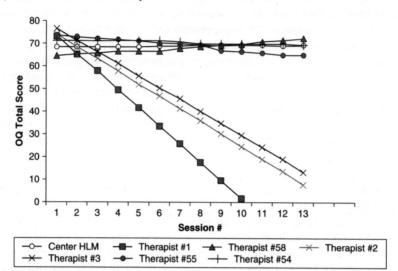

Note: The cut-off score for the Outcome Questionnaire–45 is 66. The change was assessed before each session. The decreasing score from session to session indicates improvement. The outcomes of the best three therapists improved in average dramatically, while those of the three least effective therapists did not show any improvement in averbage.

Source: J. Okiishi et al., 'Waiting for Supershrink: an empirical analysis of therapist effects', *Clinical Psychology and Psychotherapy* © 2003 John Wiley & Sons Limited. Reproduced with permission.

centre. The clients presented predominantly with mood disorders, anxiety disorders and adjustment disorders. The outcome instrument was used before each session. Okiishi et al. found significant differences between the therapists that could not be explained by the four therapist variables that were measured (experience, gender, training and orientation). The findings are poignantly illustrated on the comparison between the best three therapists and the least effective therapists (see Figure 7.1).

Though the topic of therapist effects is quite controversial (see Elkin et al., 2006b and Wampold & Bolt, 2006), the studies presented above show that at least in some studies clear differences are found, especially at the extremes of the most and least effective therapists. Not much is known yet about the characteristics of those most and least effective therapists though some studies are trying to approach this problem by studying 'master therapists' (see Chapter 13).

Aptitude-treatment Interaction and Client Characteristics

A highly popular form of current research on client and therapist variables and their influence on the effect of psychotherapy is research using the aptitude-treatment interaction design (ATI) (Snow, 1991). Typically, this research looks at the suitability of specific forms of psychotherapy, or specific therapeutic interventions, for a particular client-type. In some cases it also looks at the interaction of patient and therapist characteristics. For example, it is possible to look at whether patients with an internal locus of control react differently to directive and non-directive forms of therapy, as well as whether patients with an external locus of control react to these forms of therapy in the opposite manner (for a similar study see Beutler, Engle et al., 1991, below). Similarly, it is possible to study whether patients react differently to treatment, based on whether they are allocated a therapist with dominant or submissive behaviour.

Snow (1991) examines how to research the appropriateness of a specific type of psychotherapy in relation to the client's characteristics. He presents several approaches to ATI research. These approaches usually employ various forms of regression analysis, to accurately describe the relationship between continuous variables, of which one is dependent (therapy effect), and the other a mediating or moderating variable (a client characteristic which interferes with the therapy effect). While encouraging other ways of 'inspecting data', Snow nevertheless favours detailed examination (e.g. graphical analysis), and not the experimental testing of clients divided into various groups. While the creation of extreme groups according to a given characteristic representing two ends of a continuum can yield a statistical difference, it does not reveal the predictive value of the given characteristic in relation to the therapy effect. Such an approach would only provide very 'rough' data. Furthermore, as is demonstrated by ATI research in educational psychology (Snow, 1991), interaction of client characteristics and psychological intervention is not necessarily linear.

Snow (1991) introduces four types of research design used in ATI research. *Standard design*, which compares the regression lines of the relationship between the therapy outcome and relevant client characteristic, in the chosen therapeutic treatments. *Treatment revision design*, which, on the basis of the correlation of a given characteristic with the treatment effect, adapts the treatment procedure until it becomes effective for clients for whom it was previously ineffective. *Aptitude growth design* is used when the chosen characteristic is also the treatment target. For example, when perfectionism is the observed variable and the goal of the treatment is to decrease perfectionism, it is possible to keep adapting the treatment procedure until the level of perfectionism is significantly decreased. *Regression discontinuity design* assumes that clients with a studied characteristic (variable) that explains their lower levels of treatment success are exposed to interventions that balance out their negative prognosis. Three of the research designs (excluding the standard one) employ a series of experiments, thereby fine-tuning the optimal treatment. However, in practice psychotherapeutic research usually relies on the standard research design.

ATI research, as Snow (1991) suggests, is very complex. Many variables with distinct effects can overlap and interact with each other, thereby increasing or neutralizing their effect. This is why Snow emphasizes that uncovering the effect of treatment interaction is a difficult task, and even when such an effect is uncovered, the therapist should only use it in an heuristic manner, as other variables with a local effect can in some cases prevent this effect from manifesting itself.

While ATI research is a hot topic (e.g. APA, 2006), so far this type of research has not yet become widespread. One variable which is proving sensitive to the type of therapy employed (directive/non-directive) is client resistance (Beutler, Moleiro & Talebi, 2002). Resistance-prone clients tend to benefit more from non-directive therapy. Similarly, internalizing clients tend to benefit more from insight-oriented therapy than externalizing clients, who benefit more from symptom-oriented treatments (Beutler, Harwood et al., 2002). Stiles, Shankland, Wright and Field (1997) also showed that the differential effectiveness of psychodynamic-interpersonal and cognitive-behavioural therapy depends on how well the client's problems are formulated. When the client had clearly formulated problems, CBT was more effective than a psychodynamic-interpersonal treatment, while both were equally effective when the client's problems were not well defined.

One example of aptitude-treatment interaction research is a study by Beutler, Engle et al. (1991), who compared the effectiveness of three different types of psychotherapy: group cognitive therapy, focused-expressive psychotherapy and supportive, self-directed therapy. The authors looked into the interaction of these types of treatment with the clients' coping style (externalization) and resistance potential (defensiveness) towards the treatment. The cognitive therapy was a derivate of Beck's cognitive therapy; focused-expressive psychotherapy was a Gestalt-based manualized therapy; and supportive, self-directed therapy used minimal treatment administered by non-experts (PhD students), comprising a 30-minute telephone conversation, supplemented by suggested reading of self-help literature.

Externalizing coping style was assessed by those items from the Minnesota Multiphasic Personality Inventory (MMPI) that were the best discriminators among the 76 patients randomly assigned to one of the three treatment conditions. Similarly, the level of resistance was measured by a host of relevant items from the MMPI. Each of the therapies was administered by two psychotherapists who were experts in the respective treatment type. The psychotherapy outcome was assessed by means of BDI, SCL–90 and the Hamilton Rating Scale for Depression (HRSD). As for the differential results, supportive self-directive therapy had the lowest dropout rate, as measured after the fourth session. Covariance analysis of the aptitude-treatment interaction showed that the externalizing coping style was the best predictor for cognitive therapy while a low externalizing coping style was the best predictor for supportive, self-directive psychotherapy. The effect of focused-expressive psychotherapy was relatively independent of the level of externalizing coping. Plots on the regression lines also revealed the critical value of the externalizing coping score, marking the boundary between scores of clients who should undergo cognitive, self-directed or focused-expressive therapy. Regarding the level of clients' resistance, HRSD results showed that for low-resistance patients, focused-expressive and cognitive therapies were better than supportive, self-directive therapy; high-resistance patients showed the opposite trend.

The largest project on aptitude-treatment interaction to date is the project MATCH (Matching Alcoholism Treatment to Client Heterogeneity; Babor & Del Boca, 2003), which tested the effectiveness of three different psychotherapies for alcohol addiction, as well as for the interaction of patient characteristics with the outcome of their treatment, for different treatment types. This mammoth project involved 1,726 patients and

81 therapists. The three therapies compared were: cognitive-behavioural therapy (CBT), motivational enhancement therapy (MET, a treatment based on motivational interviewing; for a more detailed description of this treatment see Chapter 14) and twelve-step facilitation (TSF; an individual form of treatment based on the 12-step model of Alcoholics Anonymous). Each patient received a 12-week therapy with 12 sessions in the CBT and TSF condition, and only four sessions in the MET condition (in the first, second, sixth and twelfth week of treatment). The patients were treated on an outpatient basis. While 952 were recruited via advertisements offering treatment, 774 came from residential centres where they had already been treated (the average length of inpatient or daily hospital treatment before the onset of psychotherapy was 20 days). Patients were divided into two study groups for the clinical trial: those who received outpatient therapy initiated within the MATCH project (outpatient group) and those who were recruited from residential programmes (aftercare group). Within these two groups, patients were randomly assigned to one of the three experimental conditions.

As the title of the MATCH project itself suggests, not only were the outcomes of therapy tested but also a number of hypotheses about the relationship between client variables (e.g. severity of alcohol-addiction symptoms) and the differential effectiveness of CBT, motivational enhancement therapy and the 12-step facilitation. Following an intense study of the relevant literature and empirical findings, the research team carefully selected 21 mutually exclusive, clearly conceptualized variables. Available empirical evidence for these variables implied that a certain level of these variables in clients should predict differential effectiveness for the three different types of treatment.

The process of hypothesis selection was also very diligent, based on reading through all the available evidence, followed by a thorough consideration of the relevance of each and every potential hypothesis by all the team members. Since in the 21 selected variables, differences were predicted in the effect of two or sometimes even all three therapies, the resulting number of hypotheses was 31, each of them individually tested (appropriate methodological steps were taken in order to avoid the danger of experimental error because of the large number of measurements). There were primary and secondary hypotheses, based on the strength of existing empirical evidence or theoretical assumptions.

The primary hypotheses are presented in Table 7.2, along with their respective assessment tools and predictions regarding which therapy will be more effective at high levels of the given variable. Although therapy effects were measured using several assessment tools, the primary indicators were monthly percentage of days abstinent (PDA) from alcohol and the number of drinks on a day when the client did consume alcohol (monthly drinks per drinking day). These were assessed by means of a Form 90, which combined a structured assessment interview and a self-assessment scale. Since these indicators were based on the client's self-assessment, their reliability was assessed by correlating the client's self-assessment with assessment by his or her significant others and the results of liver tests. Global self-assessment proved to be a reliable measure. Testing for aptitude-treatment interaction was done on the basis of a comparison of the slope of regression lines expressing the relationship of a given client variable and the outcome of therapy for each of the three therapies individually. If there was a significant difference

Table 7.2 Variables, measurement tools and supposed differential effectiveness of the three therapies (the higher a variable value, the more effective the treatment. More effective treatment is marked '>')

Variable	Assessment tool	Supposed differential efficacy
Alcohol involvement	Alcohol Use Inventory	(CBT, TSF) > MET
Cognitive impairment	Shipley Institute of Living Scale	TSF > CBT CBT > MET TSF > MET
Conceptual level	Paragraph Completion Method	MET > TSF
Gender	Self-report questionnaire	Females (difference of means of the CBT and TSF) > males (difference of means of CBT and TSF)
Meaning seeking	Purpose in Life Scale	TSF > (MET, CBT)
Motivation	Change Assessment Scale	CBT > MET
Psychiatric severity (severity of psychopathology)	Psychiatric Severity Subscale of the Addiction Severity Index	CBT > MET CBT > TSF
Sociopathy	Socialization subscale in the California Psychological Inventory	CBT > MET TSF > MET
Support for drinking (from the social milieu)	Interview about significant people and meaningful activities	CBT > MET TSF > MET
Typology ('typical' alcoholic personality)	Combination of several assessment tools	Type B (difference of means of CBT+TSF and MET) > Type A (difference of means of CBT+TSF and MET)

Source: adapted from Kadden, Longabaugh and Wirtz, 2003, reproduced with permission of Cambridge University Press.

in the slopes of the three respective lines, as predicted by the hypothesis, the hypothesis would be confirmed.

The outcome of the three therapies was measured on a weekly basis during the treatment and every month for up to three years following treatment termination. All three therapies reached the same level of effectiveness (even the four-session long motivational enhancement therapy!) and basically remained effective during three years of follow-up, though with a moderate downtrend in the total abstinence. Those patients who came to treatment from the residential treatment centres (aftercare group) were somewhat more successful. While having roughly 20% alcohol-free days a month before the treatment, these patients had almost 100% alcohol-free days after treatment. The patients with no prior residential treatment (the outpatient group) had approximately 30% alcohol-free days before the treatment and 90% after the treatment. The results of

ATI testing were highly surprising, as almost none of the differential effects of the three treatment types was confirmed. Only three of the 31 tested hypotheses in the outpatient group were confirmed; two of these three only partially.

The most stable effect was reached with the variable 'anger', where it was shown that motivational enhancement therapy (MET) was more effective for clients with high levels of anger than CBT and the 12-step facilitation therapy (TSF), and less effective for clients with low levels of anger. Moreover, it was shown (although only in the third year of follow-up) that the TSF was more effective than MET with the clients whose social milieu supported their drinking habits. Lastly, it was shown that in the first nine months following treatment, clients with lower levels of psychiatric pathology were more successful in the 12-step facilitation than in CBT. As for the aftercare group, only one of the 31 tested hypotheses was confirmed: namely, that for the clients with lower levels of addiction, CBT was more effective than TSF, and vice versa – TSF was more effective than CBT for the patients with higher levels of addiction.

The examples of aptitude-treatment interaction studies show the potential usefulness of this type of study. However, they also indicate the complexity of this type of research and the problem of the many confounding variables that may wipe out any existing effects. Furthermore, several variables may interact with the treatment at once, so it is a very complicated procedure to find clear linear (not to mention curvilinear) trends between a relevant variable and the outcome. Still, this type of research is forcing us to think beyond the 'one package serves all' delivery of psychological treatments.

Conclusion

I have reviewed experimental and non-experimental designs as well as types of psychotherapy research according to the problem being addressed. What conclusions can be drawn from this overview? What can be claimed about the current status of psychotherapy and counselling outcome research? What characteristics define this area of research? Here are some tentative suggestions.

1. Psychotherapy outcome research is expanding It might be safe to claim that the number of outcome studies is increasing. If one briefly inspects the contents of the *Journal of Consulting and Clinical Psychology*, the flagship journal of clinical psychology in North America, one can see a vast number of studies assessing different psychological interventions. This fact is quite interesting in light of the awareness that financial resources devoted to studying psychotherapy are small in comparison to the resources available to the pharmaceutical industry. However, this can probably be explained by the general training of psychologists, who are often the ones performing psychotherapy outcome research, in research methodology.

There were 475 studies included in Smith, Glass and Miller's (1980) first meta-analysis of psychotherapy. Though their analysis covered a very long period of time, studying psychotherapy outcome has become much more common since then. There are now several hundred psychotherapy outcome studies. Psychotherapy and counselling for problems that are not really central to psychotherapy are now also rigorously studied (e.g. psychotic disorders; Tarrier et al., 2000).

2. Psychotherapy outcome research is complex I assume that previous chapters have sufficiently demonstrated the breadth of questions that must be answered when studying the effectiveness of psychological therapies and counselling. It is not just the question of whether it works, but questions such as what areas of human functioning it affects, what the duration of the effect is, for what kinds of people does it work, how many sessions are needed to bring about an effect, how a form of treatment performs in routine practice, and so on.

3. Psychotherapy outcome research uses sophisticated methodology   To be an informed consumer of psychotherapy outcome studies is becoming more and more demanding due to the level of sophistication many studies require. The designs as well as statistical procedures are tailored to addressing validity threats and at the same time bringing answers to relevant questions. Though practice-oriented research is favoured in many current training programmes, it may be limited to some types of outcome design, such as qualitative studies, naturalistic studies or case studies. Some designs, namely randomized control trials, require a level of sophistication and expertise that can be achieved only by bigger research teams that collaborate closely with practitioner services.

4. Psychotherapy outcome research requires substantial resources   If we look at the issues involved in RCTs, we realize how demanding it is to conduct such a trial. For example, if we wanted to detect moderate effects among two active psychological treatments we would need at least 60 patients in each group (Shapiro, 1995), which would be an homogeneous group and would meet inclusion criteria. Since in RCTs it is usually one-third of the screened patients that meet such criteria (Westen & Morrisson, 2001) we would need to screen 360 patients. Then we would need a group of therapists who are well trained in a treatment procedure that is well described so that the quality of its delivery can be assessed. Then we would need to have researchers to collect the data several times during the treatment and even after the treatment finishes. The reality of these demands makes some of the research designs available only to well-established research teams who may already be involved in programmatic research that further develops treatment they have already studied. This fact may prevent studies that would look at approaches that are not sufficiently studied yet, or are new.

If consumers of psychotherapy outcome studies want to use the findings they are producing, they should also be capable of critically *assessing* the methodology they use. Recommendations contained in different types of guidelines usually provide simplified conclusions about the evidence for specific forms of therapy. Closer inspection of the original studies may bring to the fore limitations of the studies on which the claims reported in the guidelines are based. For example, the effectiveness of cognitive and interpersonal therapies for depression is often taken for granted. However, closer inspection of a study such as TDCRP (see Chapter 2) shows that the effectiveness of these therapies, though proven, is quite limited (see Elkin, Shea et al., 1989; Shea et al., 1992).

Another issue that consumers of outcome research should bear in mind is that there exist a large number of studies using different forms of methodology, with both advantages and disadvantages. Therefore, it is important to assess the research evidence in its totality. No single study can resolve the question of whether therapy for a specific psychological condition works in all circumstances.

PART II

PSYCHOTHERAPY AND COUNSELLING PROCESS RESEARCH

While psychotherapy outcome research attempts to answer the question of *whether* psychotherapy works, psychotherapy process research is trying to uncover *how* it works. It is not sufficient for us to understand that some therapeutic change occurred. We need to understand what mechanisms are responsible for that change. Understanding therapeutic mechanisms may lead to further adaptations and discoveries regarding therapeutic procedures. These discoveries and adaptations may then be tested in the outcome studies.

The advantage of process research is that it does not necessarily require sizeable resources, as many outcome designs do. Therefore, it may be easier to perform meaningful process studies even with quite limited resources. Process research may be more appealing to practitioners as its procedures are often similar to those used when conducting therapy. For example, information collected after the session has ended or intensive analysis of the session transcript will certainly be familiar from therapy or supervision and may be interesting for practitioners. Furthermore, the research procedure gives an extra perspective that would otherwise be inaccessible to a practising clinician (e.g. the therapist him or herself cannot conduct independent interviews about what was helpful from the perspective of the client in the session that he or she has just completed).

Clara Hill (1991), a prominent psychotherapy process researcher, distinguishes seven areas on which psychotherapy process research focuses: ancillary behaviour such as non-verbal behaviour; verbal behaviour (its form); covert behaviours such as intentions; content of sessions; strategies such as therapist plan; interpersonal manner such as empathy; and therapeutic relationship. I will not use the same conceptualization in the following chapters, but there will be a slight overlap. We will look at the methods that are commonly used in process research. We will also look at some of the problems encountered in process research and some of the main strategies used in this type of research as well as the sorts of areas currently under investigation (for the areas that are being investigated, see also Llewelyn & Hardy, 2001).

8

Instruments Used in Psychotherapy and Counselling Process Research

In Chapter 1, I presented some of the instruments used for measuring psychotherapy outcome. Many of these instruments are not unknown to practising clinicians as they are used in routine practice either for the assessment or for the monitoring of treatment outcome. Psychotherapy process measuring instruments are less well known as they are typically not very useful for everyday practice (but there are exceptions such as the Core Conflictual Relationship Theme Method; Luborsky & Crits-Christoph, 1998).

Lambert and Hill (1994) classify psychotherapy process research instruments with regard to whether they use the client's view of the process, the therapist's view of the process or the expert's or trained observer's view of the process. Other factors they take into consideration are whether the method gathers information on the client or the therapist, what aspect of the therapeutic process it focuses on (e.g. therapeutic alliance), what type of coding or scaling it uses and what theoretical constructs it examines (e.g. transference).

Heppner, Kivlighan and Wampold (1999) differentiate methods for measuring the area that is being investigated using the seven areas delineated by Hill (1991; see above) and they add Elliott's (1991) concept of *quality* of the process. Furthermore, they distinguish whether the instrument measures one of the outlined areas on a *micro* or a *macro* level, where micro level means that the instrument measures utterances and macro level means that the unit of analysis is either the whole session or its parts.

For the purpose of this book I will utilize the simpler distinction of Greenberg and Pinsof (1986). These authors use a basic division of process methods into *participative* and *non-participative* methods. In participative methods, therapy participants, clients and therapists are the users of the instrument; while non-participative methods use independent observers.

Participative Process Methods

Participative methods assess clients' and therapists' views of their interaction and its impacts. Participative methods can be further divided according to different criteria, e.g. what aspect of the process they assess or what unit of analysis they use (see the division stated above). Here, however, I will present the methods pragmatically according to examples of the most commonly used methods.

Methods of Measuring Therapeutic Relationship (Alliance)

Several participative methods exist that measure the therapeutic relationship or therapeutic alliance. Some of them can also be used as non-participative methods by trained raters. One of the oldest participative methods is *Barrett-Lennard's Relationship Inventory* (Barrett-Lennard, 1986). This is a method that captures the facilitative relational conditions that were postulated by Carl Rogers. The instrument has 64 items in both the client and the therapist versions. The items record client perception and therapist self-perception of four dimensions: level of regard, empathic understanding, unconditionality, and congruence (see Box 8.1). Each dimension is covered by 16 items, eight of which are formulated positively and eight negatively. The Relationship Inventory can be used for measuring the provision of the above four dimensions by the therapist as seen by the client and by the therapist him or herself. It seems that the high ratings by clients on the four dimensions are predictors of good outcome (see Barrett-Lennard, 1986; and e.g. Watson & Geller, 2005).

Box 8.1   Barrett-Lennard's Relationship Inventory (Barrett-Lennard, 1986) – an example of items

The client and the therapist rate on a 6-point scale without zero point from '+3 Yes(!), I strongly feel that it is true' to '–3 No (!), I strongly feel that it is not true'.

Examples of items from the client version:
1. The therapist respects me as a person.
2. The therapist wants to understand how I see things.
12. I feel that the therapist is real and genuine with me.
27. The therapist likes certain things about me, and there are other things he/she does not like in me.

Examples of items from the therapist version:
1. I respect the client as a person.
2. I want to understand how the client sees things.
12. I feel that I am genuinely myself with the client.
27. I like the client in some ways, while there are other things about him/her that I do not like.

Source: reprinted here with permission of the author, Godfrey T. Barrett-Lennard, PhD.

The therapeutic relationship is often conceptualized as an alliance between the therapist and the client (see Horvath & Bedi, 2002). One of the methods most commonly utilized to measure the concept of therapeutic alliance is the *Working Alliance Inventory* (WAI) (Horvath & Greenberg, 1989). This method uses the conceptualization developed by Bordin (1979) that recognizes three aspects of alliance: agreement on goals of therapy, agreement on tasks of therapy, and an unspecified emotional bond between the client and the therapist. The WAI questionnaire has 36 items, 12 in each of the dimensions (see brief description in Box 8.2). Recently a new short version of the instrument was suggested (Hatcher & Gillaspy, 2006). The WAI also has a client and a corresponding therapist version. The tool has been used by independent observers as well (Safran & Muran, 1996). Alliance measured by the client's version of WAI seems to be a predictor of effectiveness of therapy (Horvath & Greenberg, 1989).

Box 8.2   Working Alliance Inventory – a brief description of the instrument

- The WAI questionnaire has 36 items, 12 in each of the dimensions (goals, tasks, and bond).
- It has a client and a corresponding therapist version.
- The items focus on whether the therapy progresses towards agreed goals, whether the way the therapy is being conducted is collaborative and whether there is a non-specific bond between the client and the therapist.
- The client and the therapist rate the items on the scale from 1 (never) to 7 (always).

Source: Horvath and Greenberg, 1989.

Session Evaluation Methods

Typical participative methods are instruments that evaluate the therapeutic session. An important cornerstone in the development of such methods was the *Therapy Session Reports* instrument of Orlinsky and Howard (1986), which inquired about different aspects of a session that had just ended. An example of a newer method is the *Comprehensive Scale of Psychotherapy Session Constructs* (Eugster & Wampold, 1996). This instrument has a patient and a therapist form and measures nine aspects of therapy that proved relevant in different studies for session evaluation: patient involvement, patient comfort, patient progress, patient real relationship (authentic relationship with the therapist), therapist involvement, therapist comfort, therapist expertise, therapist interpersonal style, and therapist real relationship (authentic relationship with the client). The instrument also includes a session evaluation. Examples of the items are shown in Box 8.3.

Box 8.3   Comprehensive Scale of Psychotherapy Session Constructs – examples of items

Respondent uses a 6-point rating scale from 1 (strongly disagree) to 6 (strongly agree).

Examples from the therapist form:
1. In this session, my patient was relaxed.
2. I took an active role in this session.
3. In this session, my patient gained some new understanding.
4. In this session, my patient was hostile.

Examples from the patient form:
1. In this session, I was relaxed.
2. My therapist took an active role in this session.
3. In this session, I gained some new understanding.
4. In this session, I was hostile.

Source: S. L. Eugster and B. E. Wampold, 'Systematic effects of participant role on evaluation of the psychotherapy session', *Journal of Consulting and Clinical Psychology*, 64, 1020–1028, 1996. Published by American Psychological Association, reprinted with permission.

An example of a method looking at specific aspects of the session is the *Session Impact Scale* or, in a later version, the *Session Reaction Scale* (Elliott & Wexler, 1994). This measures helpful and unhelpful impacts of the session as seen by clients. The method was developed on the basis of significant events identified by clients in therapy sessions (Elliott, 1985). It has three dimensions. Two basic ones are the helpful and the unhelpful impacts; helpful impacts are then divided into task-focused helpful impacts and relationship-focused helpful impacts. The client responds to the items on a Likert-type scale as to how he or she evaluates the impacts of the session. Examples of items are presented in Box 8.4. The method can be used as an instrument for assessing the outcome of the session.

Box 8.4   Session Impact Scale (Elliott & Wexler, 1994) – the items example is taken from the Revised Session Reaction Scales

The clients rate the extent to which an item fits with their reactions to the session on the scale from 1 (not at all) to 5 (very much).

An example of the Task impacts subscale item:
1. *SEEING THINGS FROM ANOTHER PERSON'S PERSPECTIVE.* As a result of this session, I have begun to see things (about myself or others) from another person's point of view, including that of my therapist.

An example of the Relationship impacts subscale item:

12. *UNDERSTOOD.* As a result of this session, I now feel understood by my therapist, either generally as a person or in specific ways; or I am impressed by how accurately my therapist understood what I was thinking, feeling or trying to say.

An example of the Hindering impacts subscale item:

13. *CRITICIZED.* As a result of this session, I now feel attacked, put down, rejected or judged by my therapist; or I feel my therapist has been critical or judgemental of me.

Source: Elliott, 1993, reprinted with permission.

A similar method is the *Session Evaluation Questionnaire* (Stiles & Snow, 1984) that measures four non-cognitive dimensions of client evaluation of the session: *depth and smoothness* of the session and *positivity and arousal* after the session. The method can be used, for example, for the evaluation of the relationship between therapist interventions and the experiencing of the session or for observing the relationship between after-session mood and overall therapy outcome.

A slightly different type of method is the *Helpful Aspects of Therapy Form* (Llewelyn, 1988), which uses not only a quantitative evaluation but also open-ended qualitative questions that the client is asked to fill in. The method is used for the identification of significant events in the therapy session. An excerpt of the method is presented in Box 8.5.

Box 8.5   Helpful Aspects of Therapy Form – excerpt of items

1. Of the events which occurred in this session, which one do you feel was the most **helpful** or **important** for you personally? (By 'event' we mean something that happened in the session. It might be something you said or did, or something your therapist said or did.)

2. Please describe what made this event helpful/important and what you got out of it.

3. How helpful was this particular event? Rate it on the following scale. (Put an 'X' at the appropriate point; half-point ratings are OK, e.g. 7.5.)

HINDERING <——————————— Neutral ———————————-> HELPFUL
1   2   3   4   5   6   7   8   9

Source: Llewelyn, 1988, reprinted with permission.

The last three methods presented use the clients' evaluation. An example of the method using the therapist's evaluation of the session is the *Experiential Therapy Session Form* (Elliott, 2003). This method serves as a means of evaluating the therapist's use of the principles and tasks of emotion-focused therapy. The session's helpfulness and important session events are also recorded.

Events Evaluation

Some participative methods focus only on small segments of therapeutic sessions. They assess the therapeutic interaction on the micro level (Heppner, Kivlighian & Wampold, 1999). Such methods may use Likert-type rating scales measuring therapist or client responses. For example, the client may be asked to review a videotape of the session and evaluate each therapist's intervention in a particular segment with regard to its helpfulness (Elliott & Shapiro, 1988; Hill, 1989). An example of such a method is *Interpersonal Process Recall* (Elliott, 1986), which uses a combination of quantitative rating scales and qualitative open-ended questions for the investigation of processes present in a significant event identified by the client. The structure of a version of this method called the *Brief Structured Recall* (Elliott & Shapiro, 1988) is presented in Box 8.6.

Box 8.6   Structure of the Brief Structured Recall method

I. **Client Recall – (Client Event Recall Form)**
    A. Helpfulness ratings (three 9-point Likert-type scales from extremely hindering to extremely helpful), descriptions of therapist and clients' contributions to event helpfulness – *quantitative and qualitative data*
    B. Description of relevant context of event (e.g. meaning of the event in client's life, context of session and previous sessions, explanation of helpfulness) – *qualitative data*
    C. Ratings of therapeutic impacts (sixteen 5-point scale items, e.g. realized something new about self; more aware or clearer about feelings, experiences; progress towards knowing what to do about problems; felt therapist understands me; felt more involved in therapy or working harder; confused or distracted), plus description of high-rated impacts; selection of most helpful impact and client comments on relevant items – *quantitative and qualitative data*
    D. Description of changes expected as result of event (client makes list of possible changes) – *qualitative data*
    E. Ratings of client intentions (seven 5-point scale items, e.g. I was trying to understand something about myself) – *quantitative data*
    F. Ratings of client feelings, other experiences (ten 5-point scale items, e.g. power/hopeful/active), plus two items about other feelings or experiences – *quantitative data (occasionally qualitative accounts)*
    G. Client rates each utterance of event for helpfulness on 9-point Likert-type scale *(this enables the researcher to locate 'peak' therapist responses in event)*

II. **Therapist Recall – (Therapist Event Recall Form)**
  A. Ratings of therapist intentions (nineteen 5-point scale items, e.g. set limits, get information), plus open-ended description of therapist manner and feelings in event – *quantitative and qualitative data*
  B. Description of relevant context of event (client characteristics, situation, therapist characteristics, previous sessions, recent life events, earlier events in session) – open-ended questions – *qualitative data*
  C. Description of client-selected 'peak' therapist responses, including immediate context and impact (open-ended questions about peaks) – *qualitative data*
  D. Description of impact of event (9-point helpfulness scale; ratings of therapeutic impacts – sixteen 5-point scale items equivalent to client version; rating of extent event was expected – 4-point scale), plus open-ended question about possible main helpful idea/feeling for client in event – *quantitative and qualitative data*
  E. Description of changes expected as result of event (therapist lists possible client changes due to event) – *qualitative data*
  F. Ratings of therapist skilfulness and degree of client 'working' in event (two 9-point scales), and one explanatory qualitative question – *quantitative and qualitative data*

Source: Elliott and Shapiro, 1988, adapted with permission.

Qualitative Methods

Qualitative methods such as different forms of interview and assisted recalls also serve as participative methods. (For assisted recalls using video or audio tapes of the session, see McLeod, 2003.) Parts of the Interpersonal Process Recall or Brief Structured Recall mentioned above are good examples of such methods. Sometimes retrospective interviews are made just after therapy has finished, or much later, to explore various aspects of the completed therapy (see, for example, a retrospective recall study of misunderstandings in therapy by Rhodes et al., 1994). Sometimes (especially in case of assisted recalls) a qualitative method is used immediately after the end of the session. An example is the study by Rennie (1992, 1994), who used a qualitative version of the Interpersonal Process Recall asking clients to comment on the process just after a psychotherapy session.

Non-participative Methods

Non-participative methods have a somewhat longer tradition than participative methods (Orlinsky & Howard, 1986). Their beginnings are associated with the development of client-centred therapy. Many non-participative methods, mostly measuring the concept of transference, were developed in the psychodynamic tradition. A large number of the non-participative methods are transtheoretical.

A typical non-participative method is the rating scale used by trained raters for rating the session transcripts. The match between raters is considered an indicator of

Table 8.1 Brief version of the Experiencing Scale

Stage	Content	Treatment
1	External events; refusal to participate	Impersonal, detached
2	External events; behavioural or intellectual self-description	Interested, personal, self-participation
3	Personal reactions to external events; limited self-descriptions; behavioural descriptions of feelings	Reactive, emotionally involved
4	Descriptions of feelings and personal experiences	Self-descriptive; associative
5	Problems or propositions about feelings and personal experiences	Exploratory, elaborative, hypothetical
6	Synthesis of readily accessible feelings and experiences to resolve personally significant issues	Feelings vividly expressed, integrative, conclusive or affirmative
7	Full, easy presentation of experiencing; all elements confidently integrated	Expansive, illuminating, confident, buoyant

Source: Klein et al., 1969, adapted with permission.

reliability. The methods are used to evaluate the clients' utterances, or therapists' utterances, or their mutual interaction. Similar to participative methods, there are different ways of dividing non-participative methods meaningfully. We will look at them on the basis of whose expression (behaviour) they evaluate.

Non-participative Methods Evaluating the Client's In-session Behaviour (Expression)

The tradition of process research methods evaluating the client's in-session expression is linked with the beginnings and development of client-centred therapy in the 1950s. Probably the most commonly used non-participative method of this tradition is the *Experiencing Scale* (Klein et al., 1969). The scale is used by trained raters who rate client utterances using session recordings or transcripts. The raters infer the depth of the client's experiencing on the basis of verbal expression. The scale recognizes seven stages of client experiencing, from impersonal to evolving and emergent (Klein et al., 1969). The stages are based on Rogers' and Gendlin's theoretical work. A brief version of the scale is presented in Table 8.1.

The scale is used consecutively by several raters, and reliability is assessed on the basis of their agreement. During the training, reliability is also assessed on the basis of agreement with the expert ratings set out in the manual. An important aspect of the rating is the size of the evaluated segment. Typically, segments lasting several minutes are rated for the peak they attain and for the pervasiveness of the experiencing mode. However, a single utterance can also be assessed. The scale is most commonly used for the evaluation of the client's experience of the therapist's intervention (e.g. Hill, 1989), at specific moments during the

Table 8.2 A brief description of the Client Vocal Quality scale

Aspects	Focused	Externalizing	Limited	Emotional
Production of accents	With loudness	With pitch	Usual balance	Not applicable
Accentuation irregular	Irregular	Extremely regular	Usual pattern	Usually
Regularity of pace	Uneven	Even	Neither even nor uneven	Usually uneven
Terminal contours	Ragged and unexpected	Expected in relation to the structure of what is said	Direction about as usual, but energy tends to peter out	Unexpected
Perceived energy	Moderate to high voice may be soft but on platform	Moderate to high; voice a bit above platform	Voice not resting on its platform	Not applicable
Disruption of speech pattern	No	No	No	Yes

session (e.g. Greenberg, 1984) or for the evaluation of the client's progress in the quality of his or her own experience in a longer-term therapeutic process (e.g. Klein et al., 1969).

The scale is used for assessing the therapeutic process of different types of therapy (see for example Weiss & Sampson, 1986; Hill, 1989; Borkovec & Costello, 1993). The authors (Klein, Mathieu-Coughlan & Kiesler, 1986) summarize early research using this scale as showing that the scale is a measure of reflective rather than expressive style; that higher levels of experiencing were found in helpful processes in different kinds of individual therapy and in developmental points of group therapy; and that there is a relationship of higher experiencing in therapy process (especially early in therapy) and therapy outcome.

The *Client Vocal Quality* scale (Rice et al., 1979) is another instrument that comes from the client-centred tradition. With this instrument trained raters assess the client's vocal expression, namely accent, pace, energy and speech pattern. The scale recognizes four different vocal qualities: focused, externalized, limited and emotional (see Table 8.2). The scale shows the presence of focused voice quality as correlating with the effect of client-centred, Gestalt and to a certain extent psychoanalytic therapy (Rice & Kerr, 1986). The scale has also been used in studies that look at relevant processes in different therapeutic episodes, such as conflict in the therapeutic relationship (see Chapter 11).

Psychodynamic theory is reflected in several instruments measuring transferential client patterns. Luborsky, Barber, Binder et al. (1993) present 15 methods (developed prior to 1993) for measuring transference (a more detailed presentation of some of them is included in a special issue of the journal *Psychotherapy Research*, 1994). I will briefly focus here on the two most commonly used methods: the *Core Conflictual Relationship Themes* method (Luborsky & Crits-Cristoph, 1990, 1998) and the *Plan Formulation* Method (Curtis et al., 1994).

The Core Conflictual Relationships Themes method is the oldest method of assessing transferential patterns of patients in therapy. The method assesses typical interpersonal patterns as presented in interpersonal accounts (relationship episodes) presented by the client in early therapy sessions. Each relationship episode is assessed from the perspective of the 'wish' (marked as W) the client wanted to have granted in the interaction, the perceived or expected 'response of the other' (RO) to that wish, and a subsequent 'response of the client's self' (RS) to that response of the other. For research purposes, the method is generally used by trained raters, who on the basis of tapes or transcripts either formulate tailor-made 'wish', 'response of other', 'response of self' categories or use the pre-existing standard set of categories (see Box 8.7). On the basis of the most prevalent patterns the Core Conflictual Relationship Themes are then formulated.

The use of this method confirmed the psychodynamic theory of transference by showing that the Core Conflictual Relationship Themes, as assessed at the beginning of therapy on the basis of the description of the interaction of the client with other people, are repeated in the relationship with the therapist later in the therapy (Fried, Crits-Christoph & Luborsky, 1990). Crits-Christoph and Luborsky (1990) also found that the Core Conflictual Relationship Themes of patients whose psychopathological symptoms receded at the end of therapy were also resolved and changed, which would correspond with psychodynamic theory, which claims that working through the transference leads to improvement in psychopathological symptoms.

Box 8.7   Example of standard categories of the Core Conflictual Relationship Themes method

Wishes:
To be understood.
To be accepted.
To be respected.

Responses from others:
Are understanding.
Are not understanding.
Are rejecting.

Responses of self:
Feel accepted.
Feel angry.
Feel depressed.

Source: adapted from Barber, et al., 1990.

A version of the Core Conflictual Relationship Themes method can also be used as a clinical tool for psychodynamic case formulation. Similarly, another well-known psycho-analytic research method, the Plan Formulation Method, can be used (Curtis et al., 1994).

This method again uses in its formulation stage the therapy transcripts from the beginning of therapy. The formulation is looking for the patient's unconscious *goals* for therapy, *obstacles* in the form of *pathogenic* beliefs that inhibit the patient in attaining these goals, *insights* that need to be achieved and '*patient's tests*' that the therapists will have to pass so that the client can achieve the goals.

The method leans on theory (Weiss & Sampson, 1986; Weiss, 1993; Curtis et al., 1994), according to which the client, in the relationship with the therapist, tests his or her pathogenic beliefs that achieving some of his or her wishes is dangerous either for the client or for other people (we will look at this theory in Chapter 12). The way the patient works in therapy on disproving his or her pathogenic beliefs is called the patient's plan (hence the name of the method). The therapist's role is to further the patient's understanding of pathogenic beliefs and to allow his or her successful disproving in the therapeutic relationship.

The method is used by several independent raters, who each compile their clinical formulation with the list of goals, obstacles, tests and insights. The length of the list depends on the individual case. The prepared list includes a formulation from all raters. The collated list is then assessed by the raters, who on a scale from 0 to 4 rate the relevance of each goal, insight, obstacle, test and insight from the list for the case. The reliability of the agreement through intraclass correlation between the raters is then assessed (ICC (3, 1) and (3, k) (Shrout & Fleiss, 1979). If the reliability is acceptable, the list is reduced by omitting those goals, obstacles, tests and insights that are below median of the average rating for each of the categories.

Research using this scale (Weiss & Sampson, 1986; Curtis et al., 1994) has shown that if the therapist passes the patient's tests in a way that is in accordance with the patient's goals, progress in therapy follows. The level of goal achievement also correlated with the effect of therapy as measured by standard outcome instruments.

An example of a transtheoretical non-participative instrument is the nominal scale of Clara Hill, the *Client Verbal Response Category System* (Hill, 1986) that categorizes client utterances in the therapy process. The instrument recognizes nine categories of client utterance on the basis of their content: simple response, request, description, experiencing, exploration of therapeutic relationship, insight, discussion of plans, silence, and other. The instrument is again used by trained raters. Reliability is assessed through their agreement. Hill (1986) presents findings from the studies using the method adopted until 1986, which showed that the client's description has a descending tendency in therapeutic process, while experiencing has an increasing tendency. Both these categories seem to be dominant in the therapeutic process.

Non-participative Methods Measuring the Therapist's In-session Behaviour

The methods focused on the therapist's in-session behaviour, like the methods that focus on the client's behaviour, are either based on a theoretical concept from a therapeutic approach

Table 8.3   Therapist Experiencing Scale – brief version

Stage	Patient (P) Content Referent	Therapist's (T) Manner
1	External events not including P	Impersonal, detached
2	External events including P; behavioural or intellectual; elaboration of P's thoughts or activities	Interested, intellectual self-referents
3	P's reactions to external events; limited or behavioural description of P's feelings	Reactive, T clearly expresses or refers to T's feelings
4	Description of P's feelings and personal experiences	Empathically involved, T elaborates or intensifies feelings and/or associations in this context
5	P's problems or propositions about feelings and personal experiences	T uses own feelings to explore P's feelings
6	Focus on P's emergent feelings and their impact	T uses own emergent feelings to affirm P's feelings
7	P's facility to move from one inner referent to another with authenticity	Expansive, with integration of all elements of the interaction, including P's feelings, T's feelings and the explicit context

Source: adapted from Klein et al., 1986 © Guilford Press.

or are transtheoretical. An example of a method based on a construct from a single theoretical orientation (client-centred) is the *Therapist Experiencing Scale* (Klein, Mathieu-Coughlan & Kiesler, 1986), a scale that corresponds with the Experiencing Scale used to evaluate the client's exploration in therapy. The Therapist Experiencing Scale recognizes seven levels of experiencing. It has two different aspects: (1) the patient content referent, to which the therapist responds; and (2) the manner in which the therapist responds. The scale is briefly introduced in Table 8.3. Client-centred theory also gave birth to other scales measuring important client-centred concepts of the therapist's behaviour (see, for example, the Accurate Empathy Scale (Truax, 1967) or the Therapist Congruence Scale (Kiesler, 1967).

A number of measures focusing on the therapist's in-session behaviour monitor whether the therapist follows theoretical principles of a specific approach as outlined in the manualized form of that treatment. These measures assess adherence to the manual and the quality of the therapist's work. Such measures are generally used in randomized control trials where they ensure validity of the study by controlling the quality of the therapist's work. An example of such a measure is the *Penn Adherence and Competence Scale for Supportive-Expressive Therapy* of Jacques Barber and Paul Crits-Christoph (1996). The rater in this scale rates on a scale from 1 to 7 the amount and quality of the therapist's interventions as postulated by supportive-expressive therapy. The scale assesses the therapeutic alliance and supportive and expressive interventions of the therapist. The scale also distinguishes the client's spontaneous engagement in the supportive-expressive mode. Examples of items from the scale are presented in Box 8.8.

Box 8.8   Examples of items from the Penn Adherence and Competence Scale for Supportive-Expressive Therapy

The rater assesses the amount and quality of the therapist's behaviour on a 7-grade scale from 1 (not at all) to 7 (very much).

Example of an item measuring general therapeutic behaviour:
1. Therapist encourages (directly or by a facilitating atmosphere) the patient's expression, i.e. to say what he or she thinks or feels.

Example of an item measuring supportive component:
11. The therapist conveys a sense of supporting the patient's wish to achieve the goals of treatment.

Example of an item measuring expressive component:
32. The therapist relates the patient's main wish to the patient's anticipated reactions of others and to the patient's responses to others' reactions and to the patient's responses to his/her wishes.

Source: Barber, J.P. & Crits-Christoph, P. (1996). Development of an adherence/competence scale for dynamic therapy: preliminary findings. *Psychotherapy Research*, 6, 81–94, and Barber, J.P., Crits-Christoph, P. & Luborsky, L. (1996). Effects of therapist adherence and competence on patient outcome in brief dynamic therapy. *Journal of Consulting and Clinical Psychology*, 64, 619–622.

Source: adapted with permission from Barber and Crits-Christoph, 1996.

An example of a transtheoretical (or atheoretical) instrument is Hill's *Verbal Response Category System* (Hill, 1986; Hill & O'Brien, 1999). This is a nominal rating scale with which trained raters assess meaning units contained in the therapist's utterances. The scale consists of the following nominal categories: approval and reassurance, closed questions, open questions, restatement, reflection of feelings, challenge, interpretation, self-disclosure, immediacy, information, direct guidance, and other. Each category is defined and raters are trained to distinguish between the categories. Reliability is assessed on the basis of agreement between raters. Clara Hill (1986) recommends the method for examining differences between different therapies, different therapy stages, different therapists, etc. She also suggests that the scale can be used for examining the relationship between different interventions and the impact they have on the client.

Methods Capturing Interaction between the Client and the Therapist

Rating scales that record the *therapeutic interaction* are typically instruments that can also be used for measuring human communication outside the therapeutic setting. An example of such methods is the *Structural Analysis of Social Behaviour* (SASB) scale (Benjamin et al., 1986; see also http://www.psych.utah.edu/benjamin/sasb/). This rating system allows each therapist or client utterance to be placed within a system of categories of social interaction. The utterance can focus on the other in the interaction, on the self, or it may be judged to come from the introjected other and respond to the self. The system consists of 34 categories defined by two axes, one representing Enmeshment (Control/Submit)–Differentiation (Emancipate/Separate) and the other capturing Love–Hate. The system is used by trained raters who evaluate each complete thought on the basis of to whom the utterance is directed and to what extent it is affiliative or controlling. It is possible to score more than one meaning in an utterance.

Benjamin, Foster, Robesto and Estroff (1986) show an example of how the method can be used to capture typical patterns of interaction in family therapy sessions. The SASB can be used in various ways for examining interaction (e.g. Safran & Muran, 1996) or treatment of oneself (Watson, Goldman & Greenberg, 2007). It can also be used as a treatment formulation tool (see Benjamin, 1996).

Qualitative Non-participative Methods

Qualitative non-participative methods focus on the therapeutic interaction in a flexible and descriptive way. Again, qualitative methods may cut across different theoretical frameworks (transtheoretical or atheoretical methods) or may endorse one particular framework. An example of a method using a framework independent of therapy theories is the *Comprehensive Process Analysis* of Robert Elliott (1989). This method is used for analysing significant events (see Chapter 11). It also has participative elements. Significant events are evaluated in the context of the therapy as a whole, as well as in the context of prior events in the therapy session. The event is assessed in relation to the process of the therapist and the client and their interaction and for the impact it has on client, therapeutic process and therapy outcome (see Box 8.9).

Box 8.9   Framework for Comprehensive Process Analysis

I.   Expansion of implicit and explicit propositions in event.
II. Contextual factors (background, pre-session context, session context, episode context).
III. Event factors (action, content, style/state, quality).
IV. Impact on client (process impact pathway, client experiencing pathway, delayed impact of event, effectiveness of event).

Source: adapted with permission from Elliott, 1989.

An example of qualitative analysis using a particular theoretical framework is the study of Hardy et al. (1999), who studied therapeutic interaction in significant events identified by clients in psychodynamic-interpersonal therapy using attachment theory (Bowlby, 1988). The events were assessed from the perspective of (1) the client attachment style in the event, (2) the presenting attachment issue, and (3) the therapist's responsiveness to the client's attachment style.

Specifics of Using Process Measures in the Group Therapy Modality

In group therapy process studies, apart from studying the interaction of the client and the therapist, it is possible to investigate the interaction of different clients and the client and the group as well. In addition to this, Burlingame, Fuhriman and Johnson (2002) show that in the case of the co-therapists, there are also relevant interactions of the therapist and the group and the therapists with each other. The specificity of group process research is illustrated by the variable of group cohesion, which covers all forms of interaction present in group therapy (therapist–client, client–client, client–group, therapist–group, and therapist–therapist) (see Burlingame, Fuhriman & Johnson, 2002). Other typical issues that are being studied in group therapy process research are the phases in the development of group dynamics, e.g. orientation, conflict, development of cohesiveness (see Kivlighan & Goldfine, 1991; Yalom & Lescz, 2005) or specific group curative factors, e.g. instillation of hope, universality, imparting information, altruism, corrective interpersonal experience (see Burlingame, MacKenzie & Strauss, 2004; Yalom & Lescz, 2005).

The fact that group therapy involves important constructs that may be typical only of group therapy means that specific instruments have been developed to measure these constructs. In other instances, the methods used in individual therapy can be adapted for group analysis purposes or there may be methods that can readily be used in several modalities (e.g. the Structural Analysis of Social Behaviour of Lorna Benjamin). Several methods available for studying the group therapy process are presented in the volume edited by Ariadne Beck and Carol Lewis (2000). Some of the issues, such as client–client interaction, pertinent to group therapy process research are also relevant to couple and family therapy process research (Sexton, Alexander & Mease, 2004; Sprenkle & Piercy, 2005).

In the previous pages we have examined examples of process research methods. It is not easy to find a compendium of process methods that would help readers to familiarize themselves with the kinds of methods available. A good example of such a compendium is an older volume by Greenberg and Pinsof: *The Psychotherapeutic Process: A Research Handbook* (1986).

9

Some Methodological Problems of Researching the Therapy Process

Before we look at some forms of process research, I focus on some of the problems encountered in this research. Many of these problems arise from the complexity of the therapeutic process, which challenges the research strategy. We will focus on six problems in psychotherapy and counselling process research:

(1) The necessity of simplifying the therapeutic process for research purposes.
(2) The importance of the context of the studied therapy for the generalizability of findings.
(3) The non-linearity of the processes involved in the therapeutic process.
(4) The issue of the responsiveness of therapy participants to the changing reality of the therapeutic process.
(5) The problem of differences between client and therapist perspectives.
(6) The ethical challenges in studying the therapeutic interaction.

Simplification

There are many variables relevant to the course of therapy and they are intermingled in the therapy process. However, when we study those variables we try to focus on just a few of them. This leads to a simplification and reduction of the therapeutic process. Because of such inevitable reduction and simplification, we need to be careful when considering how best to investigate a research problem. Otherwise we run the risk of conducting research that does not resonate with the practitioner's experience of therapy.

Similarly, we need to be careful when interpreting empirical findings. For example, if we find that the therapist's interpretations on average deepened the client's experience, we cannot automatically suppose that all interpretations result in a valuable therapeutic process regardless of the context and quality of the interpretation. An average interpretation does not exist, and homogenizing such a phenomenon may only create an artefact. It is also possible that a specific type of interpretation, or interpretations in a specific context, may lead to a flattening in experience.

Elliott and Anderson (1994) in their work on the relationship between simplification and complexity of psychotherapy process research distinguish two main forms of simplifying: (1) *simplification by non-completeness* of the research (e.g. use of only one of the possible perspectives in assessing outcome, or assessing only one type of variable), and (2) *simplification by reliance on a simple structure*. The second form of simplification manifests itself in (a) a simplification of data structure (e.g. assigning the same importance to all therapy events) or (b) a simplification of variable structure (e.g. assuming unilaterality in the therapist–client relationship: that the therapist influences the client).

Context and Generalization

Another aspect that plays an important role in the interpretation of psychotherapy process studies is the context in which the study was conducted. For example, psychotherapy is based on confidentiality achieved in the therapeutic relationship. This confidential relationship has its own dynamic, as is powerfully pointed out in many, mostly psychodynamic, theories. The fact that therapy is a part of research study certainly affects the therapeutic process. If the client is, for example, asked after each therapeutic session to review the session on the videotape and assess some of its aspects, it definitely alters the typical course of therapy. Paradoxically, such therapy will probably have extra therapeutic potential (the client may have more time to reflect on the session), but of course it may also have a hindering effect (when the client reviews something sensitive). Sometimes an intensive research strategy may lead to a specific dynamic between the researcher and the client that may interfere with therapy.

The context of the research may affect the findings. Therefore, as McLeod (2001b) emphasizes, it is important to describe the *context* of a particular study so that the reader can infer how the study relates to the context in which he or she works. Similarly, McLeod underlines the importance of reporting the researcher's own motivation for the research and the intent the researcher had when he or she conducted the study. The reader may then be freer to make his or her own judgement on the validity, relevance and applicability of the findings.

Non-Linearity

Another problem that is often mentioned in the context of process research is the problem of non-linearity of the therapeutic process. Psychotherapy is often thought of as similar to drug treatments (for the drug metaphor, see Stiles & Shapiro, 1994) in the sense that the therapeutic process includes active components which are responsible for the therapy outcome in a linear way. In such a conceptualization, psychotherapy is viewed as a homogeneous intervention and the client as a passive recipient of it. Such a conceptualization ignores the fact that the therapist tailors treatment (see responsiveness below) and the client has his or her own goals for therapy and his/her own therapeutic strategies (Bohart & Tallman, 1999).

Psychotherapy is a complex non-linear activity in which the client is a very active participant. Therapeutic interaction is also a complex process, in which one intervention relates to another and is influenced by many processes on the therapist's and client's part. So, for example, no single extremely astute interpretation exists, but therapist's interpretative interventions are a process in which one interpretation may be the right intervention at the right time. The impact of such an interaction then creates the context for other interventions.

Non-linearity of the therapy process may be causing problems for some types of process research, such as process–outcome research, which will be introduced in the following chapter. Process–outcome research attempts to identify the relationship between process variables (e.g. the level of therapeutic alliance in a specific moment of therapy) and the overall therapy outcome. Because the process is not linear, one has no certainty that selected moments of the therapeutic process will contain a quality that is representative of the studied process variable (e.g. alliance). To overcome this problem, researchers sometimes study theoretically or practically important moments of the therapeutic process (see Chapter 11).

Therapist's (and Client's) Responsiveness

A similar problem to that of non-linearity of the therapeutic process is the responsiveness of the therapist to the client and, vice versa, of the client to the therapist (Stiles, Honos-Webb & Surko, 1998). The therapist is responsive to the client in the interventions that he or she implements (see the hypothetical example in Box 9.1). This is already manifested, for example, in the selection of an appropriate form of treatment, in the strategy with which the particular form of treatment is implemented, as well as in the adaptability of the therapist's style of work from one moment to another depending on the client's actual state.

Box 9.1   Example of therapist responsiveness to the client

For example, if a psychodynamically oriented therapist works with a client who does not see much value in 'psychological' exploration, the therapist may tailor the therapy and focus it more on the coping with symptoms and supporting the client. Another therapist, let's say of predominantly CBT orientation, may work with a client interested in a deeper understanding of his/her symptoms and interpersonal functioning. Though primarily of CBT orientation, the therapist may spend less time with behavioural and cognitive techniques and more time with an empathic exploration and broadening of the understanding of the client's interpersonal functioning contributing to psychopathological symptoms.

Of course, examples like the one in Box 9.1 do not cause problems in practice and intuitively seem very practical. But they cause a problem if we want to test a neatly formulated theory. The assessment of the relationship between the therapist's activity and the client's outcome may then be threatened. However, in some sorts of process research of a descriptive nature we are able to study the flow of the therapeutic interaction as it naturally occurs, including the responsiveness of the therapist and the client. As Stiles, Honos-Webb and Surko (1998) emphasize, responsiveness is best addressed by using complex descriptive, evaluative and qualitative strategies of research.

Perspective on the Therapeutic Process

Another important aspect of process research is the perspective of an observer of this process. In Chapter 8 on process research methods, I introduced methods that use the client's and the therapist's view and instruments used by independent observers. As will be seen in some findings presented in the following pages, the perspective taken on therapeutic process matters. Different observers (clients, therapists, external observers) see things differently and their perceptions are in a different relationship to the outcomes of therapy (Orlinsky, Grawe & Parks, 1994).

It is interesting that therapists are often unaware of what is going on in the client (e.g. Hill et al., 1993). Clients keep their distance, and often conceal their real experiences (Rennie, 1990). If, for example, the client is not sure whether the therapist accepts some aspect of his or her attitudes or behaviour, then the client attentively studies the therapist's reaction to what the client reveals (Timulak & Lietaer, 2001). However, the client may do this inconspicuously, so the therapist may not be aware of it at all. In this respect it is not surprising that the client's perception of the helping aspects of the therapeutic process is a better predictor of therapy outcome than the therapist's perception (Orlinsky, Grawe & Parks, 1994).

Often the client and the therapist do not agree on what is important in the therapeutic process. Martin and Stelmaczonek (1988) state that clients and therapists, who had been asked to identify helping moments in the therapeutic process, agreed in only approximately 30% of cases. Similar discrepancies are found among therapists themselves. Walsh, Perruci and Severns (1999) found that therapists who had been asked to identify good (therapeutically valuable) moments on the videotape of the same therapeutic session, differed greatly in their evaluation.

Appropriate attention, therefore, must be dedicated to the problem of external raters (see Hill, 1991), who are often used in process studies. Raters have to be able to judge the phenomenon as defined by a rating scale. For that reason they are trained according to the expert raters ratings. Usually more raters are involved in the rating as not all of them will work with the same attention to detail. Sometimes this is discovered only after the fact. As Hill emphasizes, raters should be motivated to carry out the ratings, which is often problematic, because usually they do not know the research hypothesis. Raters should also be watched continuously because they can create their own idiosyncratic rules when rating. To examine their reasoning may prove to be important as well, so that the researcher can be confident about whether they are following the rules of rating as they should. For details of issues involving the use of raters see Hill (1991).

Research Ethics in Intensive Process Studies

Intensive research on the psychotherapeutic process (see Chapter 11) may sometimes be more demanding for the client as he or she is closer to the therapy experience than the outcome-focused research procedures. Especially demanding are research designs in which high client participation is required; for example filling out forms repeatedly or participating in assisted recalls. Although clients often value research that stimulates their experience of therapy (e.g. assisted recalls of therapeutic interaction that use therapy tapes; see McLeod, 2007), sometimes the research requirements coincide with vulnerable feelings elicited by the therapy. It must always be borne in mind that the research procedure often invades the client's privacy, and potentially intrusive requests should always be carefully considered, or avoided altogether.

Caution should be entertained by the original researchers, but also by external reviewers, researchers who may use the data later in time (by using archival data or publicly available data) or professionals who may come across some segments of therapeutic sessions in the published research studies. It is always important that the client's interest are well looked after. Clients should have the option of withdrawing from the research procedure without it affecting their therapy. Measures should be taken to ensure that future use of data is only with the full understanding and consent of the client, and the option of allowing the data to be destroyed much later after the study was completed should be allowed (see for example details in Bond, 2004).

10

Process–Outcome Research

The basic idea of research mapping the relationship between process and outcome of psychotherapy or counselling (process–outcome research) is measuring process variables and testing whether they relate to therapy outcome. The important aspect of process–outcome research is what is considered to be the outcome. For example, the outcome could be assessed within the session, after the session, after the whole therapy, or in the follow-up. However, process–outcome research is usually considered to be made up of studies linking the client's behaviour outside therapeutic sessions (usually measured at termination or at follow-up) with some process variables measured in the course of therapy (e.g. Orlinsky, Grawe & Parks, 1994). Orlinsky, Grawe and Parks (1994) also differentiate between the therapeutic process and process of change. Process–outcome research, then, primarily deals with the relationships of selected characteristics of therapy process and therapeutic change.

Research studying the relationship between the outcome and process of therapy focuses on *client* variables (e.g. the client's level of experiencing), *therapist* variables (e.g. the therapist's level of experiencing), *therapeutic intervention* variables (e.g. interpretation), and *therapeutic interaction* variables (e.g. the client's attachment style and the therapist's responsiveness to it). Orlinsky, Grawe and Parks (1994), applying Orlinsky's and Howard's Generic Model of Psychotherapy, distinguish six aspects of therapeutic process common to all therapies:

(1) The formal aspect (therapeutic contract), e.g. providing and implementing the therapeutic contract).
(2) The technical aspect (therapeutic operations), e.g. the patient's problem presentation, the therapist's understanding, the therapist's intervention and the patient's cooperation.
(3) The interpersonal aspect (therapeutic bond), e.g. the patient's cooperation or resistance or the therapist's affirmative presence.
(4) The intrapersonal aspect (self-relatedness), e.g. the patient's non-defensiveness and openness or the therapist's authenticity.

(5) The clinical aspect (in-session impacts), e.g. the client's positive evaluation of the therapist's intervention or the therapist's experience of his or her own effectiveness.
(6) The temporal aspect (sequential flow), e.g. treatment phase or length of treatment. (For more information about particular aspects see Orlinsky, Grawe & Parks, 1994.)

Orlinsky, Grawe and Parks (1994) overviewed process–outcome research taking into consideration the perspective taken on the process and outcome variable (e.g. patient, therapist or independent rater, psychometric test or objective index or the combination of perspectives). They found several process variables consistently (robustly) linked to therapy outcome (see Box 10.1). According to the authors, 'robust' meant that the process and therapy outcome were evaluated across all perspectives (patient, therapist, independent raters, objective and psychometric tests indicators) and still showed a significant link.

Box 10.1   Process variables consistently (regardless of perspective taken) linked to outcome (Orlinsky, Grawe & Parks, 1994)

Patient suitability
Patient cooperativeness versus resistance
Global therapeutic bond/group cohesion
Patient contribution to the bond
Patient interactive collaboration
Patient expressiveness
Patient affirmation of the therapist
Reciprocal affirmation
Patient openness versus defensiveness
Therapeutic realizations (in-session positive moments)
Length of therapy

Research Designs in Process–Outcome Studies

The number of process–outcome studies is substantial. They differ in their methodology: we can find correlational, descriptive, quasi-experimental and experimental studies. However, experimental studies are less frequent in process–outcome research, especially in comparison with outcome studies. The exceptions are studies that vary the therapy parameters, e.g. length, intensity, frequency of some type of intervention (see Chapter 2 on RCTs). In process research, the most frequently studied variables and their relationship to outcome are studied naturally as they appear in the psychotherapy process. Therefore, non-experimental, correlational designs dominate. An example would be an investigation of the relationship between the client-perceived therapeutic alliance at a certain point in therapy and the therapy outcome. It is also quite common to study, *ex post*, variables that were most likely to be responsible for outcome in large RCTs studies, especially if the data on a whole variety of factors that could mediate or moderate therapy outcome are collected. It is also possible to examine successful cases in more detail or probable causal processes that lead to successful therapy outcome. Process–outcome studies sometimes utilize qualitative methodology. In that case clients, therapists or independent observers are asked to establish a link between different processes in therapy and therapy outcome. The nature of qualitative studies, however, often renders their findings rather tentative.

Examples of Process–Outcome Studies

Probably the most frequently studied process variable in process–outcome research is the therapeutic alliance. We will look at two different studies analysing the relationship between therapy effectiveness and therapeutic alliance and one study looking at process variables related to premature dropout from therapy.

The Role of Theraputic Alliance in Treatment of Depression

Krupnick et al. (1996) used data from the National Institute of Mental Health Treatment of Depression Collaborative Research Program (NIMH TDCRP) to monitor the relationship between the therapeutic alliance and treatment outcome (the study was introduced in Chapter 2). Just to remind you, the original study compared the efficacy of imipramine, cognitive-behavioural therapy, interpersonal therapy and a placebo with clinical management in the treatment of depression. Krupnick et al. tested several hypotheses:

(a) that there will be a significant relationship between strength of therapeutic alliance and outcome;
(b) that the levels of therapeutic alliance will be higher in the psychotherapeutic conditions than in the pharmacotherapeutic conditions;
(c) that early alliance will predict the outcome; and
(d) that it will be the patient's contribution to the alliance that will predict outcome. (Krupnick et al., 1996: 533)

The data and outcome results from the TDCRP project were presented in Chapter 2. Two hundred and twenty-five outpatients who attended a minimum of two therapeutic sessions were the subject of this study. Therapeutic alliance was measured by a modified version of the Vanderbilt Therapeutic Alliance Scale (VTAS). The modified scale contained two dimensions: factor of patient (e.g. patient experiences therapist as understanding and supportive) and factor of therapist (e.g. therapist expresses hope and encouragement). The factor of patient dimension simultaneously consisted of items monitoring therapeutic interaction (e.g. patient and therapist agree on tasks and goals).

The scale was used by four independent raters whose ratings reached adequate reliability (agreement). The raters judged the tapes from the third, ninth and fifteenth sessions. Where the patient attended fewer sessions, fewer tapes were rated. For those who attended only two sessions, the second session was evaluated.

The main data analysis was multiple regression exploring the relationship between alliance and outcome as measured by two outcome instruments, the Beck Depression Inventory (BDI) and the Hamilton Rating Scale of Depression (HRSD), and by logistic regression studying the relationship between the alliance and the remission criterion (defined as a score below the cut-off point on the Hamilton Rating Scale of Depression). Affiliations with the experimental condition and the degree of symptoms before the treatment were considered as covariate variables. Therapeutic alliance levels were measured in two ways: *early* alliance (using evaluation of the third session) and *average* alliance (using mean alliance evaluation of the third, ninth and fifteenth sessions as rated for each client).

Krupnick et al. (1996) found that the quality of alliance was not significantly different in any of the four experimental conditions. Early alliance, average alliance and factor of patient correlated with the results on HRSD and BDI, but factor of therapist did not. The difference was, however, in the size of the relationship, with the advantage that the average therapeutic alliance showed a stronger relationship to the outcome. The interaction of the treatment condition and the early alliance appeared to be strong for three conditions: interpersonal psychotherapy, pharmacotherapy (with clinical management) and placebo (with clinical management), but weak for CBT. The interaction of the treatment condition and the average alliance and early alliance to the outcome showed no differences between the conditions. Therefore, it can be said that the relationship between the alliance and outcome was the same in each experimental condition (with the exception of the relationship of early alliance to outcome in the case of CBT). In the discussion the authors emphasized the surprisingly strong connection of the therapeutic alliance to the pharmacotherapy and placebo outcomes.

Patients' Perfectionism and Depression Treatment

Zuroff et al. (2000) again used the data from the National Institute of Mental Health Treatment of Depression Collaborative Research Program. Along with their other analyses, they examined the relationship of therapeutic alliance and the client's perfectionism with the treatment outcome. Therapeutic alliance was measured by a modified version of the Vanderbilt Scale of Therapeutic Alliance (as in Krupnick et al.'s (1996) study) in the third session (early alliance), ninth, and fifteenth sessions (late alliance). Perfectionism was measured by a self-report scale, the Dysfunctional Attitudes Scale (DAS) filled out by clients prior to treatment. The Dysfunctional Attitudes Scale has two dimensions: perfectionism, and need for approval. As the therapy outcome, the authors used a composite consisting of residual scores on the Beck Depression Inventory, Hamilton Rating Scale of Depression, SCL–90, Global Assessment Scale (GAS) and Social Adjustment Scales (SAS) (see Chapter 2).

Since the previous research studies showed that perfectionism is a negative predictor of treatment effectiveness (Blatt, Quinlan et al., 1995), Zuroff et al. (2000) tested whether perfectionism as a negative predictor can be explained (mediated) by the inability of perfectionistic patients to contribute to the therapeutic alliance between the third and the fifteenth sessions (patient alliance factor was measured). This hypothesis was partially confirmed. However, Zuroff et al. also found that the contribution of perfectionism was more than simply an inability to contribute to the relationship. Also citing work by Blatt, Zuroff, Quinalan and Pilkonis (1996), who found that the perceived quality of the emotional bond with the therapist could mitigate the negative prognosis of perfectionistic patients, Zuroff et al. concluded that the relationship between perfectionism and therapy outcome can be moderated by a positive emotional bond with the therapist and may be partially mediated by the patient's inability to contribute to the alliance.

Process Variables and Therapy Dropout

As a final example of process–outcome research, we will look at a study examining process variables predicting therapy dropouts as a specific indicator of therapy outcome. Piper, Ogrodniczuk et al. (1999) explored variables from the therapy of patients who prematurely finished (dropouts) interpretative psychodynamic therapy. Dropouts were classified as patients who finished therapy after fewer than 14 of 20 sessions without therapist recommendation. The complete research project contained 144 patients and eight therapists who provided interpretative therapy for half of the patients and supportive psychodynamic therapy for the other half. Twenty-two patients in interpretative therapy terminated therapy prematurely. For each of these patients the researchers found a matched patient who completed the treatment. Thus the authors matched 22 dropouts and 22 completers. The patients' and therapists' perceived therapeutic alliance was then studied for the two groups.

The authors used a modified version of the Vanderbilt Psychotherapeutic Process Scale (VPPS) that was used by external raters for the evaluation of session audiotapes. The scale contained five subscales (patient participation, patient hostility, patient exploration, therapist exploration, negative therapist attitude) and three additional variables (patient focus on transference, therapist focus on transference and global impression of the session). Besides that, the authors also adopted a method used by external raters that monitored two forms of therapist work, 'dynamic' and 'supportive'.

Piper, Ogrodniczuk et al. (1999) compared dropouts and completers on the ratings of the last session attended by the dropout and the same numerical session of the matched completer. They also looked at the first three sessions of the matched pairs. The alliance evaluations at the last session showed that the therapists of dropouts rated the alliance lower than those of completers (due to missing data, patients' evaluations were not compared). VPPS showed that the dropouts had a lower score on patient exploration and a higher one on the patient and therapist focus on transference. As to the early sessions, the dropouts evaluated the therapeutic alliance as lower and also had lower scores on the dynamic work. Other criteria were not different.

A qualitative analysis of the audiotapes of the dropouts' last session showed the following sequential order:

(1) The patient expressed his or her idea of dropping out.
(2) The patient expressed frustration with therapy, frequently recalling expectations that were not met and the therapist's focus on painful feelings.
(3) The therapist addressed the patient's difficulty by focusing on transference and linking the exchange to other relationships.
(4) The patient resisted the focus on transference.
(5) The therapist insisted on transference interpretations.
(6) The patient and the therapist argued with each other and seemed to engage in a power struggle.
(7) The patient remained in resistance.
(8) The session ended with the therapist encouraging the patient to continue with therapy.
(9) The patient did not appear any more. (Piper, Ogrodniczuk et al., 1999: 120)

All above examples of process–outcome studies illustrate the potential clinical and theoretical richness of this type of study. As can be seen, process–outcome studies can formulate and try to answer theoretically relevant questions. The main danger, however, is in their non-experimental nature, which may in some cases cause a problem with interpretation. This is especially true of correlational studies which may have alternative explanations, for example whether it is early alliance that improves outcome, or whether it early outcome that improves alliance (see Barber et al., 2000). Futhermore, it may not be possible to rule out the presence of some confounding variable other than early positive outcome that can explain the relationship of the alliance to the outcome (e.g. general client hopefulness may be responsible for better outcome but also for a more positive view of the relationship).

Meta-Analytic Process–Outcome Investigations

As in research on psychotherapy outcome, meta-analysis which brings together the results of several studies can be used in process–outcome research. Process–outcome meta-analysis not only allows a better estimate of the relationship between process variables and therapeutic outcome but also enables the monitoring of some other factors contributing to that relationship. For example, it is possible to monitor how the relationship studied depends on the instrument used for measuring therapeutic alliance and therapy outcome.

A good example of process–outcome meta-analysis is the study of Martin, Garske and Davis (2000), who explored the relationship between therapeutic alliance and therapy outcome. They identified 79 studies investigating this relationship. The meta-analytical procedure used contained many of the processes outlined in Chapter 4 above. For example, the entire range of variables that could have moderated the relationship between the alliance and outcome (such as the measure used or the identity of the alliance rater) were coded and examined for their relationship with the alliance–outcome link. The main result showed that the correlation between alliance and outcome was homogeneous, with an average correlation of 0.22. This homogeneity was interpreted by the authors as a sign that the alliance–outcome relationship cannot be explained by other moderators. Many variables – such as the type of publication of the original study, unpublished studies, and distortions stemming from not quoting correlations in studies that did not find a significant relationship (in such case correlation was counted as zero) – were not shown to have an influence on the size of the overall correlation. The correlation of 0.22 was interpreted by the authors as average in the context of meta-analytical study, roughly on the level of other process variables correlating with psychotherapy outcome.

Another example of process–outcome meta-analysis is a study by Bohart, Elliott, Greenberg and Watson (2002) on the relationship between empathy and therapy outcome. The authors identified 47 research studies running 190 separate tests of this relationship. The studies they included in their meta-analysis used data from 3,026 clients. Bohart et al. (2002) found that the overall average correlation of empathy and outcome oscillated between 0.26 (the lowest estimate) and 0.32 (the highest estimate) depending on the meta-analytic procedure used (for more information see Bohart et al. 2002). Bohart et al. also examined some moderating variables. For example, they found that the therapist's experience paradoxically had a negative relationship to the relationship between empathy and outcome. This could probably mean, according to the authors, that for more experienced therapists there may be factors other than empathy that contribute to therapy outcome.

Examples of process–outcome studies and of their meta-analytic reviews show the diversity and potential theoretical and clinical relevance of this type of research. In general, we could say that process–outcome research provides a lot of information about the relationship between the process and the outcome of therapy from a macro-level perspective. Though they may find some links between the process in therapy and overall outcome, they do not say much about how precisely these processes work in the course of treatment. This is probably better captured by the detailed investigations of psychotherapy and counselling process and by testing models of therapeutic change (see below).

11

Descriptive Investigation of the Therapeutic Process

Some process research strategies focus on detailed investigations of how the therapeutic process leads to therapeutic change. The most frequent methodological procedure is the descriptive approach, which we will consider in this chapter; a slightly less frequent procedure is testing theories of therapeutic change (see Chapter 12). Detailed examination of the therapeutic process is important for the development of new therapeutic approaches. The relevance of the problems studied, the use of session transcripts and clients' and therapists' views of the therapeutic process make this kind of research potentially attractive to practitioners. The relevance of this kind of research is reflected in the large number of process studies despite the fact that these are usually funded less well than outcome studies.

Descriptive investigation of the therapeutic process employs exploratory research strategy to further our understanding of therapeutic interactions. It attempts to map processes present in therapeutic sessions as well as their reflection by the client and the therapist. Sometimes it also uses comparative elements, for example a comparison of helpful versus unhelpful interactions. The descriptive investigation may focus on therapy as a whole or on its parts. Most often, recordings and transcripts of sessions are used; sometimes retrospective recalls of therapeutic interaction are used as well.

Investigation of Various Aspects of the Therapeutic Process

The simplest form of descriptive (qualitative or quantitative) process research is *monitoring the incidence of some aspects of therapy throughout entire therapy or part of it*. These could be, for example, interventions used by the therapist or the client's verbal expressions. These aspects can then be assessed by independent raters, the therapist or the client. Often the recordings and transcripts of the session are used. Sometimes they

Table 11.1 Comparing percentages of the total number of responses in each category of verbal behaviours for Rogers, Perls and Ellis for one therapeutic session with the client Gloria

Type of therapist's verbal behaviours	Rogers (%)	Perls (%)	Ellis (%)
Minimal Encourager	53	8	14
Approval/Reassurance	1	5	1
Information	7	12	30
Direct Guidance	0	19	21
Closed Question	2	6	6
Open Question	1	10	3
Restatement	11	5	5
Reflection	7	1	2
Non-verbal Referent	0	5	0
Interpretation	7	12	12
Confrontation	2	6	1
Self-Disclosure	1	1	0
Silence	2	1	0

Source: C. E. Hill et al., 'Comparison of Rogers, Perls, and Ellis on the Hill Counselor Verbal Response Category System', *Journal of Counseling Psychology*, 26(3), 198–203, 1979. Published by American Psychological Association, reprinted with permission.

serve as a base for the therapist's and client's reflections or recall. Occasionally, reflections and recalls are used without an actual tape or transcript of the session. The goal of this kind of research is a closer examination of the counselling or psychotherapy process without inevitably connecting it to the overall outcome, though immediate outcome (impact) may be assessed.

A good illustrative example of a quantitative descriptive investigation of therapeutic process is an older study by Hill, Thames and Rardin (1979). The authors evaluated recordings of a therapeutic session carried out by Rogers, Perls and Ellis with the same client, using the Hill Counselor Verbal Response Category System (Hill, 1986; see Chapter 8). (There is a well-known film presenting the work of these three therapists with this client, named Gloria.) The goal of the study was to compare the behaviour of the three famous therapists, originators of different therapeutic approaches, in one session so that the validity of the Counselor Verbal Response Category System could be assessed. The results showed that the three therapists used different types of verbal intervention consistent with their theoretical background (see Table 11.1).

Another illustrative example is the study of Hill, Thompson, Cogar and Denman (1993), who analysed how precisely therapists recognize clients' reactions to their interventions and how accurately clients read therapists' intentions behind these interventions. Nineteen therapeutic dyads in long-term therapy were asked after one of the sessions (on average the 86th session) to review that session. For the review they used the following rating scales: the Client Reactions System and the Therapist Intentions List developed by Clara Hill. The clients rated the helpfulness of each of the therapist's interventions, guessed the intentions behind the therapist's interventions (they could choose up to three of 19 possible intentions) and stated their own reactions to the respective therapist interventions (they could choose three of 21 possible reactions).

The therapists stated three of their own intentions and guessed three clients' reactions. In addition, the clients and therapists were asked to state which of the clients' reactions were covert (meaning that the clients attempted not to show them).

Hill et al. (1993) found that the therapists had on average a 45% probability of, at least to some extent, recognizing the client's reactions, which was higher than chance. The clients had a 50% probability of at least partially identifying the therapist's intention correctly. As to the concealed clients' reactions, those significantly best disguised were negative reactions.

After adding another seven clients, Hill et al. (1993) focused on what clients do not say during the session, and why. They also concentrated on whether clients had secrets in therapy, the character of these secrets, and the reasons for keeping them. Hill et al. used questionnaires with open-ended questions for obtaining the answers. They found that 65% of clients in long-term therapy left at least one thing (a relevant feeling or thought) unsaid during their sessions. The reasons were, for example, that they were too over-whelmed by emotions, they wanted to avoid dealing with disclosure, and they were worried about not being understood by the therapist. With regard to secrets, 46% of clients admitted to one or two secrets kept hidden from the therapist. Most frequently, these were related to sexuality, personal failures or mental health problems. The reasons for not revealing a secret in front of the therapist were feelings of shame or embarrassment, concerns about how to say it or fear of how the therapist would handle the disclosure.

The work of David Rennie (1990) represents an exemplary case of the qualitative approach to descriptive research. Rennie was interested in clients' representations of the therapeutic hour. In his study, 12 clients were interviewed about a therapeutic session. An assisted recall using the recording of the session was used (Interpersonal Process Recall: Elliott, 1986; see also Chapter 8). The clients reviewed the session recording together with the researcher and were instructed to stop the tape whenever they recalled what they were thinking at that specific moment. The interviews were analysed according to the grounded theory approach (Glaser & Strauss, 1971).

In line with its discovery-oriented nature, the study brought many interesting and unanticipated findings. Rennie (1990), for example, found that the clients in the session evaluated the experiencing process and regulated it. The therapist was perceived as a fig-ure in the background, if he or she did not interfere with the client's process. Part of the client's process stayed private due to the speed of the process or the fact that the client was afraid of the therapist's reaction. The client's assessment of the interaction with the therapist was made in light of the client's plan and strategy for the session. For example, one of the clients lied to the therapist in the hope that the therapist would detect the lie, as the lying was the main reason why the client had sought therapy.

In case the therapist was not in tune with the client's plan, the client's activity in the session was focused on the therapeutic relationship. Clients who generally perceived the therapeutic relationship as being okay were able to tolerate it if the therapist conducted the session not according to the client's plan. On the other hand, clients who perceived the therapist's work as incompatible with their basic plans were preoccupied with the therapeutic relationship and did not have time to pay enough attention to their own process of exploration. Altogether, the clients did everything they could not to disturb the therapists by their own problematic experience of the therapist's behaviour. This *deference* towards the therapist was one of the main findings conceptualized by Rennie. The clients, for the sake of a good relationship with the therapist, surrendered to the therapist's expertness and, due to worries about not offending the therapist, did not communicate to the therapist whether they experienced his or her interventions as inappropriate, unpleasant, inadequate, etc.

An approach similar to that used by Rennie may also be used without the session tapes. Various aspects of the therapeutic process from the client's and the therapist's perspective may be investigated in this way. Various studies of helpful and unhelpful processes in psychotherapy illustrate such investigation. (see e.g. Lietaer & Neirinck, 1986; Lietaer, 1992; Paulson, Truscott & Stuart, 1999; Paulson, Everall & Stuart, 2001; Paulson & Worth, 2002; Lilliengren & Werbart, 2005; Levitt, Butler & Hill, 2006).

Impact of the Therapist's Interventions

A specific aspect of the therapy process is the immediate impact of therapist interventions. This can be assessed either by external raters or by the client him or herself; only rarely does the therapist assess the impact of his or her own intervention (see Hill, Thompson et al., 1993). When external raters are used, the tapes and transcripts of the sessions are needed; these are generally used when the client or the therapist evaluate impact as well. When analysing impacts of therapists' interventions, the short sequence 'intervention–impact' is usually used (e.g. Hill, 1989). Sometimes, however, a longer sequential analysis is employed (Heppner, Kivlighian & Wampold, 1999). In that case, the cycles of interaction are assessed such as 'the client's utterance–the therapist's intervention–its impact–the client's utterance–the therapist's intervention', etc. Sequential analysis is, for example, used in family therapy when typical interactional patterns between particular family members are monitored (Benjamin et al., 1986).

An illustrative example of research monitoring the impact of therapists' interventions is the work of Hill et al. (1993) mentioned earlier. Hill et al., apart from exploring the therapist's perceptions of client reactions and the clients' perceptions of the therapist's intentions, also investigated how the accuracy of these perceptions correlated with the clients' and therapist's evaluation of the helpfulness of the therapist's interventions and the clients' evaluation of the session outcome (the Session Evaluation Questionnaire and Client Satisfaction Questionnaire were used). The authors, for example, found that if clients did not perceive the therapist's intention as aiming to assess them, they evaluated the intervention more positively than in situations when they correctly perceived that the therapist was assessing them.

An example of the qualitative approach to evaluating the therapist's interventions is the work of Knox, Hess, Petersen and Hill (1997). Knox et al. interviewed 13 clients (with various problems such as depression, anxiety disorders and borderline personality disorder) in long-term therapy (on average, clients attended 60 sessions) about an example of helpful therapists' self-disclosure. The clients were asked to describe one example of helpful therapist disclosure and its impact on them. Using the Consensual

Qualitative Research method (Hill, Thompson & Nutt-Williams, 1997) Knox et al. discovered that the helpful therapists' self-disclosures provided the clients with insight into how to achieve a change; they enabled the clients to see the therapist as a real person; they normalized the client's experience and in some instances the therapist served as an example for the client. Knox et al. also found that though the overall impact of therapists' self-disclosures was positive, some clients experienced, alongside the positive, negative feelings related to concerns around overstepping boundaries or unwelcome closeness with the therapist.

Since psychotherapy and counselling attempt to have a positive impact on the client, it is logical that intensive studies of the immediate impact of various interventions, or studies looking at some central or specific interventions and their broader impact on the therapy and its outcome, should be carried out. Impacts are multifaceted, so different approaches are followed looking at different aspects of the impacts and different interventions and their impacts.

Therapeutic Events Studies

Detailed investigations of the psychotherapy process can also be focused on theoretically or clinically relevant segments of the therapy process, sometimes called therapeutic episodes, change episodes or therapeutic events (Greenberg, 1986). The term *events research paradigm* is also used. This type of investigation was significantly developed by Laura Rice and Les Greenberg (1984). Events research focuses on shorter segments of the psychotherapeutic process in order to analyse change processes and the therapist's contribution to them.

One of the strategies employed in events research is a procedure called *task analysis* developed by Laura Rice (Rice & Saperia, 1984) and Les Greenberg (1984, 2007). This method consists of cyclical steps in which many research instruments are used to describe the process present in a theoretically or clinically relevant therapeutic event (e.g. use of the two chair technique in experiential therapy), so that the change model and the model of the therapist's operations in the event can be determined. For example, using task analysis, Greenberg (1984) examined processes in the two chair technique used in Gestalt therapy for resolving inner conflicts. Rice (Rice & Saperia, 1984) used the same method for studying the technique of systematic evocative unfolding for resolving clients' problematic (puzzling) reactions in client-centred therapy. In the task analysis, the authors investigated events that showed both successful and unsuccessful resolution of the task.

Using different instruments (e.g. Experiencing Scale, Client Vocal Quality Scale), Greenberg and Rice attempted to describe processes present in successful and unsuccessful events. On the basis of such description, they prepared a model for the successful resolution of a particular task (two chair dialogue or systematic evocative unfolding) and then tried the model out on a new set of events. This process was repeated several times and more refined models were established. The task-analytic approach of Greenberg and Rice was revolutionary in psychotherapy process research, inspiring other event-based approaches (e.g. Ladany, Fiedlander & Nelson, 2005; Diamond & Liddle, 1996).

One of the examples using the task-analytic method is the programmatic work of Jeremy Safran and Christopher Muran (1996) investigating conflicts in the therapeutic relationship. In their study, Safran and Muran monitored 29 cases in 20-session integrative therapy with interpersonal, cognitive and experiential elements. Patients and therapists were asked after each session to divide the session in their mind into three parts (beginning, middle and end) and evaluate each part on selected items of the Working Alliance Inventory (WAI) (see Chapter 8). On the basis of their rating, the authors selected 15 sessions in which a conflict was present and resolved at the end of the session. After intensive observation of those 15 sessions, the authors created a preliminary model of conflict resolution in the therapeutic relationship.

The model (Safran & Muran, 1996), consisting of four stages, is presented in Box 11.1. This four-stage model was a starting-point for further empirical work. Safran and Muran (1996) selected transcripts of four resolved therapeutic relationship conflicts from three cases, and three unresolved conflicts from another three cases (conflicts in which alliance improved between any of the three parts of the session were considered resolved). The authors then used eight trained raters and four scales for evaluation of the interaction in conflicts (Structural Analysis of Social Behaviour – SASB, Experiencing Scales – EXP for therapist and for patient, and Client Vocal Quality Scale – CVQ; see Chapter 8). The SASB was able to identify a marker (indicator) of patients' withdrawal. Using that marker, transcripts of sessions were assessed by another two scales (EXP and CVQ). The results were used for informing a new (second) model of conflict resolution (see Box 11.1). The cases in the unresolved sample did not follow similar stages.

Box 11.1   The evolving models of Task analysis of conflict resolution

The first model:

1. The patient (P1) expressed directly (by confronting) or indirectly (by withdrawing from the interaction) that there was a conflict in the relationship (withdrawals dominated, therefore researchers further concentrated only on such cases). The therapist (T1) responded to it by exploring and focusing the patient on the here-and-now experiencing of the therapeutic relationship.
2. The patient expressed own negative feelings towards the therapist (P2), to which the therapist reacted (T2) empathically, accepting responsibility and validating the patient.
3. The therapist (T3) probed for fears that hinder the patient's expression of conflict in the relationship and the patient explored own withdrawal (P3). The second and third stages typically overlap.
4. The patients (P4) spontaneously articulated their role in the conflict and were able to generalize from that experience to other interpersonal situations.

(Continued)

(Continued)

The second model:

1. The first stage was the same as in the model above.
2. The patient (P2) expressed negative feelings along with withdrawal conflict signs. The therapist reacted by facilitating the patient's self-assertion.
3. The third stage overlapped with the second stage. The patient (P3a) disclosed what was blocking his or her self-assertion, the therapist (T3) was probing to label the block and the patient (P3b) explored the block more.
4. The patient in the last stage asserted his or her own view of the conflict (P4) and the therapist validated and supported the patient (T4).

Source: Safran and Muran, 1996.

The refined model (Safran & Muran, 1996) was then tested on three new resolved and three unresolved cases. Patients and therapists were asked to report the presence of a problem or tension in the therapeutic relationship and localize it in the session. Again the scales mentioned above were used. The authors tested a hypothesized sequence on the basis of findings on rating scales confirming the model. For example, in the first stage the patients used an externalized or limited voice quality and in the fourth stage (of the patients from the resolution group) an emotional or focused voice quality. With regard to the patients' experience, in the first stage, the experiencing was ≤2 of the seven stages of the Experiencing Scale (experiencing is measured from very superficial to very elaborate). The experiencing in the fourth stage was ≥4 on a seven-level scale, where 1 is shallow quality of experience and 7 is a deep experience.

Safran and Muran (1996) further refined the model using the conceptual framework of the Core Conflictual Relationship Themes method (CCRT – see Chapter 8; Luborsky & Crits-Christoph, 1990). They conceptualized the fourth stage as the expression of the patient's wish (assertion) and the second stage as the patient's response (irritation) to the perceived reaction of the therapist. The third stage (avoidance) was characteristic of the patient's response to the expected reaction of the therapist (anger). The use of task analysis by Safran and Muran (1996) is a good illustrative example of the method. It demonstrates the richness of process research as well as its usefulness for informing therapeutic practice (see also Chapter 14).

Investigation of therapeutic episodes is also possible without the use of session transcripts. Retrospective recall of the therapeutic process may be used. Again, this strategy may either focus on theoretically or clinically interesting events (e.g. Rhodes et al., 1994) or on events that proved to be significant in the therapy process (e.g. Levitt, Butler & Travis, 2006). An example of such work is the investigation of misunderstanding events between the client and the therapist by Renee Rhodes and her colleagues (Rhodes et al., 1994).

The team of researchers distributed 70 questionnaires asking clients (also professionals who underwent personal therapy) questions about a major misunderstanding event in the relationship with their therapist. The questions focused on areas such as when, in the course of therapy, the event happened; how they experienced the misunderstanding, and whether the experience changed over time; whether the event was resolved; whether they voluntarily revealed their dissatisfaction to the therapist; how did the event affect the therapy, etc. Nineteen participants filled out the questionnaire. Nineteen events were then assessed as to the resolution of misunderstanding. Eleven were considered to be resolved and eight events were considered unresolved. The questionnaires were then analysed using the Consensual Qualitative Research method (Hill, Thompson & Nutt-Williams, 1997). The two groups of events, resolved and unresolved, differed for example in the fact that the clients in resolved events assertively expressed their point of view more often. In addition, the resolved events were characterized by a mutual process of working on the resolution of misunderstanding. In comparison, in the unresolved events, therapists often insisted on their point of view or were unaware of or unresponsive to the client's dissatisfaction.

Significant Events Research

A specific form of event paradigm research is significant events research (Elliott, 1985; Timulak, 2007). In this kind of research, session events identified by clients as significantly helpful or unhelpful are investigated. Significant events research explores what events clients determine as helpful or unhelpful, what processes are present in these events and what impact they have on therapy outcome. In many significant events studies, recall interviews are conducted (Elliott, 1986), looking for the perspectives of the client and the therapist on a significant event. A framework including transcripts of sessions and the recalls is usually followed (Elliott & Shapiro, 1988).

Robert Elliott (1984), for example, studied insight events in therapy using the Comprehensive Process Analysis method that he developed (see Chapter 8). He analysed four insight events from various types of therapy (exploratory, psychodynamic and cognitive). The events were identified as significantly helpful by both clients and therapists, during the Interpersonal Process Recall (see Chapter 8). The Comprehensive Process Analysis used 11 sources of data focusing on the client process in the event and 11 focusing on the therapist process in the event. Some of the data were collected through quantitative measures (e.g. Client Vocal Quality scale, Experiencing Scale) and some through qualitative (e.g. Client Conversational Mode). On the basis of all available data, Elliott provided a general description of common characteristics of the four insight events.

He found that the clients, before the key intervention, were trying to understand a problematic experience and indirectly wanted the therapist to help them with it. The therapist's target intervention was thus an interpretation that focused on a core interpersonal issue of the client. The interpretation was complex, relating to material from previous sessions or various parts of the current session. It was usually delivered in several parts, sensitively and in a warm and friendly manner. The interpretation also contained imperfections and inaccuracies, which the clients tolerated. The client subsequently or concurrently with the interpretation worked internally and further processed information contained in the interpretation. This resulted in an insight that was characterized by the experience of newness, accuracy and relief, and by the feeling that the therapist had been helpful (the clients were noticeably more friendly towards the therapists). After the insight the clients continued to work with the interpretation; the cognitive stimulation led to further self-exploration and self-interpretation.

Events paradigm research was presented for the first time in the early 1980s (e.g. Elliott, 1983; Rice & Greenberg, 1984). Despite its potential, and its definite relevance to practice, studies did not take off as one might have expected. Nevertheless, the potential of this type of study is clearly present in the interesting examples above. The studies can not only enrich our understanding of therapeutic micro-processes, but may also lead to the development of therapeutic approaches, as Les Greenberg, Laura Rice and Robert Elliott (1993) showed well in the development of emotion-focused therapy.

Intensive (Systematic) Case Studies

A special form of descriptive psychotherapy process research is the *intensive case study*. Intensive case studies employ comprehensive data collection. Typically, researchers work with tape recordings of sessions and their transcripts as well as many other instruments that collect clients' and therapists' views on therapy and its process (see, for example, Hill, 1989; Elliott, 2002a). An advantage of intensive exploration of a case is that the researchers may draw on information from various resources (e.g. session transcripts, interviews about therapy, process and outcome measures collecting views of the therapist and the client). An example of an intensive case study is the Hermeneutic Single-Case Efficacy Design (Elliott, 2002a), which was considered in Chapter 3 when presenting the outcome studies. An important feature of intensive case studies is that they often focus on successful cases or compare successful and unsuccessful cases (e.g. Honos-Webb, Stiles et al., 1998). Such a strategy can help to delineate processes that contributed to the success of therapy, or prevented it. Intensive case studies may also be used in testing a particular change theory (e.g. Honos-Webb, Stiles et al., 1998) or even competing theories of change (Weiss & Sampson, 1986; see below). Their advantage then can be, as Stiles (2006) following Campbell's previous suggestion indicates, the fact that they may provide good evidence for the evaluation of a theory of therapy on the basis that they match this theory in 'precise or unexpected detail' (Stiles, 2006: 60). On the other hand, they can also contribute to theory building by paying attention to details that, if summarized across several cases, may lead to the formulation of a theory.

Case studies can be considered a mixture of process and outcome studies, as they usually look at both the process and the outcome of therapy. As pointed out in Chapter 3, they have special value for the development of established therapies as well as for the development of new approaches, thanks to the fact that they can allow themselves to focus on the details of the therapy process and how these are linked to the outcome. I presented intensive case studies in Chapter 3, and further examples focusing on the testing of therapeutic change theories are given in Chapter 12, so we will not look at them in greater detail here.

The examples of descriptive process research provided above show the potential informativeness of descriptive studies as well as their value for practitioners. Many of the studies presented here have implications that can readily inform the reader's practice. The main advantage is that the procedures employed provide perspectives that otherwise would not be accessible to the practitioner in routine practice. The discovery-oriented nature of most descriptive studies also encourages new ways of conceptualizing therapy. This is often fostered by giving clients the opportunity to express their views and talk about their experiences.

12

Testing Theories of Therapeutic Change and Therapeutic Processes

Another type of process research focuses on testing theories of therapeutic change and mechanisms that lead to change. Theories may well be informed by practical experience, but also derive from empirical findings from previous, usually exploratory, descriptive and intensive studies. Theories may also be informed by theoretical reasoning and empirical findings from areas outside counselling and psychotherapy (mostly general psychological research).

Testing theories of therapeutic change often requires investigation of whether a specific type of therapeutic interaction has therapeutically beneficial impacts in the short-term as well as the long-term perspective. Sometimes a spontaneous change in the client is observed and attributed to the relationship as a result of the conditions created by the therapist. Sometimes theoretically postulated mechanisms such as transference are tested for their presence in the actual therapy. Especially interesting are investigations that test competing theories (see Weiss & Sampson, 1986).

Testing psychological theories of therapeutic change allows us to assess postulated principles of how therapy works. Delineating these principles may inform therapeutic practice relatively independently of 'grand' therapeutic theories, which are often full of jargon and ideological bias. Recently, the edited book of Beutler and Castonguay (2005), mentioned in Chapter 5, had a similar goal.

Testing Transtheoretical Theories of Therapeutic Change

The theories of therapeutic change that we test may be linked to a particular therapeutic approach or may cut across several therapeutic approaches ('transtheoretical approaches'). Transtheoretical approaches view therapy as one, more or less unified, activity regardless of the different emphases of different theoretical approaches (see e.g. Prochaska & Norcross, 2003). Transtheoretical approaches see the differences between different therapies on a continuum, depending on what aspects of psychological functioning they address. Such theories provide a platform for integration of different therapeutic approaches or provide an explanation of mechanisms present in different therapeutic approaches.

One of the popular transtheoretical macro-level concepts is a stage model of change (DiClemente & Prochaska, 1982; Prochaska & DiClemente, 1983; more recently see Prochaska & Norcross, 2002). This model postulates six stages of behavioural change (see Box 12.1). The model is, according to its authors, non-linear and clients fluctuate from one stage to another. It was derived from empirical investigations of smoking cessation programmes and later of similar programmes for other addictions (Prochaska & DiClemente, 1983; Prochaska, DiClemente & Norcross, 1992; see also Prochaska & Norcross, 2002).

Box 12.1   Model of behavioural change (DiClemente & Prochaska, 1982; Prochaska & DiClemente, 1983; Prochaska & Norcross, 2002)

1. Pre-contemplation (the client has no intention of changing problematic behaviour).
2. Contemplation (the client is aware of a problem and need of change).
3. Preparation (the client is preparing for a change).
4. Action (the client is changing his or her behaviour).
5. Maintenance (the client is consolidating changes and works on the prevention of relapse).
6. Termination (a stable behaviour change is achieved).

In their wider theoretical work Prochaska and Norcross (2003) prescribe which therapeutic processes should be stimulated at different stages of change. For example, in pre-contemplation stage they suggest the provision of nurturing presence (Prochaska & Norcross, 2002). The stages of change model, though popular, has not yet been tested in the detailed process research, only in larger outcome studies (see for example MATCH project presented in Chapter 7). It was evaluated rather on a macro level, e.g. by assessing what therapy is most suitable for different stages of change or at what stage clients tend to terminate therapy prematurely (see an overview in Prochaska & Norcross, 2002).

An example of a transtheoretical formulation that has attracted much attention in intensive process research is the theory of assimilation of problematic experiences in therapeutic process developed by W. B. Stiles (2002) and his colleagues. The theory postulates that the process of therapeutic change is visible in the client's progress in working through the problems brought to therapy. It recognizes eight stages of assimilation of problematic experience (see Box 12.2).

Box 12.2   Assimilation of Problematic Experience Scale (APES)

0. Warded off/dissociated. Client is unaware of the problem. Affect is minimal.
1. Unwanted thoughts/active avoidance. Client avoids experience. Affect is intensively negative (episodic).
2. Vague awareness/emergence. Client is aware of a problematic experience but cannot formulate the problem clearly. Affect includes acute psychological pain.
3. Problem statement/clarification. Client clearly states the problem. Affect is negative but manageable.
4. Understanding/insight. The problematic experience is formulated and understood. Affect may be mixed.
5. Application/working through. The understanding is used to work on a problem. Affect is positive, optimistic.
6. Resourcefulness/problem solution. The formerly problematic experience has become a resource, used for solving problems. Affect is positive, satisfied.
7. Integration/mastery. Client automatically generalizes solutions. Affect is positive or neutral.

Source: adapted and shortened from Stiles, 2002, by permission of Oxford University Press, Inc.

The theory was built gradually, first on the basis of significant events research (Elliott, 1985; Stiles, Elliott et al., 1990) and then in a series of case studies (see overview in Stiles, 2002). It was tested by assessing whether different forms of therapy address problems in differents stage of assimilation, i.e. exploratory therapies in lower stages of the continuum vs. prescriptive at higher levels (Stiles, 2002).

An example of the use of assimilation theory is the work of Honos-Webb, Surko, Stiles and Greenberg (1999). The authors studied transcripts of 16-session-long emotion-focused (process-experiential) therapy (EFT) for depression (for more about the therapy see Chapter 14). The client, a 42-year-old female, improved on four outcome measures (Beck Depression Inventory, SCL–90, Inventory of Interpersonal Problems and Rosenberg's Self-Esteem Scale). For example, the score on the BDI before therapy was 30 and in the six-months follow-up 0; the Global Severity Index of the SCL was 1.79 before therapy and 0.07 at six-months follow-up. The results for the client far exceeded the average results of other clients in the larger study of EFT for depression. The researchers in the study applied the assimilation analysis, consisting of four steps:

1. Cataloguing (two researchers read transcripts of all sessions and recorded all topics that were worked on in therapy).
2. Identifying themes (researchers identified a new understanding of events in regard to the central themes of 'superwoman' and 'good girl').
3. Selecting passages (researchers identified all passages related to the two themes: a total of 43 segments).

4. Assigning assimilation ratings (researchers and later blind independent raters rated the assimilation level in 43 segments using an extended version of the Assimilation of Problematic Experiences Scale).

The results showed that both central themes were progressing in therapy relatively linearly along the levels of assimilation of problematic experiences as predicted by assimilation theory.

Stiles and his colleagues used a similar approach in other studies in which, for example, they compared cases with successful outcome versus cases with unsuccessful outcome. They found that unsuccessful cases, by contrast with successful ones, do not make progress in the assimilation of problematic experiences (Honos-Webb, Stiles et al., 1998; Shapiro, 1997). Stiles and his colleagues also studied the assimilation theory in different therapies (CBT, psychodynamic, experiential) (see the overview in Stiles, 2002). They studied cases in which progress was minimal due to the severity of the problematic experiences (e.g. work with severely traumatized refugees; Varvin & Stiles, 1999). The Assimilation of Problematic Experiences Scale was also used for studying critical factors responsible for progress from one level of assimilation to another (see Honos-Webb, Lani & Stiles, 1999).

Both examples, the stages of change model and the assimilation model, provide an empirically derived framework that can be applied to various therapeutic approaches. The models have not only explanatory and observational power but can be very informative in leading therapists to apply differential strategies to work with clients at various stages of the respective models. Incorporating both models into everyday practice may help practitioners to meet the clients where they currently are.

Testing Monotheoretic Theories of Therapeutic Change

Despite the developments in psychotherapy integration, monotheoretic approaches are still alive and well. An advantage of monotheoretic, as opposed to transtheoretic, approaches is that they are more specific. This may be beneficial in detailed studies of the therapeutic process. Investigations of theories of therapeutic change are typical, especially of psychodynamic and experiential approaches. I will focus here on two examples of testing psychodynamic theories.

The first example presents the Core Conflictual Relationship Theme method (CCRT; Luborsky & Crits-Christoph, 1990) that was introduced in Chapter 8. Paul Crits-Christoph and Lester Luborsky studied changes in the pervasiveness of the CCRT over the course of therapy. Just to remind you, Core Conflictual Relationship Themes are gathered through observation of repeated interactional patterns in the relationship episodes described by the client in the process of therapy. The repeated patterns are formulated into the Core Conflictual Relationship Theme(s) (usually one or two). A Core Conflictual Relationship Theme consists of the wish (W) the patient had in the relationship episodes, response(s) of others to that wish (RO), and response of the self to their response(s) (RS). For example: 'I want to be understood' (W: wish); 'They do not understand me' (RO: response of others); 'I am depressed about that' (RS: response of the self). Responses of others do not have to be perceived responses; they may also be expected responses and sometimes it may even be an internal process where the response of the other is a response from the introjected other, now the self.

In one of the studies, Crits-Christoph and Luborsky (1990) studied a sample of 33 patients (with depression, generalized anxiety disorder and personality disorders) in psychodynamic therapy. The pervasiveness of the Core Conflictual Relationship Theme (CCRT) established for each client was assessed by two independent raters. Pervasiveness was assessed on the basis of the proportion of all of the client's relationship episodes taken up by the CCRT. The raters assessed episodes from the beginning and end of therapy (therapy lasted from 21 to 149 sessions).

Crits-Christoph and Luborsky (1990) found that the wishes included in the CCRTs were the ones that appeared most often in the assessed episodes (more than 60% of assessed episodes contained them) and their pervasiveness did not change from the beginning to the end of therapy. The pervasiveness of expected negative reactions of others and negative reactions of the self declined significantly during the therapy process (from about 40% to 28% and 23%, respectively). Pervasiveness of positive responses of others and the self increased from about 10% to about 20%. The authors also found that the size of positive change in the CCRTs correlated with positive change in the outcome as assessed by the SCL–90. The authors concluded that the core conflictual patterns presented in psychodynamic therapy change and have a positive relationship with the change in psychopathological symptoms as postulated by psychodynamic theory.

In another study, Fried, Crits-Christoph and Luborsky (1990) tested the psychodynamic theory of transference on 35 patients in psychodynamic therapy. For each patient a Core Conflictual Relationship Theme was formulated on the basis of relationship episodes described by the patient that did not contain the therapist (the authors called these core relationship themes the other person CCRT). The other person CCRTs were then compared with the relationship episodes concerning the therapist (therapist episodes). A group of therapist episodes from one case was then paired either with the other person CCRT from that case (a matched pair) or with other person CCRTs from seven different cases (mismatched pairs). A larger number of mismatched pairs was used, to minimize the chance that relationship episodes from different cases would accidentally be similar in the matched pair. Three independent raters then rated the groups of relationship episodes and the CCRT components, matched and mismatched pairs (without knowing whether they were matched or mismatched), on a Likert-type scale from 1 = no similarity to 7 = high similarity.

The results showed that the CCRT components and the relationship episodes from the same case (matched pairs) were considered by the independent raters more similar than CCRT components and relationship episodes from different cases (mismatched pairs). The authors interpreted this finding as pointing to the presence of the transference mechanism in the clients' relationships to the therapists, as the clients' central problematic relationship patterns were also enacted in their relationship with the therapist.

Another example of testing a theory of therapeutic change is work evaluating the theory of unconscious testing of the patient's pathogenic belief in the relationship with the therapist (Weiss & Sampson, 1986; Weiss, 1993). Joseph Weiss, Harald Sampson and their colleagues tested, in a series of studies, two alternative psychoanalytic theories of change: the theory of automatic functioning (rooted in Freud's original writing) and the theory of higher mental functioning. According to the first theory (automatic functioning), psychopathological functioning is rooted in longing for the fulfilment of an unconscious wish, the frustration of which resulted in psychopathology. According to the second theory (higher mental functioning), at the centre of psychopathology are pathogenic beliefs based on interpersonal experiences connected with the fulfilment of wishes. According to the first theory, psychoanalytic therapy works through an interpretation of unconscious motives. According to the second one, therapy works by disproving the pathogenic beliefs in the therapeutic relationship.

The theory of higher mental functioning – in other words, the theory of the testing of pathogenic beliefs – assumes that the patient in childhood either (a) had to suppress the satisfaction of some impulse due to the fear of loosing his or her bond with the parents, or (b) experienced guilt due to linking satisfaction of an impulse with a traumatic event concerning his or her significant others, for which the patient felt responsible. These experiences then led to the formulation of pathogenic beliefs related to their wishes that hinder the patient's functioning as he or she fears that certain behaviours will lead to the loss of the other or to the patient's traumatization.

The theory of higher mental functioning assumes that the patient creates greater safety in the relationship with the analyst through disproving his or her own pathogenic beliefs by testing them in the relationship with the analyst. Mastery of the beliefs is, in a longer-term perspective, more gratifying than satisfaction of a suppressed impulse. If the therapist passes the tests, it leads to further and more direct testing. According to Weiss (1986), the patient tests the analyst through the transferential repeating of his or her own way of relating to significant others or through turning the passive into the active, meaning that the patient treats the analyst in the way the patient was treated by his or her significant others. While doing this the patient unconsciously hopes that the analyst's behaviour will be different from that expected in the pathogenic belief. The patient thus basically tests whether satisfying some wish is threatening either to the patient or the therapist. According to Weiss, the analyst passes the tests usually by staying in his or her usual therapeutic mode. If the therapist does not pass the test, the patient, according to Weiss, usually adapts the test to make it easier for the therapist to pass. The patient may also help the therapist to pass the test.

Sampson (1986) conceptualizes testing the two alternative hypotheses. He postulates that in the case of validity of the automatic functioning theory, if the patient presses the analyst to satisfy his or her wish, the therapist's refusal will lead to an increase in anxiety and conflict between the wish and its satisfaction. If the higher mental functioning theory is valid, the therapist's refusal will lead to a decrease in anxiety and better engagement in therapy, because the patient will experience disproof of the feared pathogenic belief that the following of his or her own wishes threatens the therapeutic relationship or the therapist. Disconfirmation of the pathogenic belief in the interaction may also open a space for exploration of this belief.

A series of empirical studies tested the hypothesis of testing pathogenic beliefs. Joseph Caston (1986) developed a version of the Plan Formulation Method (see Chapter 8). Using a similar procedure to that outlined in Chapter 8, the team of researchers formulated patients' goals, obstacles that prevent their fulfilment, expected tests that patients will apply in the relationship with the therapist (including an estimate of the valence of the test) and the behaviour of the therapist that would be considered compatible with the test.

George Silberschatz (1986) investigated, in a case study, the hypothesis that the therapist's passing of the patient's test results in a more productive therapeutic process. The patient in the study was a female client with obsessive-compulsive disorder in long-term psychoanalysis. Independent raters were asked to select, from the first 100 hours of therapy, the episodes in which the patient seemed to be searching for some response from the analyst. The assumption here was that such episodes are quite likely instances of testing the analyst. Eighty-seven of such episodes were assessed by three analysts with regard to their relevance for the case formulation. The analysts used a prepared formulation (the process is outlined in Chapter 8). Forty-seven tests were identified as the key tests. Four different analysts then assessed whether the therapist passed the test on a scale from 0 to 6. Different groups of analysts then assessed segments before the tests and after the tests. They assessed level of experiencing (using the Experiencing Scale; see Chapter 8), boldness in tackling problems (the boldness rating scale), level of relaxation (the relaxation scale) and the presence of affective states such as love, satisfaction, anxiety and fear in the segments. The analysts did not know whether the segments they were assessing were from before the test or after the test. The results showed that the level of passing the patient's test significantly correlated with deeper experiencing, greater boldness and relaxation, as well as with the emotion of love. The level of passing the test correlated negatively with levels of anxiety and fear. This corresponded with Weiss' theory (Weiss, 1986, 1993) that lack of fulfilment of the wish does not have to lead to frustration.

A direct test of the above competing psychoanalytic hypotheses was performed by Silberschatz, Sampson and Weiss (1986), who studied one psychoanalytic case and collaborated with analysts who were proponents of the competing hypothesis of automatic functioning. The proponents of each theory selected episodes in which the patient made a demand of the analyst, assuming that it represented either the need for gratification of a wish (automatic functioning) or the testing of pathogenic belief (higher mental functioning). Thirty-four segments were deemed by both teams to be central to their respective formulations of the case. The results showed that those segments that seemed to represent optimal frustration of the patient's wish (from the perspective of the supporters of automatic functioning theory) were at the same time instances of optimal passing of the patient's test by the analyst. The scales used by Silberschatz (1986) showed that the patient, after an optimal frustration or the analyst passing a test, increased the exploration of problematic experiences, was more relaxed and less anxious, which corresponded more with the higher mental functioning theory. The finding and the methodology were very interesting as they showed that though the two teams representing opposing theories agreed on an optimal way of working, the theory of one team explained the patient's in-session behaviour better.

The examples of the testing of monotheoretic theories of therapeutic change show their informative richness for practice and their potential for theory development (in the case of higher mental functioning theory). They show that even sophisticated psychotherapeutic theories may be empirically tested in relatively typical practice conditions (the only difference is the use of tape recording and having consent for the research).

Conclusion

Psychotherapy process research is an extremely broad area of research. It looks at what actually happens behind the therapist's door from different angles. In the previous pages we briefly scanned different types of psychotherapy and counselling process research. What can be said about it as a summary?

1. Process research is characterized by a great variety of often original methodological approaches This type of research is often innovative, providing new perspectives on what is happening in therapy. As the process of therapy is very complex, researching it provides a challenge that needs to be addressed by the use of sophisticated methodological approaches. To keep process research meaningful, researchers must combine scientific rigour and practical relevance. In the previous pages, I have tried to show that this is possible.

2. Process research can readily inform therapeutic practice The richness of information provided by process research can inform everyday practice much better than outcome research, which is relatively 'distant' from practice. The immediate impact as well as the great detail captured by process research provide practising therapists with an often otherwise inaccessible perspective that can enrich their understanding of the therapeutic process. Process research can inform both new, evolving therapeutic approaches and modifications of established ones.

3. Process research often uses the client's view of therapeutic process The fact that some sorts of process research allow the client's voice to be heard may be another strength of this type of research. Clients are not only consumers of psychological therapy, but also active collaborators in making therapy work (Bohart & Tallman, 1999), so to hear their view of the therapeutic process is very valuable to therapists and researchers. Their 'lay' perspective may also be informative because of its independence from mainstream psychotherapeutic theories, thus providing a fresh look at concepts that are often taken for granted simply because of tradition.

4. Process research may be less dependent on the availability of resources Many types of process research presented in this part of the book used quite small resources (at least in comparison to large RCTs). This may make some types of process research appealing to PhD students, practitioners, and academics who lack large financial resources. On the other hand, though financial resources may not always be a prerequisite of embarking on a process study, the problem may be the demands this type of research makes on the researcher (especially its time-consuming nature). Many process studies, for example, focus on the evaluation of therapy transcripts and tapes. Ethical issues in conducting process research may also be more complex, because of the often intensive involvement of participants.

Psychotherapy and counselling process research may offer a pleasant surprise for practitioners who are unfamiliar with the research. Many practitioners may enjoy reading case presentations without being aware that they often represent process research (though often not in a very systematic and rigorous way). Many process studies may, therefore, be familiar to the practitioner-reader as they may resemble traditional process and case reports. Process studies represent a very similar approach to what happens in the process of therapy and how change does or does not come about.

PART III

CONTEXT AND PRACTICE

Psychotherapy and counselling research is broader than simply outcome and process research. In Chapter 13, I will briefly outline what else can be covered by the umbrella of research in psychotherapy and counselling.

There is another issue that I will focus on in this part of the book: an issue I have alluded to throughout the book. It is the research–practice link. Though there are different partial goals of psychotherapy and counselling research, the ultimate objective of research in psychotherapy and counselling is to improve therapeutic practice and thus achieve better outcomes for clients. I will discuss this area in Chapter 14.

13

Research on the Context of Psychotherapy and Counselling

Besides outcome and process research, in research in psychotherapy and counselling there are a number of studies which can be assigned to neither outcome nor process studies. Usually this kind of research focuses on the context of psychotherapy and counselling. We will now look at some examples of the areas pertinent to therapy that are being studied and what issues are being explored.

Studying the Utilization of Psychotherapy and Counselling

It is certainly interesting to know some facts about how psychotherapy is conducted in everyday practice. Studies mapping patterns of mental health utilization, types of service available, professionals offering psychological therapy and counselling as well as the type of clients attending therapy (see Howard, Cornille et al., 1996) are – alongside epidemiological studies – an important tool allowing the creation of a more precise picture of the types of therapy offered as well as showing gaps that could be filled. Examining the differences found between prevalence of disorders and actual clients or patients seeking treatment are a first step in reasoning why some clients do not use therapy and what kind of help could be provided to them. It is important to know how clients who seek psychotherapy differ from those with similar problems who do not seek it. It is also interesting to know on what basis clients choose their therapists.

Comprehensive overviews of studies looking at the use of psychotherapy are provided by Garfield (1994) and Clarkin and Levy (2004). Their overviews show, for example, that therapy is usually practised in brief forms and clients also expect therapy to be brief; that clients are more often women than men, younger people than older; and that accessibility of social support can be a determinant of help-seeking behaviour. Concerning the selection of a psychotherapist, see, for example, Worthington and Sandage (2002), who draw mainly on their own work on religious affiliations and selection of therapists to conclude that highly religious clients prefer similar therapists and that their behaviour in therapy is influenced by the religious beliefs of the therapist (e.g. when religious views are not strong the clients censor what they say with regard to religious issues).

An example of an epidemiological study with findings relevant to the provision of psychotherapy is the work of Narrow, Rae, Robins and Regier (2002), who re-analysed two large epidemiological studies of the adult population in the USA (the two pro-grammes were the National Institute of Mental Health Epidemiologic Catchment Area Program and the National Comorbidity Survey). Taking into consideration the clinical significance and the lower prevalence found in both studies, Narrow et al. consider, as a conservative estimate, that approximately 18.5% of the adult population suffers from a mental disorder in the course of one year.

The question of why some people do not seek treatment even though they could ben-efit from it is yet to be properly addressed, though there are studies that focus on this problem, such as Meltzer et al.'s work (2003). Meltzer et al. undertook a survey of house-holds in Britain and identified individuals with neurotic disorders (altogether they included more than 10,000 adults, of whom around 1,500 had a neurotic disorder). Approximately 25% of those with a disorder did not seek help. Symptom severity, social dysfunction and consumption of alcohol were negative predictors of seeking help. Among the reasons given for not seeking help, thoughts such as 'did not think anybody could help' and 'One should be able to cope with a problem' dominated. Similar studies would certainly be welcomed. An important aspect may be the general public's attitudes to mental health problems and mental health treatments to which specific stigma is attached.

Research on Psychotherapists

Another interesting area of research that provides a context relevant to the provision of psychotherapy is research focusing on psychotherapists. The problems studied vary; they may include theoretical orientation (see Orlinsky, Ronnestad et al., 1999), style of interpersonal relating (Bruck et al., 2004), development over the years of practice (Orlinsky, Ronnestad et al., 1999), and therapists' values and attitudes (Jensen & Bergin, 1988; Bergin & Jensen, 1990).

The psychotherapist's personality is a central variable. As we saw in Chapter 7, thera-pists may differ quite dramatically in their effectiveness. Also, studies of therapists' values and attitudes and their impact on the client show that clients tend to adopt certain ther-apists' values, namely those they see as relevant to mental health (Beutler, Machado & Neufeldstat, 1994).

An exemplary case of a programmatic study of psychotherapists is the collaborative work of Orlinsky, Ronnestad et al. (1999). Orlinsky et al.'s study is definitely the largest project on psychotherapists ever conducted. It began at the end of the 1980s and it is still in progress. The first data, which included more than 3,800 psychotherapists from more than 12 countries, was published in 1999. The project uses a common instrument, the Development of Psychotherapists Common Core Questionnaire. This questionnaire gathers data on psychotherapists' training, professional practice, professional development, experiences from their own personal therapy, theoretical orientation, modality used in their practice, their own experiences in therapeutic work, and in their personal life (see the outline of the questionnaire in Box 13.1). One version of the questionnaire also asks about religious affiliation and the influence of religious views and spirituality on the therapist's identity (Smith, 2004).

Orlinsky, Ronnestad et al. (1999) presented the first findings from the project concerning psychotherapists' professional development. For example, they found that the majority of therapists rate their development as substantial in comparison to their early years of practice, but that less than half rate themselves high on competence. The evaluation of their professional development positively correlates with the evaluation of the quality of their work and also with positive experience in their own therapeutic work.

The project led to a book, which presented broader findings (Orlinsky & Ronnenstad, 2005) from almost 5,000 therapists. The authors focused on patterns of work experience, recognizing either healing involvement (e.g. characterized by feelings of being effective, committed, skilful) or stressful involvement (e.g. feelings of anxiety, avoidance of therapeutic engagement, professional self-doubt). They found that 50% of therapists perceived themselves as 'effective' in their practice, meaning that they are highly 'healingly involved' and have little stress. The work of 23% of the therapists could, according to Orlinsky and Ronnestad (2005), be labelled as challenging (high on healing involvement as well as on stressful involvement); 17% were disengaged in their practice (low on healing involvement and low on stressful involvement); and 10% were distressed in their work (low on healing involvement and high on stressful involvement). The authors also found that healing involvement was explicable by variables such as currently experienced growth, sense of overall career development, or theoretical breadth. In contrast, stressful development was explicable by currently experienced depletion, dissatisfaction with work as a therapist, etc.

Box 13.1 Main domains of the Development of Psychotherapists Common Core Questionnaire (according to Orlinsky et al.)

Types of professional psychotherapeutic training (23 items ascertaining, for instance, academic background, professional certification, current supervision, etc.)

Professional experience (21 items asking, for instance, about number and variety of clients, supervising or treating other therapist, etc.)

Overall development as a therapist (51 items concerning, for instance, possible change in theoretical orientation, change in quality of work, etc.)

Experience of personal therapy (7 items asking, for instance, about benefits of personal therapy)

Orientation of therapeutic work (52 items asking questions relating to the therapist's theoretical beliefs)

Current development as a therapist (35 items asking about everyday experience of therapeutic work)

(Continued)

(Continued)

Forms of practising (43 items asking, for instance, whether therapist practises group or individual therapy, with what clientele, etc.)

Experienced quality of therapeutic work (96 items asking, for instance, about fields of expertise, personal limitations in work, etc.)

Personal life and self-experience of therapist (42 items covering, for instance, current self-concept, etc.)

Source: adapted with permission from Orlinsky et al., 1999.

The work of Orlinsky, Ronnestad and their colleagues is an exciting venture that looks cross-culturally at such an important variable as the therapist. The breadth, comprehensiveness and level of international collaboration of this study deserve commendation. Probably the strongest feature of this project is its international nature, allowing for comparisons among therapists from different countries.

A different type of study examining psychotherapists is the work of Jennings and Skovholt (1999). Because this research was so original, we will look at it in more detail. The authors asked therapists in the Midwest community in the USA to nominate the best therapists among their colleagues. The selection followed the 'snowball' principle, i.e. three known therapists were asked to nominate three they thought were master therapists (excellent therapists); these then nominated another three, and so on. The nomination should follow these criteria: (a) the nominated person should be a master therapist; (b) one would refer a close person to this therapist; and (c) one would have full confidence in seeing this therapist for one's own personal therapy.

The procedure led to the selection of the ten therapists who received the most nominations (from a total number of 103 nominated at least once). These therapists were interviewed using 16 open-ended questions (for examples see Box 13.2). After two months, the researchers carried out a follow-up interview, in which the respondents had the chance to comment on the preliminary results.

Box 13.2   Examples of questions for master therapists

How do you differ from when you started your career?
What distinguishes a good therapist from a great therapist?
What is particularly 'therapeutic' about you?
How does your emotional health impact the therapy you do?
How does the person you are impact the therapy you do?
How do you know when you are doing a good job with a client?
How does psychotherapy heal?

Source: Jennings and Skovholt, 1999.

Eventually, Jennings and Skovholt (1999) presented nine themes, which arose from the interviews and which were mentioned by at least eight of the ten therapists. These concerned three domains: cognitive, emotional and relational. The cognitive domain included themes which referred to the fact that 'master therapists' are voracious learners; they use their accumulated experience as a resource; and they value the cognitive complexity and ambiguity of the human condition. The emotional domain covered the facts that master therapists are non-defensive, open to feedback, reflective; are mature and mentally healthy; and aware of how their emotional health affects the quality of their work. The relational domain showed that master therapists possess strong relationship skills and that they use them in therapy; a strong working alliance is, according to them, the foundation of therapeutic change.

Skovholt and Jennings (2004) used the sample of master therapists for a few other studies. For example, they looked at how master therapists construe the therapeutic relationship, how they build emotional wellness and resilience, and what ethical values they pursue. They gathered their data over a period of seven years. Finally, they attempted to paint a portrait of master therapists (see Skovholt, Jennings & Mullenbach, 2004) on the basis of the analysis of several studies they conducted. They did this in several ways. They listed paradoxical characteristics (e.g. a drive to mastery, yet never the sense of having fully arrived), identifying characteristics (e.g. maximum use of personal life experiences as food for growth; humility is present while grandiosity is kept at bay; accepts self as having professional limitations), word characteristics (e.g. alive, congruent, committed), and central characteristics (e.g. cognitive characteristics such as embraces complex ambiguity; emotional characteristics such as deep acceptance of self; and relational characteristics such as being able to engage others intensively).

The work of Jennings and Skovholt shows an original approach to the problem of establishing who are the most skilful therapists. Though one may object that the therapists in their studies were selected on the basis of word-of-mouth rather than on the basis of effectiveness measured by established outcome measures, the major strength is the in-depth analysis of the experiences and perspectives of the selected therapists.

The studies on psychotherapists, as shown in the above examples, help us to know who is offering therapy, what psychotherapists experience when they conduct therapy, or what contributes to therapists' productivity. As therapists can differ dramatically in their effectiveness, it is important to know something about them. Also, if we are thinking in terms of continuous professional development, it is worthwhile understanding what the potential needs of therapists are.

Research on Psychotherapy and Counselling Training

Psychotherapy training is not a very widely researched area. Very little is known empirically about how to teach psychotherapy and counselling, what to teach, how long to teach, what an education in therapy should consist of, what is optimal supervision, what place individual therapy plays in training, what place psychotherapy research plays in training, etc. The majority of psychotherapy and counselling training models are based on tradition: they evolved in a gradual manner, building on the experiences and reflections of professionals involved in developing training. Though there exists some general consensus on what and how future psychotherapists should learn, not much of it is based on empirical foundations.

The same applies to continuous professional development. Traditionally, for example, supervision when in training as well as continuous supervision after training are key for practitioners conducting therapy. Similarly, personal therapy when in training and afterwards is emphasized. Both activities are central to the therapist's training and are very highly regarded by generations of therapists. However, not much is known about the impact of personal therapy and ongoing supervision on the therapists. Research on training in psychotherapy and counselling is trying to provide us with knowledge in this regard.

An example of sophisticated well-conducted research on the effectiveness of psychotherapy training is the study of Guthrie et al. (2004). The authors used an interesting format of training in psychodynamic-interpersonal therapy (PI). Twenty-four counsellors working in primary care in the UK (mainly using the person-centred approach) were trained in psychodynamic-interpersonal therapy. The main measure assessing the level of adherence to the PI model of treatment, i.e. outcome of the training, was the Sheffield Psychotherapy Rating Scale. This scale was used in the Sheffield research studies (see Chapter 2) comparing the effectiveness of psychodynamic-interpersonal and CBT therapy for depression. The scale enables psychodynamic and CBT therapy modes to be differentiated by assessing videotapes of actual therapist behaviour.

In the study, the counsellors were first asked to carry out a 20-minute session with a role-playing client. Each counsellor saw one client simulating depression, one simulating somatization problems and one simulating suicidal tendencies. Afterwards, the counsellors completed an intensive one-week training course in psychodynamic-interpersonal therapy. After the training, they again did the role-play sessions. Then, for a period of three months, the counsellors provided psychodynamic-interpersonal therapy with at least two real patients with various problems. They completed eight sessions with each patient and during that time they received supervision in small groups (3–5 counsellors). Finally, after three months of providing supervised psychodynamic therapy, they again did a therapeutic session with a role-playing client.

Using the Sheffield rating scale, the authors showed that the counsellors learned the skills of psychodynamic-interpersonal therapy, but did not lose their basic counselling skills. The counsellors showed adequate levels of adherence to the psychodynamic-interpersonal model in simulated as well as real therapeutic sessions. In addition, the psychodynamic therapy that they performed led to positive outcomes as measured by the CORE–OM questionnaire (see Chapter 1). The evaluation of the effect of three-month therapy with the real patients showed that 50% of patients of the counsellors providing psychodynamic-interpersonal therapy achieved clinically significant change.

Guthrie et al.'s (2004) study is a nice example of a sophisticated design showing that trainees–professionals are capable of picking up new skills, however complex, in a very brief time and competently and effectively use them in practice. The design is also interesting because it not only assesses the level of skills acquired by trainees but also their validity as tested by the outcomes achieved in everyday practice. This level of sophistication is extremely rare in the studies of psychotherapy training.

The Role of Personal Therapy

Another area of research relevant to training in psychotherapy and counselling is research on the role of personal therapy in training and clinical work. This type of research looks at the impact personal therapy has on trainees, but it can also focus on the therapists who provide such therapy (e.g. Norcross, Geller & Kurzawa, 2000).

An example of research looking at the importance of personal therapy is the work of Macran, Stiles and Smith (1999), who were interested in how personal therapy influenced the clinical work of seven practising therapists. The study in question looked at therapists with at least three years' practice. Each of the therapists studied attended therapy for a couple of years. They usually had more than one therapist, mainly of psychodynamic orientation. Two to three semi-structured interviews were conducted with the therapists about reasons for seeking therapy, the meaning of individual therapy, helpful and unhelpful aspects of therapy, and how therapy had helped their own clinical work.

Twelve themes appeared as a result of qualitative analysis. For example, the therapists realized what uneasy feelings the client can have in therapy. They saw how important it was for those who practise therapy to have their wounds healed. They also realized that it was human to need therapy. Another feature was that their own therapists served as role models for them: they imitated their therapists when they practised therapy. Therapy also taught them to be more open with others and work on a deeper level.

Studying the personal therapy of therapists is an area that will probably need more attention in the future. Though quite a lot is known about how many therapists have experience of personal therapy (either due to training requirements or for personal reasons) (Norcross & Guy, 2005; Orlinsky, Botermans et al., 2005), how therapists usually experience personal therapy (Orlinsky, Norcross et al., 2005), how it affects their practice (Orlinsky, Norcross et al., 2005), how therapists select their own therapy, or why they hesitate to seek therapy (Norcross & Grunebaum, 2005; Norcross & Connor, 2005), not much has been established about how personal therapy affects the way one conducts therapy (Orlinsky, Norcross et al., 2005). The importance of studying personal therapy is rooted in the fact that traditionally, and in many contexts still predominantly, attending personal therapy is an essential requirement for therapists. However, it still is not known exactly how the variation (or potential variation) in exposure to personal therapy affects one's development as a therapist.

Supervision

Another component of psychotherapists' training is supervision. Supervision research often utilizes its own methods (e.g. Supervision Questionnaire – Worthington & Roehlke,

1979; Supervision Expectations Questionnaire – Bahrick, Russell & Salmi, 1991; Role Conflict and Role Ambiguity Inventory – Olk & Friedlander, 1992). Supervision research can be roughly divided into outcome and process research as well. Though research on supervision contains a huge number of studies, they mainly focus on satisfaction with supervision and factors contributing to it (see Wheeler, 2003) or on the contribution of supervision to the development of the skills of trainee therapists (see Lambert & Ogles, 1997). There are almost no studies that assess the actual impact of supervision on outcomes of supervised therapy (however, there are exceptions to this rule, as I show in the example below). There are also virtually no studies on how supervision impacts the effectiveness of established practitioners (Wheeler, 2003), even though it is often recommended – if not required – that therapists are in regular supervision.

It is a similar situation with regard to supervision process research. A limited number of studies (Wheeler, 2003) look at the empirical foundations of diverse models of supervision. Supervision process research is more concerned with identifying helpful or unhelpful factors in supervision. In particular, research focusing on characteristics that are valued by supervisees in their supervisors, or that influence supervisees' behaviour, is quite well established (see overview in Allsteter-Neufeldt, Beutler & Banchero, 1997).

An example of a uniquely sophisticated research design is the work of Bambling, King, Raue, Schweitzer and Lambert (2006). Bambling et al. studied 127 therapists providing brief, eight session-long, problem-solving treatment for 127 clients with a diagnosis of major depression. The therapists were randomly assigned to three groups: unsupervised (n = 38), in process-focused supervision (n = 34), and in skills-focused supervision (n = 31). The supervision was provided by 40 supervisors trained in the respective models of supervision. Process-focused supervision concentrated on helping the therapist to develop an understanding of interpersonal dynamics in order to improve the therapeutic alliance. Skills-focused supervision centred on the alliance as well; however, through the means of direct guidance of working with goals, tasks, and bond aspects of the alliance. Supervision lasted eight sessions, so it matched the length of the treatment provided.

Two main measures were used to assess the effect of supervision on outcome. The Working Alliance Inventory (WAI) (Horvath & Greenberg, 1989) assessing the client's perceived alliance in the first, third and eighth sessions and the Beck Depression Inventory (BDI) (Beck et al., 1988) used to evaluate pre-post outcome. WAI evaluations showed scores indicating a stronger alliance for the supervised groups in comparison to the unsupervised group. BDI scores also showed a larger improvement in the supervised groups in comparison to the unsupervised group. There were no differences between the two supervised groups. Especially surprising was the difference in retention rates. While 35% of clients did not finish therapy in the unsupervised group, only 3% and 6%, respectively, of the clients did not finish therapy in the supervised groups.

This study really has no parallel among other studies on supervision, in level of sophistication. Though there were some limitations to the study (e.g. allegiance), of which the authors were well aware, one important safeguard was the fact that the clients did not know whether their therapist was in the active supervision or the control condition. This type of study may well be the future of research on supervision, if we want to establish a more direct link between supervision and its outcomes.

An example of supervision process research is the work of Gray, Ladany, Walker and Ancis (2001). Using long qualitative interviews with 13 psychotherapy trainees, Gray et al. examined their experience of a counterproductive event that occurred in individual supervision. The trainees were doctoral students in counselling psychology. They had seen on average 65 clients and had received on average 19 months of supervision. The supervision, which was the focus of the research interview, lasted an average of 15 weeks, with sessions approximately once a week. The interview, based on previous studies, consisted of questions focused on several areas, for example: description of the counterproductive event; perception of supervisor experience before, during and after the event; desired supervisor response; influence of the event on further supervision; presence of parallel process; dreams related to event and so on.

The researchers found that counterproductive events were related to the supervisor's dismissal of the trainee's thoughts or feelings; lack of understanding of the trainee; denial of the trainee's request; or the supervisors' telling the trainee to behave differently. They also found that often supervisors subsequently did not listen to the trainee, challenged the trainee or pushed their own agenda. That often led the trainees into confusion, negative thinking about themselves and about the relationship with the supervisor. Often it was a pattern quite typical for the entire supervision (but not always: sometimes it was a negative exception). The supervisors were often not aware of the trainees' experience. The trainees would prefer empathic and supportive reactions, perhaps even a discussion of the counterproductive event. This event usually led to the increased defensiveness of the trainee, his or her guardedness or withdrawal and non-disclosure. Some trainees disclosed their negative experience, which led in some cases to a supportive response from the supervisior. Some trainees reported a negative influence of the event on their supervision and some also admitted to a negative impact on their work with clients.

Gray et al.'s (2001) study is a nice example of a qualitative study that can inform one's practice as a supervisor in the context of postgraduate training. The vividness of the examples used in the original study may even provide interesting reading for practising supervisors. Though the study did not use transcripts of the supervision and therefore it is hard to establish to what extent the retrospective recall captures what actually happened in the session, an important strength of the study is that it gives a voice to the supervisee, which can inform people involved in providing supervision.

Both of these examples of supervision studies provide the reader with an idea of what interesting problems can be addressed when studying supervision and how relevant they can be for everyday practice as a supervisor, but also for the therapist. The examples show again that the diverse features of psychotherapy research, such as experimental (e.g. RCT) methodology or qualitative in-depth interviewing focusing on participants' experience, may also be found in supervision research. The only distinction is, as is shown in Bambling et al.'s study, that supervision research may add another layer to the impact of the intervention being investigated. It affects not only the direct recipient of the intervention (therapist–supervisee), but also the client. This complexity is probably responsible for the fact that most supervision studies are in reality not investigating supervisee's clients.

As we have seen in this chapter, psychotherapy and counselling research are not limited only to outcome and process research. There is a whole context of psychotherapy involving patients (clients) and potentially also their families, therapists, the training of therapists, supervision, the institutional context of therapy, and even the research context of psychotherapy. All of these are legitimate areas of interest to therapists and researchers, all can have potentially important impacts on the delivery and outcomes of counselling and psychotherapy services. It is important to bear in mind that different aspects of the therapy context have specific elements that affect the methodology used in them, ranging from surveys and interviewing when investigating the attitudes and views of potential clients or therapists to thorough experimental designs that can assess the impact of training or supervision on therapist performance and client outcomes.

14

The Link between Research and Practice

Though the previous chapters have focused mainly on presenting different areas of psychotherapy research, the relevance of different kinds of research to therapeutic practice was often mentioned as well. In this chapter I will try to elaborate on the relevance of psychotherapy research for constantly developing therapeutic practice and I will also discuss some successful examples of using research in informing therapeutic practice. I will specifically present examples of empirically informed therapies from different theoretical approaches.

Outcome Research and Practice

There are several ways in which outcome studies can influence therapeutic practice. For example, they may contribute to the therapist's *stability*. The therapist who is informed about the effectiveness of an intervention he or she uses will have realistic expectations about the extent to which the intervention may be helpful, or to what extent it may be decisive as part of an overall treatment 'package' (see dismantling studies in Chapter 2). Such a therapist should also be able to estimate the predictors that will impact on the intervention for a particular client, depending on the client's characteristics. The therapist may also be able to estimate the number of sessions needed to increase the likelihood of a positive impact.

The therapist can also use outcome studies to check his or her own effectiveness against that reported in empirical studies. Outcome research is then used as a form of feedback about the therapist's own effectiveness. Where effectiveness is lower than reported in the outcome studies, the therapist can examine these for potential variables that might be responsible for the difference (e.g. different types of client without co-morbid disorders, the possibility of intensive supervision, etc.) or can reflect on whether the interventions used in the studies that report better outcome differ from the ones he or she is using. If so, the therapist can focus on developing his or her own practice, for instance by undergoing further training.

Awareness of therapy effectiveness may also be used as an intervention in the process of psychotherapy. In interpersonal therapy for depression, for example, information about outcomes, typically reported in the outcome studies investigating this type of therapy, is usually communicated to the client at the beginning of therapy (Gillies, 2001). The client has thus a chance to form realistic expectations about what benefits therapy can have, but also of the potential limitations of the therapy.

Another way of applying outcome research is to use studies focused on the dose–effect relationship of therapy (Howard, Kopta et al., 1986) to obtain a picture of the number of therapy sessions needed, or to apply the new form of dose–effect research, i.e. an ongoing *monitoring* of the effectiveness of a specific case and benchmarking this against the expected curve of recovery based on a relevant referential data set (see Whipple et al., 2003; Ogles, Lambert & Fields, 2002; Chapter 6). The monitoring may be supplemented by providing feedback to the clinician on the effectiveness of a specific case as well as providing tips to inform treatment strategy (Whipple et al., 2003). Such an approach may even be tailored for a specific therapist by using his or her own previous clients' outcomes as a data set for benchmarking the effectiveness of every new client. Several instruments (e.g. CORE–OM, OQ–45, and Outcome Rating Scale) are currently available in an online or software form that can be readily used by therapists for monitoring the course of therapy of a specific client and benchmarking it against relevant data sets. The ongoing monitoring of therapy outcome may also be a good base for supervision, as therapy that does not progress as expected can be explored by the therapist in supervision (Ogles, Lambert & Fields, 2002).

Outcome research can also inspire practising therapists to use a simpler form of monitoring a routine pre-post evaluation of their effectiveness that can then be benchmarked against the findings from different types of outcome study. Applying a routine outcome assessment is good practice when evaluating the usefulness of services. It is important not only for the therapists themselves, but also for their former and prospective clients, insurance companies, community or state authorities. Therefore, it comes as no surprise that implementation of outcome evaluation is becoming a natural component of psychotherapeutic practice. Guidelines for implementing routine evaluation are available for practitioners (see e.g. a practical book by Ogles, Lambert and Fields, *Essentials of Outcome Assessment* (2002)).

Outcome research is also important politically as it may show that psychotherapy and counselling are bringing some benefits to clients and to society as a whole. Thus outcome studies have a direct influence on how therapy is practised, and many therapists working in different contexts may well be aware of this as different stakeholders may dictate what they expect of therapy on the basis of their understanding of the findings of outcome studies. A knowledge of and critical evaluation of findings generated by outcome studies may then help practising therapists to justify their view on the nature of therapy they provide.

Process Research and Practice

There is an obvious link between process research and therapeutic practice. The nature of this type of research makes it very similar to everyday practice, so as the therapists learn from their work, they can learn from process research in a very similar way. Furthermore, research brings a rigour that increases the value of learning.

An example of process research that nicely illustrates the link between this kind of research and practice is the work of Jeremy Safran and Christopher Muran (1996, 2000) on conflicts in the therapeutic alliance (mentioned in Chapter 11). Safran and Muran carried out a series of studies on conflict in the therapeutic alliance that they transformed into recommendations for practitioners who encounter conflict in their relationship with the client (Safran & Muran, 2000). They summarized their recommendations in the form of working models that therapists can try to follow when working with a rupture in the therapeutic alliance. They specifically described models for working with an open confrontation coming from the client as well as for working with the client's withdrawal from the therapeutic process. The model for working with confrontation is presented in Box 14.1.

Box 14.1   Model of therapeutic work with the client's confrontation

1. **Identification of confrontation marker** (confrontation can be present in the client's complaints about the therapist as a person, or professional, threatening premature termination of therapy, complaints about parameters of therapy – i.e. time schedule, complaints about the lack of progress in therapy).
2. **Disembedding** (the therapist interrupts confrontation – the therapist may admit own contribution to the problematic interaction, the therapist re-establishes the 'analytical' space, provides feedback, facilitates greater explicitness in the client's demands, meta-communicates about the interaction, discloses the impact of the client's confrontation, supports a direct expression of confrontation and critique, etc.).
3. **Exploration of construal** (the therapist facilitates the expression of the patient's needs, expectations, wishes, perceptions present in the conflict, etc.).
4. **Avoidance of aggression** (the client avoids direct expression of anger because of own anxiety and guilt; it may make the aggression indirect; the therapist should facilitate the client's awareness of this fact).
5. **Avoidance of vulnerability** (the therapist facilitates the client's awareness of the fact that the anger prevents an awareness of own vulnerability triggered by therapeutic interaction).
6. **Vulnerability** (if the therapist showed willingness to take seriously reasons for the client's anger, admitted own contribution to it, and was able to contain the client's aggression, it leads to the client's expression of vulnerable feelings and wishes, which are often connected to hopelessness. However, now it is not hopelessness communicated cynically and aggressively, but truly).

Stages 3 and 4 and 3 and 5 run in parallel (they present the process of experiencing or the process of avoiding the experiencing). Stage 6 follows directly either after stage 3 or 5.

Source: adapted from Safran and Muran, 2000.

Box 14.1 well illustrates how programmatic process research can be transformed into a formulation that may inform practice. The series of studies that preceded the construction of this model form an empirical base that makes such a model sounder than mere clinical observations. In the same way, process studies on other important phenomena can be translated into principles that can inform therapeutic practice. In their discussion section, most process studies make recommendations for therapeutic practice. Some lead to the production of specialized papers or books that translate research findings into step-by-step approaches to working with specific processes in therapy (a good example is emotion-focused therapy, which is based on the studies of therapeutic episodes in client-centred and Gestalt therapy; see Greenberg, Rice & Elliott, 1993). Good examples of the relevance of process research for psychotherapeutic and counselling practice may also be found in review papers (see example in Box 14.2).

Box 14.2   Example of empirically based conceptualization: work by Charles Gelso and Jeffrey Hayes (2002) who reviewed research conducted on countertransference

- There exists empirical evidence pointing to the harmful effect of acting out countertransference.
- There exists empirical evidence that countertransference management based on the therapist's
  - self-integration,
  - self-insight,
  - anxiety management,
  - empathy, and
  - conceptualizing ability
  is helpful.
- There exists empirical evidence for the importance of admitting own mistakes by the therapist in the therapeutic process as well as for a good use of theory in the context of good personal awareness for managing countertransference optimally.

The above are just small examples of the wealth of process research that can inform therapeutic practice. The examples show how process research can be translated into recommendations for practice (Grawe, 1997). Many practitioners, who consider psychotherapy research irrelevant to their work and prefer papers and books presenting clinical experience and reflections on it, might be surprised to find that summaries of process research and synthesizing reviews do not differ so dramatically from clinical papers in accessibility and richness of information.

Examples of Research-informed Psychotherapy and Counselling

Psychotherapy research informs therapeutic practice in many ways. As I outlined above, this may be done through different process and outcome studies. Some of these studies are done programmatically so that they can feed into the development of a specific therapeutic intervention. Several therapies were either substantially informed by outcome studies which assessed their efficacy, and the efficacy of their components, or were significantly informed by process research on the mechanisms of their functioning. We will look now at some successful examples from different theoretical backgrounds.

Empirically Informed Psychodynamic and Interpersonal Approaches

Though psychodynamic therapies are still the most widely practised therapies internationally, to find distinct coherent psychodynamic interventions that are significantly informed by research is not as common as one would expect, given the tradition and prevalence of this form of therapy. The first example that comes to mind is supportive-expressive psychoanalytic therapy (Luborsky, 1984; Luborsky & Luborsky, 2006). This is a therapy that evolved from the approach practised in the Menninger Clinic and was manualized by the well-known psychoanalytical researcher, Lester Luborsky (1984; Luborsky & Luborsky, 2006).

Supportive-Expressive Psychoanalytic Psychotherapy

Supportive-expressive psychoanalytic psychotherapy (Luborsky, 1984; Luborsky & Luborsky, 2006) is one of the first manualized psychodynamic therapies. Significantly, it was empirically informed by process studies using the Core Conflictual Relationship Themes method (see Chapter 8; Luborsky, & Crits-Christoph, 1990, 1998) that distils the main interpersonal problematic patterns of the client. Indeed, the method is used as a tool for clinical conceptualization in this manualized version of psychodynamic therapy. Supportive-expressive psychoanalytic therapy was tested in efficacy trials of methadone patients' treatment as well as in the treatment of cocaine addiction (see Woody et al., 1983; Luborsky, Woody et al., 1995; Crits-Christoph et al., 1999). More satisfactory results for this therapy were achieved in the case of methadone patients. Preliminary tests were also carried out in the treatment of depression and anxiety disorders (Crits-Christoph et al., 1995; Luborsky, Mark et al., 1995). Therapies related to supportive-expressive psychoanalytic therapy were also tested in personality disorder treatment (see Piper, Joyce et al., 1998).

Supportive-expressive psychoanalytic psychotherapy focuses on increasing patients' understanding of symptoms in the context of the Core Conflictual Relationship Themes (psychopathological symptoms are seen as compromised resolutions of problematic interpersonal patterns). Increased understanding is believed to help in the resolution of symptoms and in changing the core interpersonal schemes. The therapy uses a combination of supportive (e.g. communicating understanding) and expressive (interpretative) techniques centred on the patient's Core Conflictual Relationship Themes. In therapy, the patient has an ally in the therapist, who helps the patient to develop the capacity for reflection and exploration of the Core Conflictual Relationship Themes. This approach also emphasizes the need for preparation for therapy in the form of a socialization interview in which patients learn about how therapy works.

Supportive-expressive therapy is an empirically informed treatment that uses no impenetrable psychoanalytic jargon and therefore is easily understood by non-psychonanalytic professionals. It can thus inform the practice of many therapists whose work is influenced by other than psychoanalytic theories. The main strength of this treatment is probably its efficient, easy-to-learn and empirically based conceptualization of the problematic patient relationships that are symptoms of distress themselves as well as the cause of many other psychological symptoms. Extensive process studies using the Core Conflictual Relationship Themes method (see Chapter 8) and several outcome studies (Woody et al., 1983; Luborsky, Woody et al., 1995) contribute to the confidence that the process of this therapy is based on sound principles and is worth offering to clients.

Interpersonal Psychotherapy for Depression

Another example of an empirically informed therapy that is quite similar to psychodynamic therapies is *interpersonal psychotherapy* (Klerman et al., 1984; Weissman, Markowitz & Klerman, 2000). Interpersonal psychotherapy was first tested in the late 1970s, and in 1984 was presented in a manualized form (Klerman et al., 1984). The successful dissemination of this therapy is linked to the fact that it was one of the two therapies tested in the National Institute of Mental Health Treatment of Depression Collaborative Research Program (see Chapter 2). Interpersonal therapy did very well in that study. Since then, it has been tested in many other studies (see review in Weissman, Markowitz & Klerman, 2000; and Gillies, 2001), which have examined its effectiveness for a broader range of problems (e.g. eating disorders).

Interpersonal therapy for depression (IPT) (Weissman, Markowitz & Klerman, 2000) is a short-term therapy (12–16 sessions), usually conducted in an outpatient setting for depressed patients who do not suffer from a co-morbid psychotic disorder. It is recommended that the therapist specializes in the treatment of depression. Therapy focuses on one issue, which is established early in the treatment by the therapist and the patient as relevant to the patient's depression (Weissman, Markowitz & Klerman, 2000; Gillies, 2001). This issue may be from one of the following four problem areas: grief, interpersonal disputes, role transitions and interpersonal deficits. The focus is usually an emotionally loaded problem that is selected collaboratively by therapist and patient.

Where the focus of treatment is on *grief*, the therapeutic work consists of reactivation of the mourning process, support, the interpretative linking of depression symptoms to the loss, and exploration of related feelings during the sequence of events surrounding the loss. Later in the therapy, involvement with others is promoted. Where the focus is on the area of *interpersonal disputes*, the therapist helps to clarify the connection between a dispute and depressive symptoms, the stage of disputes, role expectations involved in the dispute, etc. The therapist also tries to help to identify the issues in the disputes, explore them and work on potential change, explore communication styles, differences in values, expectations and goals, etc. If the focus of the therapy concerns the client's *role transition* as a result of life events, the therapist tries to facilitate mourning for the loss of the previous role and acceptance of the new one. Depressive symptoms are looked upon here as relating to problems in the role transition. The therapist explores positive and negative aspects of the new as well as of the old role, and also the feelings connected to the roles. The development of new skills that are needed is also supported. When the focus of therapy is on the area of *interpersonal deficits* (social isolation), the prognosis is slightly worse than for the other areas (Weissman et al., 2000). Depression symptoms are explored here in the context of social isolation. Therapy is then focused on an exploration of the relationship patterns, including the context of the relationship with the therapist (for more details, see Weissman et al., 2000).

Interpersonal therapy for depression is an example of highly successful and empirically supported treatment from a non-behavioural tradition. Its applications are now explored for other problems and disorders too, such as eating disorders, substance abuse and anxiety disorders. In addition, IPT is often used as a maintenance therapy following termination of the main therapy (Frank, 1991). As to the research that informs this therapy, it is mostly outcome research and randomized control trials, although there is also substantial evidence from *post hoc* analysis of the process data from RCT trials such as the NIMH TDCRP project about important process variables (such as alliance) and predictors (e.g. perfectionism) of the treatment (see also Chapter 10).

Interpersonal therapy is not precisely a psychodynamic therapy even though it resembles mainstream psychodynamic therapy to an extent. I chose this example because of its success in gaining empirical support. There are other psychodynamic therapies that are attracting attention thanks to research activity around them. Two examples could be the psychoanalytic mentalization-based treatment of Bateman and Fonagy (2004; see also Allen & Fonagy, 2006) for borderline personality disorder and the psychodynamic-interpersonal therapy of Hobson (1985), which acquired research support from the Sheffield studies conducted in the 1990s by Shapiro and his colleagues (e.g. Shapiro, Barkham et al., 1994).

Empirically Informed Cognitive-Behavioural Approaches

The labels empirically supported therapies and cognitive-behavioural therapies are often synonymous, as many cognitive-behavioural therapies have gathered evidence that is being recognized by different bodies collating evidence on the effectiveness of psychotherapy (see Chapter 5). Traditionally, proponents of CBT and behaviour therapy carry out RCTs and experimental single-case studies, though naturalistic studies are also used.

Cognitive-behavioural therapies are often presented in the form of therapeutic manuals; this contributes to their dissemination, as the manuals are often easy to follow and self-explanatory. Manualization also supports outcome research as the procedure is well described and therapists can work in a similar way so that therapy rather than a therapist can be assessed (see Chapter 2). Thus, cognitive-behavioural therapies are not only easily disseminated treatments, but often effective treatments as well (see e.g. Nathan & Gorman, 2007).

As there is a large number of empirically supported cognitive-behavioural therapies, it is hard to choose just a few successful examples. I have picked two therapies that have proved to be either significantly effective, as in the case of panic control treatment (Craske & Barlow, 2007), or were among the first successful manualized treatments to be relatively effective for widespread disorder, for example cognitive therapy for depression (Beck, Rush et al., 1979).

Cognitive Therapy for Depression

Cognitive therapy for depression (Beck, Rush et al., 1979) is probably the most researched form of therapeutic procedure in relation to its outcome (see Hollon & Beck, 2004). For example, it was also researched in the NIMH Treatment of Depression Collaborative Research Program (Elkin, 1994; see Chapter 2). Alongside interpersonal therapy, cognitive therapy is currently considered to be the standard of psychotherapeutic care in depression (see Nathan & Gorman, 2007). Nowadays, cognitive therapy is applied across a whole range of psychological and psychiatric problems (e.g. panic disorder, hypochondriasis: see Hollon & Beck, 2004).

Cognitive therapy gave an important stimulus to the formation of broadly defined cognitive-behavioural therapy. Though cognitive in name, it utilizes many behavioural procedures. On the other hand, the method of cognitive restructuring that originated in cognitive therapy is probably used in some form in all cognitive-behavioural therapies nowadays.

Cognitive therapy is based on the cognitive model of depression (Beck, Rush et al. 1979), which postulates the following concepts that play a role in the development and maintenance of depression: the cognitive triad (negative self-view, negative interpretation of experiences, negative view of the future), cognitive schemes (stable cognitive patterns influencing the processing of experience) and cognitive errors in information processing. The cognitive model of depression (Beck, Rush et al., 1979) also postulates that people may have a predisposition to depression on the basis of early experiences that created a negative self-concept and negative thinking about the future and the external world. This predisposition may then be precipitated by a current life situation.

The therapist, in cognitive therapy, tries to forge a solid therapeutic alliance characterized by collaborative work. Therapy is structured and planned by the therapist as to the content of the sessions, tasks, techniques, homework, etc. The early sessions focus on basic symptoms (affective, motivational, cognitive, behavioural and physiological) and on problematic information processing. Different behavioural techniques (e.g. activity planning, graded task assignment, assertiveness training) and cognitive techniques (such as automatic thoughts detection, automatic thoughts testing, searching for alternative solutions) are used. In the later phase, the therapy focuses on depressogenic assumptions, which are the source of automatic thoughts, on their identification and modification (by the generation of alternatives). Cognitive errors are also addressed (e.g. through testing of assumptions).

Cognitive therapy for depression is an incredible success story. It is probably the most widely recognized therapy currently among professionals in psychiatry and psychology. Its success is due to the huge emphasis it has placed on the empirical evaluation since its inception. Though cognitive therapy was developed on the basis of clinical experience and then tested in numerous trials (Hollon & Beck, 2004), it was also subject of some process studies (Hollon & Beck, 2004).

Panic Control Treatment

Panic control treatment is a form of cognitive-behavioural therapy for panic disorder with or without agoraphobia (Craske & Barlow, 2001, 2007). The effectiveness of this treatment is one of the highest achieved in a trial examining psychological therapy and counselling (see Westen & Morrison, 2001). It is still a 'relatively' new treatment, so only the future will tell whether its excellent results stand up to further trials (psychotherapy research is often enthusiastic about the effectiveness of a newly developed treatment, but this is followed by a more sober assessment; see Lambert, Garfield & Bergin, 2004).

Panic control treatment is very similar to other CBT therapies for anxiety disorders. It uses a cognitive-behavioural conceptualization (Craske & Barlow, 2001) of panic disorder which assumes that the patient has a trait of anxiety sensitivity (e.g. perceives anxiety as being harmful, especially its bodily symptoms). In this conceptualization it is assumed that the patient estimates bodily symptoms poorly and that the first panic attack is connected to various feelings of threat. Maintenance factors that contribute to the patient's problem include certain beliefs, for example strong beliefs and fears linked to negative bodily feelings. The unpredictability of panic attacks leads to the avoidance of any places that might trigger the attack. The goals of treatment are then the management of the acute fear of bodily feelings, elimination of the chronic anxiety associated with panic attacks and the overcoming of agoraphobic avoidance.

Panic control treatment (Craske & Barlow, 2001, 2007) starts with a thorough examination of anxiety status. After this complex examination, therapy proceeds sequentially, introducing new steps that build on the previous ones. Mainly this consists of carrying out tasks and using techniques in approximately the following order (Craske & Barlow, 2001): explaining the principles of therapy; exploring panic attacks; monitoring panic attacks; explaining panic attacks; retraining breathing, cognitive restructuring (catastrophizing is often used); interoceptive exposure (gradual); *in vivo* cognitive restructuring; exposure in imagination; and *in vivo* exposure (gradual, using a hierarchy of agoraphobic situations, and also using the patient's significant others). Individual techniques build on each other, are performed or discussed in the sessions, and homework is set often throughout treatment. Panic control treatment usually lasts for 15 sessions, and maintenance sessions are also used (see Craske, Barlow, 2001).

Panic control treatment is the prototype of an empirically derived and tested therapeutic approach that is relatively easy to learn and therefore has great potential for dissemination and accessibililily to patients with panic disorder. Furthermore, as pointed out above, this form of treatment has one of the highest success rates achieved in psychotherapy or counselling trials. Together with Beck's cognitive therapy for depression, it presents an excellent example of currently used, empirically informed interventions. The two therapies mentioned here represent only a small part of the vast number of empirically informed CBT therapies; these are well presented in various handbooks (e.g. Barlow, 2007; Fisher & O'Donohue, 2006; Nathan & Gorman, 2007).

Empirically Informed Experiential (Humanistic and Existential) Approaches

Proponents of humanistic and existential approaches (increasingly referred to as experiential approaches in North America) often argue against therapy manualization (see Bohart, O'Hara & Leitner, 1998); this relates to the fact that few of these approaches were examined in randomized trials that require a certain level of manualization (see Chambless & Hollon, 1998). Despite this, research that examines this kind of therapy is being conducted. This fits well with the research tradition, particularly in client-centred therapy, which is very rich and historically has been one of the most dominant forms of therapy, especially in the area of process research in the 1950s and 1960s.

Here I will briefly introduce two therapeutic approaches that are well informed by research and which are current expressions of humanistic and existential thinking. I will look at emotion-focused therapy (also known as process-experiential therapy) (Greenberg, Rice & Elliott, 1993) and motivational interviewing (and its particular form, motivational enhancement therapy) (Miller & Rolnick, 1991, 2002). One may wonder why I include motivational interviewing here as a form of humanistic and existential therapy, when many authors (probably its authors too) see it as a behavioural treatment. Indeed, motivational interviewing was developed as a form of behavioural therapy (see Miller, 1983); however, it also emphasizes (together with transtheoretical theory of change, cognitive dissonance theory and self-perception theory) its 'client-centred' nature and the influence of Carl Rogers' work (Miller & Rollnick, 2002: 25).

Emotion-Focused Therapy

Emotion-focused (process-experiential) therapy is an integrative therapy built on the client-centred and Gestalt therapy traditions and to a smaller extent also on existential approaches (Greenberg, Rice & Elliott, 1993; Greenberg, 2002; Elliott, Watson et al., 2004). A variant of this therapy, emotionally focused couples therapy, is one of the best researched forms of couple therapy (Greenberg & Johnson, 1988; Johnson, 2004).

Individual emotion-focused therapy is researched mainly as a therapy for depression (Greenberg & Watson, 1998, 2005; Watson, Gordon et al., 2003). It has also been studied in relation to other problems (see review in Elliott, Watson et al., 2004). An important feature of this approach is that it was extensively informed by programmatic process research that investigated different techniques used in the therapy, such as the two chair technique for conflict splits (Greenberg, 1984) or systematic evocative unfolding for problematic reactions (Rice & Saperia, 1984). Many of the studies that informed this type of therapy are summarized in Elliott, Greenberg and Lietaer (2004) and Elliott and Greenberg (2002). Examples of these studies are also presented in Chapter 11.

Emotion-focused therapy (Greenberg, Rice & Elliott, 1993; Elliott et al., 2004) uses conceptualization, in which emotions (emotion schemes) and dialectical-constructivistic theory of self play an important role. Emotion schemes are understood as complex biosocial integrations of perceptions, cognitions, affects, bodily experiences and motivations with acting tendencies, which function automatically. In emotion-focused therapy it is important to distinguish between primary adaptive, primary maladaptive, secondary, and instrumental emotions (Greenberg & Safran, 1987, 1989), with the focus on primary adaptive emotions as a resource for resolving emotional difficulties.

The psychological dysfunction that this approach attempts to address lies either (1) in the process of meaning-creation that makes sense of emotional experiencing brought to awareness, or (2) in the automatic activation of emotion schemes that are problematic, i.e. do not correspond well with reality. The goal of emotion-focused therapy is to support the dialectical constructive processing and reworking of the automatic emotion schemes. Emotion-focused therapy uses various types of therapeutic task (Elliott, Watson et al., 2004) focused on empathic exploration, the therapeutic relationship (e.g. alliance repair), experiencing (e.g. experiential focusing), reprocessing (e.g. systematic evocative unfolding), and enactment (two-chair dialogue). The process of change in this therapy proceeds through several phases (see Box 14.3).

Box 14.3   Process of change in emotion-focused therapy (Greenberg, Rice & Elliott, 1993)

1. Relationship building (in this phase therapy focuses on forming a good working relationship).
2. Empathic exploration (in this phase therapy provides a general empathic environment).
3. Task initiation (at the appropriate 'marker' an experiential task is suggested).
4. Evocation/arousal (the task often has an evocative character).
5. Experiential exploration (deep exploration is followed during the task).
6. Emotion scheme change or resolution (change of an emotion-scheme is achieved in the task).
7. Carrying-forward (an action is planned that would consolidate the change in the emotion-scheme).

Emotion-focused therapy is an example of empirically informed humanistic therapy that evolved from the programmatic research of its developers. It combines the pragmatic and evidence-based nature of CBT therapies with the ethos of traditional humanistic and existential approaches. It provides proof that therapies that traditionally have been less congruent with the dominant mental health establishment can talk the language of this establishment without losing their own distinct voice. Emotion-focused therapy illustrates that humanistic and existential approaches can not only be understandable to the mainstream medical world, but can also provide evidence that cannot be ignored.

Motivational Interviewing

Motivational interviewing (MI) is 'a client-centred, directive method for enhancing intrinsic motivation to change by exploring and resolving ambivalence' (Miller & Rollnick, 2002: 25). Motivational interviewing is nowadays one of the most popular approaches used in treatment for alcohol and other drug abuse. There is a large number of outcome studies, mostly RCTs (Burke, Arkowitz & Dunn, 2002), and recently process studies as well (e.g. Moyers & Martin, 2006), examining its effectiveness and the processes involved in it. A version of motivational interviewing, motivational enhancement therapy, was also examined in the largest project studying the effectiveness of psychological treatment for alcohol abuse (Project MATCH – Babor & Del Boca, 2003; see also Chapter 7).

Motivational interviewing (Miller & Rollnick, 2002) and motivational enhancement therapy (Miller, 1995) are based on several general principles, such as the therapist's expressed empathy, development of discrepancy in where the client is and where he or she wants to be, avoidance of argumentation by the therapist trying not to convince the client of the need for change, rolling with the client's resistance to change, and supporting the client's self-efficacy. In the first phase of treatment, the therapist and the client work together on building motivation for change. In the second phase, the therapist together with the client, concentrates on strengthening commitment to change. When the therapist considers the client ready to try to implement change in drug-taking behaviour, together they draw up a plan that should help the client to succeed. The client plays a major role in drawing up the plan, with the therapist contributing his or her own knowledge about combating drug usage. In the third phase of treatment, the therapist and the client together monitor the client's progress and try to renew motivation. Significant others are often used as well. More information on this treatment can be found in the work of Miller (1995).

Motivational interviewing is another success story with regard to treatment development. It spread quickly to other areas beyond drug abuse treatment. Its effectiveness has been examined for a wide variety of problems, such as eating disorders, HIV risk behaviour, diet, exercise and lifestyle changes (see overview of research findings in Burke, Arkowitz & Dunn, 2002). The fact that it can be used as a form of pre-therapy and that it is a very brief intervention lasting from one to four or five sessions makes it a very good candidate for experimental RCT-type research. Process research on

MI has recently started (e.g. Moyers & Martin, 2006), which hopefully will illuminate the powerful effect of this brief intervention. Though this therapy cannot be perceived as totally humanistic as it also uses concepts and interventions more typical of other, mostly behavioural, therapies, its emphasis on client-centred skills, and the client's ultimate role and active engagement in the treatment, makes it a clear bearer of the legacy of Carl Rogers for psychotherapy. It also fits well with the original emphasis on empirical research in the early days of client-centred therapy. It shows that treatments that are non-behavioural can be examined in the context of experimental, RCT-type trials.

Empirically Informed Eclectic and Integrative Approaches

Integrative psychotherapeutic approaches attempt to combine theoretically two or more therapeutic approaches or to build a generic theory of psychotherapy (Grawe, 2004; Norcross & Goldfried, 2005). Assimilative integration (Lampropoulous, 2001; Messer, 2001), in which practices of other approaches are incorporated into the original theoretical approach of the therapist or theorist, is also becoming more common. One may also encounter terms similar to integrative therapy, such as eclectic psychotherapy, which stands for a pragmatic combination of interventions coming from different theoretical orientations without the construction of an overlapping integrative theory.

Some of the integrative and eclectic therapies to a great extent build on research evidence that has the advantage of looking at evidence from different therapeutic approaches. We will look at two good examples of therapies informed by a wide range of empirical evidence.

Prescriptive Therapy for Depression

Prescriptive therapy (Beutler & Harwood, 2000; the other name for this approach is Systematic Treatment Selection – Beutler, Clarkin & Bongar, 2000) is a pragmatic and systematic eclectic therapeutic approach informed by a collated knowledge of the whole area of psychotherapy research. It can be used by therapists of different theoretical orientations, as it focuses on empirically derived principles that can be adopted by any theoretical orientation (see Castonguay & Beutler, 2005). One of its applications is collected in 'prescriptive' recommendations for depression treatment (Beutler, Clarkin & Bongar, 2000). Beutler, Clarkin and Bongar (2000) prepared recommendations based on their own research as well as on that of others. They looked at patients' characteristics, treatment characteristics, and their combination. They divided depression treatment into basic and optimal principles of therapy for depression (see Box 14.4), which can be used by therapists regardless of their therapeutic orientation. These principles were further elaborated into a manual in the form of a guide for the therapist in practice (Beutler & Harwood, 2000).

Box 14.4 Example of basic and optimal principles of depression treatment

Example of basic principles:
- The likelihood of the patient's improvement is a positive function of the patient's social support level and a negative function of the patient's functional impairment
- Patients with complex and chronic problems have worse prognosis, but social support enhancement may increase the likelihood of good outcome in their therapy
- Likelihood of better outcome increases in therapy of patients with complex (chronic) problems, when their significant others are also involved in the treatment
- Suicide risk and self-harm tied to depression may be reduced by a careful assessment of risk
- Risk may be reduced and patient compliance increased when the treatment includes family intervention
- Risk may be reduced and patient compliance increased when the patient is realistically informed about the length and effectiveness of the treatment and when s/he has a clear understanding of the role and activity expected of him/her

Example of optimal principles:
- Therapeutic change is most likely when the patient is exposed to the objects or targets of behavioural and emotional avoidance
- Therapeutic change is greatest when the relative balance of interventions either (1) favours the use of skill building and symptom removal, among those patients who externalize, or (2) favours the use of insight and relationship-focused procedures among internalizers
- Therapeutic change is most likely when the initial focus of treatment is on building skills and symptoms change
- Therapeutic change is most likely when the therapeutic procedures do not evoke patient resistance
- Therapeutic change is greatest when the directiveness of the interventions either (1) inversely corresponds to the patient's current level of resistance, or (2) authoritatively prescribes a continuation in the symptomatic behaviour
- Therapeutic change is most likely when the patient's level of emotional stress during therapy is moderate (neither excessively high nor excessively low)
- Therapeutic change is most likely when the patient is stimulated to emotional arousal in a safe environment until problematic responses diminish or vanish

---

Source: adapted from Beutler, Clarkin and Bongar, 2000: 183–184, 204–205.

Prescriptive therapy represents a unique perspective cutting across theoretical school and potentially indicating the direction of psychotherapy of the future. The work of Beutler, Clarkin and Bongar (2000) was followed by an edited volume (Castonguay &

Beutler, 2005) that invited leading experts to review the research evidence and prepare guidelines for mood disorders, anxiety disorders, personality disorders, and substance abuse (see Chapter 5) that would be based on this evidence. This excellent idea of formulating all of the research evidence as recommendations that can be used by practitioners of any theoretical orientation has, however, from my perspective, one important disadvantage. The level of abstraction of some of the principles makes them too general and hard to translate into moment-to-moment interaction with clients.

Psychological Therapy

Klaus Grawe (2004), a Swiss psychologist, worked for several years on the concept of generic psychotherapy, later known simply as psychological therapy. The name 'psychological therapy' was supposed to indicate that it is based on findings from basic psychological research. The therapy was extensively presented in *Psychological Therapy*, an English translation of which appeared in 2004.

Though Grawe (2004) presents a comprehensive theory of psychopathology and normal human psychological functioning, his conceptualization of therapeutic mechanisms is summarized in a simple three-component model of integrative, empirically informed, 'effective' psychotherapy. The first component of effective psychotherapy, according to Grawe, is the *activation of resources* of the patient: empirically found early improvements in therapy can be attributed to the activation of what is functional in the patient as well as to the support provided by the therapeutic relationship. Especially important are the patient's experiences of personal control in influencing his or her well-being. These can be achieved in therapy by allowing the patient to influence the therapeutic process in line with his or her motivational schemata (needs). A significant role here is also played by positive interpersonal experiences with the therapist. For this purpose the therapist should offer a 'complementary' relationship that would allow 'the patient to have experiences consistent with important but unfulfilled motivational schemata' (Grawe, 2004: 436). The relationship as well as positive control experiences should contribute to experiences that enhance self-esteem, which in an optimal case will boost the client's well-being. The activation of resources may lead to experiences which may interfere with the assumed motivational structure, and this may participate in the creation of psychopathological symptoms.

The second component of Grawe's psychological therapy is the focus on the *destabilization of parameters of psychological disorders through specific interventions*. Grawe's conceptualization assumes that psychological disorders develop as a result of the constellation of specific parameters but then live on their own (the concept of attractors from dynamic systems theory). Therefore, the disorder as such must be tackled if it is to be overcome. Interventions directly targeting the disorder are used. These may focus on problematic experiencing, problematic cognitions or problematic behaviour. However, they must be carried out in accordance with the patient's motivational schemata and needs. They also have to activate any negative emotions embedded in problematic experiencing.

The third component of successful psychotherapy is, according to Grawe (2004), reduction of conflicting functioning through the *modification of motivational schemata* that led to the development of the disorder. Motivational schemata are characterized by their stability, automatic functioning and self-perpetuation, as their enactment contributes to their maintenance. They are also difficult to change intentionally as they include avoidance of awareness, and of certain experiences and behaviour. Typically, problematic motivational schemata do not allow the patient to satisfy important needs because the schemata are unclear. Interventions in psychological therapy should therefore also focus on the modification of problematic motivational schemata by providing clarification and corrective experiences.

In its practical application, Grawe's model combines strategies from several theoretical orientations. It offers a structured case conceptualization that follows an articulated theory and also draws on a variety of tasks and techniques from experiential, psychodynamic and cognitive-behavioural therapies. For example, a change in motivational schemata often requires a person-centred and/or psychodynamic way of working, whereas changing psychopathological symptoms and problems draws on cognitive-behavioural interventions tailored to specific problems.

Grawe's theoretical framework attempts to coherently marry knowledge from basic psychological research as well as psychotherapy research. The model is quite well known, especially in German-speaking countries and the psychotherapy research community. In his last book before his death, Grawe (2007) enriched his conceptualization of psychological therapy by findings from neuroscience. The book not only provides an explanation of what is happening on a biological level in the brain during psychotherapy, but also offers tips to the therapists as to what could be tried out so that lasting changes are more likely to occur.

The six therapies I briefly introduced here show how the final product of research-informed therapies can look. Many therapists in practice are unaware of the research efforts that underlie the development of particular approaches. Some of the approaches presented here are built mostly on outcome studies (e.g. cognitive therapy, panic control treatment), some grew out of tradition and programmatic research on the therapeutic process (e.g. supportive-expressive psychoanalytical therapy, emotion-focused therapy), while others use general evidence from psychotherapy research (e.g. prescriptive therapy) supplemented by basic psychological research (e.g. the psychological therapy of Grawe) for the development of conceptualizations that integrative therapists can use to inform their practice.

Conclusion

This book is not the definitive text on psychotherapy and counselling research. Many areas are not covered in detail and are merely mentioned to the reader. Some aspects of research are emphasized more than others. Since I wrote the Slovak version of this text (in autumn 2004) several books on psychotherapy and counselling research have been published (e.g. Dallos & Vetere, 2005; Lebow, 2006; Lepper & Riding, 2006) that complement the good introduction *Doing Counselling Research* by John McLeod (1994, 2003).

In this book, I wanted to focus on the field in its entirety and discuss some examples of what good studies focus on and what they can bring to the reader or potential future researcher. I wanted the book to be simple, so that it can be followed by the reader who has a basic understanding of research methodology. I hope this text will not only present the field of psychotherapy and counselling research, but will also stimulate interest in using research literature to inform one's practice. Psychotherapy research will certainly play a more and more important role in the future development of professions that use psychotherapy and/or counselling. It is difficult to imagine a therapist of the future who would not describe his or her own practice as *research-informed*.

I hope that this book will also stimulate some interest in conducting new research on psychotherapy and counselling. I hope it will be used in training programmes as a tool for informing students' choice of which area of research they could contribute to through their dissertations and research projects. I also hope the book may stimulate an interest among practising therapists in examining their local problems by conducting practitioners' research (McLeod, 1999). Many methodological approaches presented in this book are very valuable for that.

I also hope that the book will provide an overview for practising therapists and trainees that will make them more informed consumers of research findings. Sometimes research evidence is used 'politically', when evidence that supports particular practices is embraced while evidence that would speak against them or that would support different approaches goes unnoticed. This is probably often unintentional, since – as in other human activities – people can feel very passionate about the things that are close to them (and spending several years in mastering a specific therapeutic approach makes such an approach very important).

Sometimes evidence is incorporated into the language used to describe psychological therapies and so it can happen that some approaches, such as cognitive or behavioural or their combinations, are thought of as synonymous with evidence-based therapy and others, such as humanistic or psychodynamic therapy, as its opposite. Certainly cognitive and behavioural approaches are to be commended for their scientific rigour and the emphasis they place on conducting RCTs and experimental case studies, but as many examples used throughout the book have shown, other approaches are being studied from different angles too.

Furthermore, it may happen for some reason that certain therapeutic procedures are considered to be empirically supported because of a study or series of studies conducted on them. However, a closer look sometimes shows that the actual study that is being cited produced quite different results than recommendations based on it claim. An example would be the TDCRP study on depression that has been used as an example throughout the book. Though the interpretations of this study often lead to many controversies (e.g. Craighead et al., 2007) quite often it is cited as an example of the effectiveness of *brief* cognitive and interpersonal therapy, while the original authors (Shea et al., 1992), after conducting a follow-up examination of the results of this project, concluded that because of the modest results from the longer-term perspective, brief cognitive or interpersonal therapy may not be optimal for depressed patients (this is not to say that the same applies to medication, the usage of which is now recommended for a significantly prolonged time). Despite that finding, the recommended length of these therapies is still short (see National Collaborating Centre for Mental Health & National Institute for Clinical Excellence guidelines for depression, 2007). It seems that some research studies are becoming part of a psychotherapy culture and their actual results are getting lost beneath layers of different arguments that were made on the basis of them.

Anyway, the main message that this book has tried to convey is that research in psychotherapy and counselling is broad and its different strands are trying to answer different, but altogether mutually complementary issues of whether therapy (or rather, a specific therapeutic procedure) works and how it works. My intent here has been to present the diversity of psychotherapy research and the importance of its different components as my experience has been that some practising therapists are unaware of different types of research and are cognizant only of RCTs because they are politically influential; on the other hand, some practising therapists, preferring 'soft data', are often aware only of qualitative studies and thus ignore the rich potential of other research approaches. I hope that this book will persuade proponents of both camps that their approaches can be more embracing.

Glossary

Adherence measures – measures used for evaluating whether the therapist follows a prescribed manual or theoretical principles of delivered therapy.

Analysis of covariance – analysis of difference between groups that statistically controls for confounding or **interfering variables**.

APA – American Psychological Association; the biggest psychological society in the USA.

Aptitude treatment interaction – research design looking at the interaction of particular client characteristics and a specific form of treatment.

Bona fide therapy – therapy conducted by the therapist who considers it to be therapeutic.

Cohen's *d* – an index expressing the magnitude of **effect size** for differences between two groups (e.g. treatment vs. control).

Composite outcome – the outcome averaged across several measures.

Construct – a term used in psychological research depicting the phenomenon studied (e.g. depression); often explained by its definition.

Construct validity – can have two meanings: in regard to construct validity of an instrument, it reveals how well the instrument correlates with other instruments measuring similar constructs (convergent validity) and whether or not it correlates with dissimilar and independent constructs (divergent validity); in terms of research design, construct validity talks about how well the investigated construct is measured – usually by utilizing several instruments measuring the same or similar constructs.

Descriptive studies – research designs that do not use experimental manipulation but observe a phenomenon (or the relationship of independent and dependent variables) in its natural course.

Dodo bird verdict – alludes to the bird Dodo in *Alice in Wonderland*. The Dodo said, 'All have won and all must have prizes'. It is a mataphor used in psychotherapy research to point to the fact that different therapies are approximately equally effective. The phrase was first used by Rosenzweig in the 1930s.

Dose–effect research – a type of outcome research that examines the relationship between the number of therapy sessions and outcome.

DSM–IV – *Diagnostic and Statistical Manual* of the American Psychiatric Association, 4th edition; contains descriptions, diagnostic and differential diagnostic features of all psychiatric disorders. It also provides information on prevalence and the typical course of illness.

Dysfunctional population (sample) – clinical population; usually scores obtained on psychological instruments by patients seeking psychological or psychiatric treatment.

Effect size – in the context of measuring psychotherapy outcome it is usually a numerical expression of the difference between the means of two or more compared groups as measured by an outcome measure. *See also* Colen's *d*

Empirically supported (validated) treatments – psychological therapies considered by the APA Society of Clinical Psychology as having empirical evidence of their effectiveness.

Error of measurement – an index expressing the magnitude of variance from true score in a measurement.

Experiment-wise error – in cases when several significance tests are conducted (e.g. measuring outcome on several measures) there is an increased chance to detect change even though it may be just an artefact of the fact that several tests were conducted (the chance of obtaining significance is inflated with repeated testing). As we usually accept a 5% chance of error in research, if we run more tests, there is an increased likelihood that such an error may occur.

Experimental case study – a case study that uses experimental manipulation and control.

Experimental designs – research designs utilizing experimental manipulation with an independent variable (in psychotherapy research it is psychotherapy) and experimental control to establish a causal link between an independent variable (psychotherapy) and the dependent variable (the client's state after therapy).

Expert rated scales – psychometrically sound rating scales used by trained observers for assessing verbal or non-verbal behaviour in therapy.

External validity – an aspect of research design addressing the generalizability of findings (the match between research and real-life conditions).

Factor analysis – a statistical technique used to explain variability in responses to items in terms of variation in hypothetical variables (factors) that are believed to be responsible for the responses.

Functional population (sample) – non-clinical population; data gathered from healthy participants.

Hierarchical linear modelling – statistical analysis looking at the explanation of variance in a dependent variable on more hierarchical levels. An extension of multiple regression, it is used with data structured hierarchically, i.e. data in which subgroupings (e.g. therapists, hospitals, regions) exist within the data.

Independent variable – a variable influencing the dependent variable in research designs; in experimental designs this variable is manipulated by the researcher so that its impact can be causally interpreted.

Interfering variable – a variable that may have an influence on the observed dependent variable; it needs to be controlled for so that the link between the manipulated independent (therapy) and the dependent (clients' state) variable can be established. An example could be the variable of therapist quality when we want to assess a specific set of techniques such as CBT techniques.

Internal validity – an aspect of experimental design capturing the strength of causal interpretation of the relationship between the independent and the dependent variable.

Intraclass correlation – reliability coefficient assessing the agreement between two or more experts using interval scales (see also **expert rated scales**).

Logistic regression – statistical analysis in which a dichotomous dependent variable (e.g. readmitted to hospital vs. not readmitted) is predicted by one or more variables. The results are presented in the form of odds ratios (e.g. those with a history of deliberate self-harm are five times more likely to be readmitted than those with no history of deliberate self-harm).

Mediator – a variable explaining how the independent variable has the effect on the dependent variable.

Meta-analysis – a quantitative tool allowing a quantitative overview of findings across several studies by converting findings of individual studies to a common metric (usually **effect size**).

MMPI – Minnesota Multiphasic Personality Inventory – one of the most commonly used personality inventories; it assesses psychopathological features across several domains.

Moderator – a variable that influences the effects of the independent variable on the dependent variable.

Naturalistic studies – in the context of psychotherapy and counselling research, these are studies that look at the therapy intervention as it occurs in everyday practice.

Non-participative methods – methods used in process research employing trained raters for the evaluation of session material.

Normal distribution (Gaussian distribution) – a distribution of the variable values that has a symmetrical bell-curve shape and is defined by the mean and the variance parameters. The normal distribution of the variable is usually an assumption for conducting parametrical tests (e.g. t-test, F-test).

Normative data – data gathered from referential samples (e.g. non-clinical population; clinical population) often following normal distribution. They can be used for benchmarking.

Participative methods – the methods used in process research in which the clients and the therapists are used as raters of a studied aspect of therapeutic process.

Patient-focused research – research developed by Michael Lambert and his colleagues that focuses on the establishment of normative curves of positive progress in therapy in reference to which it is possible to benchmark an individual client.

Phase model of change – a theoretical model based on empirical findings developed by Ken Howard and his colleagues; the model predicts that therapeutic change first occurs in the domain of subjective well-being, then in psychopathological symptoms and then in broader social and interpersonal functioning.

Predictor – a variable predicting scores on the dependent variable.

Preferential trials – quasi-experimental designs assessing the outcome of therapy that take into account the client's choice of a specific treatment.

Probit analysis – Similar to logistic regression, it is a statistical method analysing the relationship of levels of dose of an independent variable (e.g. number of therapeutic sessions attended) and a dichotomous outcome (e.g. readmitted or not readmitted to hospital).

Quasi-experimental designs – research designs with limitations in the experimental manipulation that weaken the interpretation of a causal link between the independent variable (therapy) and the dependent variable (clients' state after therapy).

Randomized control trial – an experimental design using (1) randomization when allocating participants to compared groups and (2) a sophisticated experimental control ruling out other influences than studied psychotherapy intervention.

Reactivity – respondents' response not to the measure they are filling in but to the context of using that measure; for example, if the therapist administers an instrument, the client may be aware that the therapist will see the responses and therefore provides answers depending on how he or she wants to appear in the therapists' eyes.

Regression analysis – a correlational data analysis technique looking at the relationship between several independent variables (and, if necessary, their combinations) and the dependent variable.

Regression equation – an equation based on correlations among variables that allows prediction of scores on a dependent variable based on the scores obtained on the independent variable(s).

Regression line – a line depicting the linear relationship between the dependent variable and the independent variable(s).

Reliability – the consistency of measurement of a specific psychometric instrument.

Reliable Change Index – an index delineating the size of pre-post change that would be considered reliable, not random.

Remission – recovery from the disorder.

Residual scores – a deviation of observed scores from the predictions made on the basis of the regression equation in regression analysis.

Rosenzweig *see* **Dodo bird verdict**

Sensitivity to change – an aspect of a measurement instrument that indicates whether the instrument is likely to capture changes if they occur.

Single-case experiments – experimental research designs focused on a limited number of participants using them as their own controls for experimental manipulation. The causal link between an independent variable (therapy) and a dependent variable (client's state after therapy) may be well controlled and therefore safely interpreted; however, there are limits to the generalizibility of findings.

SPR – International Society for Psychotherapy Research; an international body for psychotherapy researchers.

Standard deviation – a parameter of variability that, together with the mean, describes the distribution of data.

Statistical conclusion validity – an aspect of research design that considers whether statistical analyses are properly used and interpreted.

Statistical power – an index that expresses the probability with which the statistical test detects the difference between the experimental and the control group, if a difference exists.

Survival analysis – a statistical technique modelling of the time needed for an event to occur (in psychotherapy research, often recovery).

Type I error – a probability that we claim that a statistically significant difference exists between the compared groups while in reality it does not exist.

Variable – an assessed construct in a specific study or studies; the term 'variable' indicates that the observed values of the construct in a specific study vary.

References

Achenbach, T. M. (1999). The Child Behavior Checklist and related measures. In M. E. Maruish (ed.), *The Use of Psychological Testing for Treatment Planning and Outcomes Assessment* (2nd edn, pp. 1247–1275). Mahwah, NJ: Lawrence Erlbaum Associates.

Ahn, H., & Wampold, B. E. (2001). Where oh where are the specific ingredients: a meta-analysis of component studies in counseling and psychotherapy. *Journal of Counseling Psychology, 48(3)*, 251–257.

Allen, J. G. & Fonagy, P. (eds) (2006). *The Handbook of Mentalization-based Treatment*. Hoboken, NJ: John Wiley & Sons.

Allstetter-Neufeldt, S., Beutler, L. E. & Banchero, R. (1997). Research on supervisor variables in psychotherapy supervision. In C. E. Watkins (ed.), *Handbook of Psychotherapy Supervision*. New York: John Wiley.

American Psychiatric Association (2001). *Diagnostic and Statistical Manual of Mental Disorders* (4th edn, Text revision). Washington, DC: American Psychiatric Association.

American Psychological Association (APA) (2002). Criteria for evaluating treatment guidelines. *American Psychologist, 57*, 1052–1059.

American Psychological Association (2006). Evidence-based practice in psychology. *American Psychologist, 61*, 271–285.

APA, Division 29 (2002). *Task Force on Empirically Supported Therapy Relationships*. Washington, DC: American Psychological Association.

APA, Division 32 (1997). *Task Force for the Development of Practice Recommendations for the Provision of Humanistic Psychosocial Services*. Washington, DC: American Psychological Association.

Arnkoff, D. B., Glass, C. R. & Shapiro, S. J. (2002). Expectations and preferences. In J. C. Norcross (ed.), *Psychotherapy Relationships that Work: Therapist Contributions and Responsiveness to Patients* (pp. 335–356). New York: Oxford University Press.

Asay, T. P., Lambert, M. J., Gregersen, A. T. & Goates, M. K. (2002). Using patient-focused research in evaluating treatment outcome in private practice. *Journal of Clinical Psychology, 58*, 1213–1225.

Atkins, D. C., Bedics, J. D., McGlinchey, J. B. & Beauchaine, T. P. (2005). Assessing clinical significance: does it matter which method we use? *Journal of Consulting and Clinical Psychology, 73(5)*, 982–989.

Babor, T. F. & Del Boca, F. K. (eds) (2003). *Treatment Matching in Alcoholism.* Cambridge: Cambridge University Press.

Bahrick, A. S., Russell, R. K. & Salmi, S. W. (1991). The effects of role induction on trainees' perceptions of supervision. *Journal of Counseling and Development, 69*, 434–438.

Bambling, M., King, R., Raue, P., Schweitzer, R. & Lambert, E. W. (2006). Clinical supervision: its influence on client-rated working alliance and client symptom reduction in the brief treatment of major depression. *Psychotherapy Research, 16(3)*, 317–331.

Barber, J. P. & Crits-Christoph, P. (1996). Development of an adherence/competence scale for dynamic therapy: preliminary findings. *Psychotherapy Research, 6*, 81–94.

Barber, J. P., Connolly, M. B., Crits-Christoph, P., Gladys, L. & Siqueland, L. (2000). Alliance predicts patients' outcome beyond in-treatment change in symptoms. *Journal of Consulting and Clinical Psychology, 68(6)*, 1027–1032.

Barber, J. P., Crits-Christoph, P. & Luborsky, L. (1990). A guide to the CCRT standard categories and their classification. In L. Luborsky & P. Crits-Christoph, *Understanding Countertransference: The Core Conflictual Relationship Theme Method* (pp. 37–50). New York: Basic Books.

Barkham, M., Connell, J., Stiles, W. B., Miles, J. N. V., Margison, J., Evans, C. & Mellor-Clark, J. (2006). Dose-effect relations and responsive regulation of treatment duration: the good enough level. *Journal of Consulting and Clinical Psychology, 74*, 160–167.

Barkham, M., Margison, F., Leach, C., Lucock, M. & Mellor-Clark, J. (2001). Service profiling and outcomes benchmarking using the CORE-OM: toward practice-based evidence in the psychological therapies. *Journal of Consulting and Clinical Psychology, 69(2)*, 184–196.

Barkham, M. and Mellor-Clark, J. (2000). Rigour and relevance: the role of practice-based evidence in the psychological therapies. In N. Rowland & S. Goss (eds), *Evidence-based Counseling and Psychological Therapies: Research and Applications* (pp. 127–144). London: Routledge.

Barlow, D. H. (ed.) (2007). *Clinical Handbook of Psychological Disorders: A Step-by-Step Treatment Manual* (4th edn). New York: Guilford Press.

Barrett-Lennard, G. (1986). The relationship inventory now. In L. S. Greenberg & W. Pinsof (eds), *The Psychotherapeutic Process* (pp. 439–476). New York: Guilford Press.

Bateman, A. & Fonagy, P. (2004). *Psychotherapy for Borderline Personality Disorder: Mentalization-Based Treatment.* New York: Oxford University Press.

Battle, C. G., Imber, S. D., Hoehn-Saric, R., Stone, A. R., Nash, E. R. & Frank, J. D. (1966). Target complaints as criterion for improvement. *American Journal of Psychotherapy, 20*, 184–192.

Bauer, S., Lambert, M. J. & Nielsen, S. L. (2004). Clinical significance methods: a comparison of statistical techniques. *Journal of Personality Assessment, 82*, 60–70.

Beck, A. P. & Lewis, C. M. (2000). *The Process of Group Psychotherapy: Systems for Analyzing Change.* Washington, DC: American Psychological Association.

Beck, A. T., Rush, A. J., Shaw, B. F. & Emery, G. (1979). *Cognitive Therapy of Depression.* New York: Guilford Press.

Beck, A. T., Steer, R. A. & Garbin, M. G. (1988). Psychometric properties of the Beck Depression Inventory: twenty-five years of evaluation. *Clinical Psychology Review, 8,* 77–100.

Beck, Sohel, et al.

Benjamin, L. S. (1996). *Interpersonal Diagnosis and Treatment of Personality Disorders* (2nd edn). New York: Guilford Press.

Benjamin, L. S., Foster, S. W., Roberto, L. G. & Estroff, S. E. (1986). Breaking the family code: analysis of videotapes of family interactions using structural analysis of social behaviour (SASB). In L. S. Greenberg & W. Pinsof (eds), *The Psychotherapeutic Process* (pp. 391–438). New York: Guilford Press.

Bergin, A. E. (1971). The evaluation of therapeutic outcomes. In A. E. Bergin & S. L. Garfield (eds), *Handbook of Psychotherapy and Behavior Change* (pp. 217–270). New York: John Wiley.

Bergin, A. E. & Garfield, S. L. (eds) (1994). *Handbook of Psychotherapy and Behavior Change* (4th edn). New York: John Wiley. (First published 1971.)

Bergin, A. E. & Jensen, J. P. (1990). Religiosity of psychotherapists: a national survey. *Psychotherapy, 27,* 3–7.

Beutler, L. E. & Castonguay, L. G. (2005). The task force on empirically based principles of therapeutic change. In L. G. Castonguay & L. E. Beutler (eds), *Principles of Therapeutic Change that Work.* New York: Oxford University Press.

Beutler, L. E., Castonguay, L. G. & Follette, W. C. (2005). Integration of therapeutic factors in dysphoric disorders. In L. G. Castonguay & L. E. Beutler (eds), *Principles of Therapeutic Change that Work.* New York: Oxford University Press.

Beutler, L. E., Clarkin, J. F. & Bongar, B. (2000). *Guidelines for the Systematic Treatment of the Depressed Patient.* New York: Oxford University Press.

Beutler, L. E., Engle, D., Mohr, D., Daldrup, R. J., Bergan, J., Meredith, K., et al. (1991). Predictors of differential response to cognitive, experiential, and self-directed psychotherapeutic procedures. *Journal of Consulting and Clinical Psychology, 59(2),* 333–340.

Beutler, L. E. & Harwood, T. M. (2000). *Prescriptive Psychotherapy: A Practical Guide to Systematic Treatment Selection.* New York: Oxford University Press.

Beutler, L. E., Harwood, T. M., Alimohamed, S. & Malik, M. (2002). Functional impairment and coping style. In J. C. Norcross (ed.), *Psychotherapy Relationships that Work: Therapist Contributions and Responsiveness to Patients* (pp. 145–170). New York: Oxford University Press.

Beutler, L. E., Machado, P. P. & Allstetter-Neufeldt, S. (1994). Therapist variables. In A. E. Bergin & S. L. Garfield (eds), *Handbook of Psychotherapy and Behavior Change* (4th edn, pp. 229–269). New York: John Wiley.

Beutler, L. E., Malik, M., Alimohamed, S., Harwood, T. M., Talebi, H., Noble, S., et al. (2004). Therapist variables. In M. J. Lambert (ed.), *Bergin's and Garfield's Handbook of Psychotherapy and Behavior Change* (5th edn, pp. 227–306). New York: John Wiley.

Beutler, L. E., Moleiro, C. M. & Talebi, H. (2002). Resistance. In J. C. Norcross (ed.), *Psychotherapy Relationships that Work: Therapist Contributions and Responsiveness to Patients* (pp. 129–143). New York: Oxford University Press.

Blatt, S. J., Quinlan, D. M., Pilkonis, P. A. & Shea, M. T. (1995). Impact of perfectionism and need for approval on the brief treatment of depression: the National Institute of Mental Health Treatment of Depression Collaborative Research Program revisited. *Journal of Consulting and Clinical Psychology, 63(1)*, 125–132.

Blatt, S. J., Sanislow III, C. A., Zuroff, D. C. & Pilkonis, P. A. (1996). Characteristics of effective therapists: further analyses of data from the National Institute of Mental Health Treatment of Depression Collaborative Research Program. *Journal of Consulting and Clinical Psychology, 64(6)*, 1276–1284.

Blatt, S. J., Zuroff, D. C., Quinlan, D. M. & Pilkonis, P. A. (1996). Interpersonal factors in brief treatment of depression: further analyses of the National Institute of Mental Health Treatment of Depression Collaborative Research Program. *Journal of Consulting and Clinical Psychology, 64(1)*, 162–171.

Bohart, A. C., Elliott, R., Greenberg, L. S. & Watson, J. C. (2002). Empathy. In J. C. Norcross (ed.), *Psychotherapy Relationships that Work: Therapist Contributions and Responsiveness to Patients* (pp. 89–108). New York: Oxford University Press.

Bohart, A. C., O'Hara, M. & Leitner, L. (1998). Empirically violated treatments: disenfranchisement of humanistic and other psychotherapies. *Psychotherapy Research 8*, 141–157.

Bohart, A. C. & Tallman, K. (1999). *How Clients Make Therapy Work*. Washington, DC: American Psychological Association.

Bond, T. (2004). *Ethical Guidelines for Researching Counseling and Psychotherapy*. Rugby: British Association for Counselling and Psychotherapy.

Bordin, E. S. (1979). The generalizability of the psychoanalytic concept of the working alliance. *Psychotherapy: Theory, Research and Practice, 16*, 252–260.

Borkovec, T. D. & Costello, E. (1993). Efficacy of applied relaxation and cognitive-behavioral therapy in the treatment of generalized anxiety disorder. *Journal of Consulting and Clinical Psychology, 61(4)*, 611–619.

Bower, P., Byford, S., Sibbald, B., Ward, E., King, M., Lloyd, M. et al. (2000). Randomized controlled trial of non-directive counseling, cognitive-behavior therapy, and usual general practitioner care for patients with depression. II: Cost effectiveness. *British Medical Journal, 321*, 1389–1392.

Bower, P. & King, M. (2000). Randomized controlled trials and the evaluation of psychological therapy. In N. Rowland & S. Goss (eds), *Evidence-based Counseling and Psychological Therapies: Research and Applications* (pp. 79–109). London: Routledge.

Bower, P. & Rowland, N. (2006). Effectiveness and cost effectiveness of counselling in primary care. *Cochrane Database of Systematic Reviews, 3*.

Bowlby, J. (1988). *A Secure Base: Parent–Child Attachment and Healthy Human Development*. London: Basic Books.

Brent, D. A., Holder, D., Kolko, D., Birmaher, B., Baugher, M., Roth, C. et al. (1997). A clinical psychotherapy trial for adolescent depression comparing cognitive, family, and supportive therapy. *Archives of General Psychiatry, 54*, 877–885.

Bruck, E., Aderholt, S., Muran, J. C., Gorman, B. & Winston, A. (2004, June). Patient and therapist personality, therapeutic alliance, and overall outcome in short-term dynamic and cognitive-behavioral therapies. Paper presented at 34th Annual Conference of International Society for Psychotherapy Research, Rome, Italy.

Burke, B. L., Arkowitz, H. & Dunn, C. (2002). The efficacy of motivational interviewing. In W. R. Miller & S. Rollnick (eds), *Motivational Interviewing: Preparing People for Change* (2nd edn) (pp. 217–250). New York: Guilford Press.

Burlingame, G. M., Fuhriman, A. & Johnson, J. E. (2002). Cohesion in group psychotherapy. In J. C. Norcross (ed.), *Psychotherapy Relationships that Work: Therapist Contributions and Responsiveness to Patients* (pp. 71–87). New York: Oxford University Press.

Burlingame, G. M., MacKenzie, K. R. & Strauss, B. (2004). Small-group treatment: evidence for effectiveness and mechanisms of change. In M. J. Lambert (ed.), *Bergin's and Garfield's Handbook of Psychotherapy and Behavior Change* (5th edn, pp. 647–696). New York: John Wiley.

Burlingame, G. M., Mosier, J. I., Gawain Wells, M., Atkin, Q. G., Lambert, M. J., Whoolery, M. & Latkowski, M. (2001). Tracking the influence of mental health treatment: the development of the Youth Outcome Questionnaire. *Clinical Psychology and Psychotherapy, 8,* 361–379.

Caston, J. (1986). The reliability of the diagnosis of the patient's unconscious plan. In J. Weiss & H. Sampson (eds), *The Psychoanalytic Process: Theory, Clinical Observations, and Empirical Research* (pp. 256–266). New York: Guilford Press.

Castonguay, L. G. & Beutler, L. E. (eds) (2005). *Principles of Therapeutic Change that Work.* New York: Oxford University Press.

Chadwick, P. D. J. & Lowe, C. F. (1990). Measurement and modification of delusional beliefs. *Journal of Consulting and Clinical Psychology, 58,* 225–232.

Chambless, D. L. & Hollon, S. D. (1998). Defining empirical supported therapies. *Journal of Consulting and Clinical Psychology, 66(1),* 7–18.

Chambless, D. L., Sanderson, W. C., Shoham, V., Bennett Johnson, S., Pope, K. S., Crits-Christoph, P., Baker, M., Johnson, B., Woody, S. R., Sue, S., Beutler, L., Williams, D. A. & McCurry, S. (1996). An update on empirically validated therapies. *The Clinical Psychologist, 49,* 5–18.

Chambless, D. L., Baker, M. J., Baucom, D. H., Beutler, L. E., Calhoun, K. S., Crits-Christoph, P., Daiuto, A., DeRubeis, R., Detweiler, J., Haaga, D. A. F., Bennett Johnson, S., McCurry, S., Mueser, K. T., Pope, K. S., Sanderson, W. C., Shoham, V., Stickle, T., Williams, D. A. & Woody, S. R. (1998). Update on empirically validated therapies, II. *The Clinical Psychologist, 51,* 3–16.

Clarkin, J. F. & Levy, K. N. (2004). The influence of client variables on psychotherapy. In M. J. Lambert (ed.), *Bergin's and Garfield's Handbook of Psychotherapy and Behavior Change* (5th edn, pp. 194–226). New York: John Wiley.

Clinical Psychologist (1998). An Update on Empirically Validated Therapies. *The Clinical Psychologist,* Special issue.

Cohen, J. (1988). *Statistical Power Analysis for the Behavioral Sciences* (2nd edn). Hillsdale, NJ: Erlbaum.

Craighead, W. E., Sheets, E. S., Brosse, A. L. & Illardi, S. S. (2007). Psychosocial treatments for major depressive disorder. In P. E. Nathan & J. M. Gorman (eds), *A Guide to Treatments that Work* (3rd edn). New York: Oxford University Press.

Craske, M. G. & Barlow, D. H. (2001). Panic disorder and agoraphobia. In D. H. Barlow (ed.), *Clinical Handbook of Psychological Disorders: A Step-by-step Treatment Manual* (3rd edn, pp.1–59). New York: Guilford Press.

Craske, M. G. & Barlow, D. H. (2007). *Mastery of Your Anxiety and Panic: Therapist Guide*. (4th edn). New York: Oxford University Press.

Crits-Christoph, P., Crits-Christoph, K., Wolf-Palacio, D., Fichter, M. & Rudick, D. (1995). Brief supportive-expressive psychodynamic therapy for generalized anxiety disorder. In J. P. Barber & P. Crits-Christoph (eds), *Dynamic Therapies for Psychiatric Disorders (Axis I)* (pp. 43–83). New York: Basic Books.

Crits-Christoph, P. & Gallop, R. (2006). Therapist effects in TDCRP and other psychotherapy studies. *Psychotherapy Research, 16*, 178–181.

Crits-Christoph, P. & Luborsky, L. (1990). Changes in CCRT pervasiveness during psychotherapy. In L. Luborsky & P. Crits-Christoph, *Understanding Countertransference: The Core Conflictual Relationship Theme Method* (pp. 133–146). New York: Basic Books.

Crits-Christoph, P., Siqueland, L., Blaine, J. et al. (1999) Psychosocial treatments for cocaine dependence: National Institute on Drug Abuse collaborative cocaine treatment study. *Archives of General Psychiatry, 56*, 493–502.

Curtis, J. T., Silberschatz, G., Sampson, H. & Weiss, J. (1994). The plan formulation method. *Psychotherapy Research, 4(3&4)*, 197–207.

Dallos, R. & Vetere, A. (2005). *Researching Psychotherapy and Counselling*. Maidenhead: Open University Press.

Department of Health (2001). *Treatment Choice in Psychological Therapies and Counseling: Evidence-Based Clinical Practice Guideline*. London: HMSO.

Derogatis, L. R. (2000). Symptom Checklist – 90 – Revised (SCL-90-R). In American Psychiatric Association, *Handbook of Psychiatric Measures* (pp. 81–84). Washington, DC: Author.

Derogatis, L. R., Lipman, R. S. & Covi, L. (1973). SCL-90: an outpatient psychiatric rating scale – preliminary report. *Psychopharmacology Bulletin, 9*, 13–28.

Diamond, G. & Liddle, H. A. (1996). Resolving a therapeutic impasse between parents and adolescents in multidimensional family therapy. *Journal of Consulting and Clinical Psychology, 64(3)*, 481–488.

DiClemente, C. C. & Prochaska, J. O. (1982). Self-change and therapy change of smoking behavior: A comparison of processes of change in cessation and maintenance. *Addictive Behaviors, 7*, 133–142.

Durlak, J. A. & Lipsey, M. W. (1991). A practitioner's guide to meta-analysis. *American Journal of Community Psychology, 19*, 291–332.

Elkin, I. (1994). The NIMH Treatment of Depression Collaborative Research Program: where we began and where we are. In A. E. Bergin & S. L. Garfield (eds), *Handbook of Psychotherapy and Behavior Change* (4th edn, pp. 115–139). New York: John Wiley.

Elkin, I., Falconnier, L. Martinovich, Z. & Mahoney, C. (2006a). Therapist effects in the NIMH Treatment of Depression Collaborative Research Program. *Psychotherapy Research, 16*, 144–160.

Elkin, I., Falconnier, L., Martinovich, Z. & Mahoney, C. (2006b). Rejoinder to commentaries by Stephen Soldz and Paul Crits-Christoph on therapist effects articles. *Psychotherapy Research, 16*, 182–183.

Elkin, I., Shea, M. T., Klett, C. J., Imber, S. D., Sotsky, S. M., Collins, J. F., et al. (1989). National Institute of Mental Health Treatment of Depression Collaborative Research Program: general effectiveness of treatments. *Archives of General Psychiatry, 46*, 971–982.

Elliott, R. (1983). '"That in your hands...': A comprehensive process analysis of a significant event in psychotherapy. *Psychiatry, 46*, 113–129.

Elliott, R. (1984). A discovery-oriented approach to significant events in psychotherapy: interpersonal process recall and comprehensive process analysis. In L. Rice and L. Greenberg (eds), *Patterns of Change* (pp. 249–286). New York: Guilford Press.

Elliott, R. (1985). Helpful and nonhelpful events in brief counseling interviews: an empirical taxonomy. *Journal of Counseling Psychology, 32*, 307–322.

Elliott, R. (1986). Interpersonal process recall (IPR) as a psychotherapy process research method. In L. S. Greenberg & W. M. Pinsof (eds), *The Psychotherapeutic Process: A Research Handbook* (pp. 249–286). New York: Guilford Press.

Elliott, R. (1989). Comprehensive process analysis: understanding the change process in significant therapy events. In M. Packer & R. B. Addison (eds), *Entering the Circle: Hermeneutic Investigation in Psychology* (pp. 165–184). Albany, NY: State University of New York Press.

Elliott, R. (1991). Five dimensions of therapy process. *Psychotherapy Research, 1*, 92–103.

Elliott, R. (1993). *The Revised Session Reaction Scale*. Toledo, OH: University of Toledo.

Elliott, R. (1998). Editor's introduction: a guide to the empirically-supported treatment controversy. *Psychotherapy Research, 8*, 115–125.

Elliott, R. (2002a). Hermeneutic single case efficacy design. *Psychotherapy Research, 12*, 1–21.

Elliott, R. (2002b). The effectiveness of humanistic therapies: a meta-analysis. In D. Cain & J. Seeman (eds), *Humanistic Psychotherapies: Handbook of Research and Practice* (pp. 57–82). Washington, DC: American Psychological Association.

Elliott, R. (2003). *CSEP-II Experiential Therapy Session Form*. Toledo, OH: University of Toledo Department of Psychology.

Elliott, R. & Anderson, C. (1994). Simplicity and complexity in psychotherapy research. In R. L. Russell (ed.), *Reassessing Psychotherapy Research* (pp. 65–113). New York: Guilford Press.

Elliott, R. & Greenberg, L. S. (2002). Process-experiential psychotherapy. In D. Cain & J. Seeman (eds), *Humanistic Psychotherapies: Handbook of Research and Practice* (pp. 279–306). Washington, DC: American Psychological Association.

Elliott, R., Greenberg, L. S. & Lietaer, G. (2004). Research on experiential psychotherapies. In M. J. Lambert (ed.), *Bergin's and Garfield's Handbook of Psychotherapy and Behavior Change* (5th edn, pp. 493–539). New York: John Wiley.

Elliott, R., Mack, C. & Shapiro, D. A. (1999). *Simplified Personal Questionnaire Procedure*. Toledo, OH: University of Toledo.

Elliott, R. & Shapiro, D. A. (1988). Brief structured recall: a more efficient method for studying significant therapy events. *British Journal of Medical Psychology, 61*, 141–153.

Elliott, R., Slatick, E. & Urman, M. (2001). Qualitative change process research on psychotherapy: alternative strategies. *Psychologische Beiträge, 43(3)*, 69–111. [Reprinted in: J. Frommer and D. L. Rennie (eds), *Qualitative Psychotherapy Research: Methods and Methodology* (pp. 69–111). Lengerich, Germany: Pabst Science Publishers.]

Elliott, R., Watson, J. C., Goldman, R. & Greenberg, L. S. (2004). *Learning Emotion-focused Therapy: The Process-experiential Approach.* Washington, DC: American Psychological Association.

Elliott, R. & Wexler, M. M. (1994). Measuring the impact of session in process-experiential therapy of depression: the session impacts scale. *Journal of Counseling Psychology, 41(2)*, 962–969.

Endicott, J., Spitzer, R. L., Fleiss, J. L. & Cohen, J. (1976). The Global Assessment Scale: a procedure for measuring overall severity of psychiatric disturbance. *Archives of General Psychiatry, 33*, 766–771.

Eugster, S. L. & Wampold, B. E. (1996). Systematic effects of participant role on evaluation of the psychotherapy session. *Journal of Consulting and Clinical Psychology, 64*, 1020–1028.

Evans, C., Connell, J., Barkham, M., Marshall, C. & Mellor-Clark, J. (2003). Practice-based evidence: benchmarking NHS primary care counselling services at national and local levels. *Clinical Psychology & Psychotherapy, 10*, 374–388.

Even, C., Siobud-Dorocant, E. & Dardennes, R. M. (2002). Critical approach to antidepressants trials: blindness protection is feasible, necessary, and measurable. *British Journal of Psychiatry, 177*, 47–51.

Eysenck, H. J. (1952). The effects of psychotherapy: an evaluation. *Journal of Consulting Psychology, 16*, 319–324.

First, M. B., Spitzer, R. L., Gibbon, M. & Williams, J. B. W. (1996). *Structured Clinical Interview for DSM-IV Axis I Disorders.* New York: New York State Psychiatric Institute.

Fisher, J. E. & O'Donohue, W. (eds) (2006). *Practitioners' Guide to Evidence Based Psychotherapy.* New York: Springer Publishing.

Frank, E. (1991). Interpersonal psychotherapy as a maintenance treatment for patients with recurrent depression. *Psychotherapy, 28*, 259–266.

Franklin, M. E., Abramowitz, J. S., Kozak, M. J., Levitt, J. & Foa, E. B. (2000). Effectiveness of exposure and ritual prevention for obsessive-compulsive disorder: randomized compared with nonrandomized samples. *Journal of Consulting and Clinical Psychology, 68*, 594–602.

Fried, D., Crits-Christoph, P. & Luborsky, L. (1990). The parallel of the CCRT for the therapist with the CCRT for other people. In L. Luborsky & P. Crits-Christoph, *Understanding Countertransference: The Core Conflictual Relationship Theme Method* (pp. 147–157). New York: Basic Books.

Fuhriman, A. & Burlimgame, G. M. (eds) (1994). *Handbook of Group Psychotherapy: An Empirical and Clinical Synthesis.* New York: John Wiley.

Garfield, S. L. (1994). Research on client variables in psychotherapy. In A. E. Bergin & S. L. Garfield (eds), *Handbook of Psychotherapy and Behavior Change* (4th edn, pp. 190–228). New York: John Wiley.

Garfield, S. L. (1996). Some problems associated with 'validated' forms of psychotherapy. *Clinical Psychology: Science and Practice, 3*, 218–229.

Gelso, C. J. & Hayes, J. A. (2002). The management of countertransference. In J. C. Norcross (ed.), *Psychotherapy Relationships that Work: Therapist Contributions and Responsiveness to Patients* (pp. 267–283). New York: Oxford University Press.

Gilbody, S. & Sowden, A. (2001). Systematic reviews in mental health. In N. Rowland & S. Goss (eds), *Evidence-based Counselling and Psychological Therapies: Research and Applications* (pp. 147–170). London: Routledge.

Gillies, L. A. (2001). Interpersonal psychotherapy for depression and other disorders. In D. H. Barlow (ed.), *Clinical Handbook of Psychological Disorders: A Step-by-step Treatment Manual* (3rd edn, pp. 309–331). New York: Guilford Press.

Glaser, B. G. & Strauss, A. (1971). *The Discovery of Grounded Theory: Strategies for Qualitative Research* (2nd edn). Chicago: Aldine Press.

Goldman, A. & Greenberg, L. (1992). Comparison of integrated systemic and emotionally focused approaches to couples therapy. *Journal of Consulting and Clinical Psychology, 60(6)*, 962–969.

Goldstein, A. & Brown, B. W. (2003). Urine testing in methadone maintenance treatment: applications and limitations. *Journal of Substance Abuse, 25*, 61–63.

Goodman, W. K., Price, L. H., Rasmussen, S. A., Mazure, C., Fleischmann, R. L., Hill, C. L., Heninger, G. R. & Charney, D. S. (1989). The Yale–Brown obsessive-compulsive scale. I. Development, use and reliability. *Archives of General Psychiatry, 46*, 1006–1011.

Grawe, K. (1997). Research-informed psychotherapy. *Psychotherapy Research, 7*, 1–19.

Grawe, K. (2004). *Psychological Therapy*. Göttingen: Hogfrege & Huber Publ.

Grawe, K. (2007). *Neuropsychotherapy: How the Neurosciences Inform Effective Psychotherapy*. Mahwah, NJ: Lawrence Erlbaum.

Grawe, K., Donati, R. & Bernauer, F. (1994). *Psychotherapie im Wandel: Von der Konfession zur Profession*. Göttingen: Hogrefe.

Gray, L. A., Ladany, N., Walker, J. A. & Ancis, J. R. (2001). Psychotherapy trainees' experience of counterproductive events in supervision. *Journal of Counseling Psychology, 48*, 371–383.

Greenberg, L. S. (1984). A task analysis of interpersonal conflict resolution. In L. N. Rice & L. S. Greenberg (eds), *Patterns of Change* (pp. 67–123). New York: Guilford Press.

Greenberg, L. S. (1986). Research strategies. In L. S. Greenberg & W. Pinsof (eds), *The Psychotherapeutic Process: A Research Handbook* (pp. 707–734). New York: Guilford Press.

Greenberg, L. S. (2002). *Emotion-focused Therapy: Coaching Clients to Work through Feelings*. Washington, DC: American Psychological Association.

Greenberg, L. S. (2007). A guide to conducting a task analysis of psychotherapeutic change. *Psychotherapy Research, 17*, 15–30.

Greenberg, L. S. & Johnson, S. (1988). *Emotionally Focused Therapy for Couples*. New York: Guilford Press.

Greenberg, L. S. & Pinsof, W. (eds) (1986). *The Psychotherapeutic Process: A Research Handbook*. New York: Guilford Press.

Greenberg, L. S., Rice, L. N. & Elliott, R. (1993). *Facilitating Emotional Change: The Moment-by-moment Process*. New York: Guilford Press.

Greenberg, L. S. & Safran, J. D. (1987). *Emotion in Psychotherapy: Affect, Cognition and the Process of Change*. New York: Guilford Press.

Greenberg, L. S. & Safran, J. D. (1989). Emotion in psychotherapy. *American Psychologist*, *44*, 19–29.

Greenberg, L. S. & Watson, J. C. (1998). Experiential therapy of depression: differential effects of client-centered relationship conditions and process experiential interventions. *Psychotherapy Research, 8*, 210–224.

Greenberg, L. S. & Watson, J. C. (2005). *Emotion-focused Therapy of Depression*. Washington, DC: American Psychological Association.

Gurman, A. S. & Jacobson, N. S. (2003). *Clinical Handbook of Couples Therapy* (3rd edn). New York: Guilford Press.

Guthrie, E., Margison, F., Mackay, H., Chew-Graham, C., Moorey, J. & Sibbald, B. (2004). Effectiveness of psychodynamic interpersonal therapy training for primary care counsellors. *Psychotherapy Research, 14*, 161–175.

Haaga, D. A. & Stiles, W. B. (2000). Randomized clinical trials in psychotherapy research: methodology, design, and evaluation. In C. R. Snyder & R. E. Ingram (eds), *Handbook of Psychological Change* (pp. 14–39). New York: John Wiley.

Hamilton, M. (1960). A rating scale for depression. *Journal of Neurology, Neurosurgery, and Psychiatry, 12*, 56–62.

Hardy, G. E., Aldridge, J., Davidson, C., Rowe, C., Reilly, S. & Shapiro, D. A. (1999). Therapist responsiveness to client attachment styles and issues observed in client-identified significant events in psychodynamic-interpersonal psychotherapy. *Psychotherapy Research, 9*, 36–53.

Harmon, S. C., Lambert, M. J., Smart, D. M., Hawkins, E., Nielsen, S. L., Slade, K. & Lutz, W. (2007). Enhancing outcome for potential treatment failures: therapist–client feedback and clinical support tools. *Psychotherapy Research, 17*, 379–392.

Hatcher R. L. & Gillaspy, J. A. (2006). Development and validation of a revised short version of the Working Alliance Inventory. *Psychotherapy Research, 16*, 12–25.

Henggeler, S. W., Melton, G. B., Brondino, M. J., Scherer, D. G. & Hanley, J. H. (1997). Multisystemic therapy with violent and chronic juvenile offenders and their families: the role of treatment fidelity in successful dissemination. *Journal of Consulting and Clinical Psychology, 65*, 821–833.

Henry, W. P. (1998). Science, politics, and the politics of science: the use and misuse of empirically validated treatment research. *Psychotherapy Research, 8(2)*, 126–140.

Heppner, P. P., Kivlighian, D. M., Jr & Wampold, B. E. (1999). *Research Design in Counseling* (2nd edn). Belmont, CA: Brooks/Cole–Wadsworth.

Hersen, M. (2004). *Psychological Assessment in Clinical Practice: A Pragmatic Guide*. New York: Brunner-Routledge.

Hill, C. E. (1986). An overview of the Hill Counselor and Client Verbal Response Modes Category Systems. In L. S. Greenberg & W. Pinsof (eds), *The Psychotherapeutic Process* (pp. 131–160). New York: Guilford Press.

Hill, C. E. (1989). *Therapist Techniques and Outcomes: Eight Cases of Brief Psychotherapy*. London: SAGE.

Hill, C. E. (1991). Almost everything you ever wanted to know about how to do process research on counseling and psychotherapy but didn't know who to ask. In C. E. Watkins

& L. J. Schneider (eds), *Research in Counseling* (pp. 85–118). Hillsdale, NJ: Lawrence Erlbaum.

Hill, C. E. & O'Brien, K. (1999). *Helping Skills: Facilitating Exploration, Insight, and Action*. Washington, DC: American Psychological Association.

Hill, C. E., Thames, T. B. & Rardin, D. K. (1979). Comparison of Rogers, Perls, and Ellis on the Hill Counselor Verbal Response Category System. *Journal of Counseling Psychology, 26(3)*, 198–203.

Hill, C. E., Thompson, B. J., Cogar, M. C. & Denman III, D.W. (1993). Beneath the surface of long-term therapy: therapist and client report of their own and each other's covert processes. *Journal of Counseling Psychology, 40(3)*, 278–287.

Hill, C. E., Thompson, B. J. & Nutt-Williams, E. (1997). A guide to conducting consensual qualitative research. *The Counseling Psychologist, 25*, s. 517–572.

Hobson, R. F. (1985). *Forms of Feeling: The Heart of Psychotherapy*. London: Tavistock.

Hollon, S. D. & Beck, A. T. (2004). Cognitive and cognitive-behavioral therapies. In M. J. Lambert (ed.), *Bergin's and Garfield's Handbook of Psychotherapy and Behavior Change* (5th edn, pp. 447–492). New York: John Wiley.

Honos-Webb, L., Lani, J. A. & Stiles, W. B. (1999). Discovering markers of assimilation stages: the fear-of-losing-control marker. *Journal of Clinical Psychology, 55*, 1441–1452.

Honos-Webb, L., Stiles, W. B., Greenberg, L. S. & Goldman, R. (1998). Assimilation analysis of process-experiential psychotherapy: a comparison of two cases. *Psychotherapy Research, 8(3)*, 264–286.

Honos-Webb, L., Surko, M., Stiles, W. B. & Greenberg, L. S. (1999). Assimilation of voices in psychotherapy: the case of Jane. *Journal of Counseling Psychology, 46(4)*, 448–460.

Horowitz, L. M., Rosenberg, S. E., Baer, B. A., Ureno, G. & Villasenor, V. S. (1988). Inventory of Interpersonal Problems: psychometric properties and clinical applications. *Journal of Consulting and Clinical Psychology, 56(6)*, 885–892.

Horvath, A. O. & Bedi, R. P. (2002). The alliance. In J. C. Norcross (ed.), *Psychotherapy Relationships that Work: Therapist Contributions and Responsiveness to Patients* (pp. 37–69). New York: Oxford University Press.

Horvath, A. O. & Greenberg, L. S. (1989). Development and validation of the Working Alliance Inventory. *Journal of Counseling Psychology, 36*, 223–233.

Hotopf, M. (2002). The pragmatic randomised controlled trial. *Advances in Psychiatric Treatment, 8*, 326–333.

Howard, K. I., Cornille, T. A., Lyons, J. S., Vessey, J. T., Lueger, R. J. & Saunders, S. M. (1996). Patterns of mental health service utilization. *Archives of General Psychiatry, 53*, 696–703.

Howard, K. I., Kopta, S. M., Krause, M. S. & Orlinsky, D. E. (1986). The dose-effect relationship in psychotherapy. *American Psychologist, 41*, 159–186.

Howard, K. I., Lueger, R. J., Maling, M. S. & Martinovich, Z. (1993). A phase model of psychotherapy outcome: casual mediation of change. *Journal of Consulting and Clinical Psychology, 61*, 678–685.

Howard, K. I., Moras, K., Brill, P. L., Martinovich, Z. & Lutz, W. (1996). Evaluation of psychotherapy: efficacy, effectiveness, and patient progress. *American Psychologist, 51(10)*, 1059–1064.

Howe, D. (1996). Client experiences of counseling and treatment interventions: a qualitative study of family views of family therapy. *British Journal of Guidance and Counselling, 24(3)*, 367–375.

Hunter, J. E. & Schmidt, F. L. (2004). *Methods of Meta-analysis: Correcting Error and Bias in Research Findings* (2nd edn). Newbury Park, CA: SAGE.

Jacobson, N. S. & Truax, P. (1991). Clinical significance: a statistical approach to defining meaningful change in psychotherapy research. *Journal of Consulting and Clinical Psychology, 59(1)*, 12–19.

Jennings, L. & Skovholt, T. M. (1999). The cognitive, emotional, and relational characteristics of master therapists. *Journal of Counseling Psychology, 46*, 3–11.

Jensen, J. P. & Bergin, A. E. (1988). Mental health values of professional therapists: a national interdisciplinary survey. *Professional Psychology: Research and Practice, 19*, 290–297.

Johnson, S. M. (2004). *The Practice of Emotionally Focused Marital Therapy: Creating Connection* (2nd edn). New York: Brunner/Mazel.

Kächele, H., Kordy, H., Richard, M. & Research Group TR-EAT (2001). Therapy amount and outcome of inpatient psychodynamic treatment of eating disorders in Germany: data from a multicenter study. *Psychotherapy Research, 11(3)*, 239–257.

Kadden, R. M., Longabaugh, R. & Wirtz, P. W. (2003). The matching hypotheses: rationale and prediction. In T. F. Babor & F. K. Del Boca (eds), *Treatment Matching in Alcoholism* (pp. 81–102). Cambridge: Cambridge University Press.

Kaplan, R. M. & Sacuzzo, D. P. (2005). *Psychological Testing: Principles, Applications, and Issues*. (6th edn). Pacific Grove, CA: Brooks/Cole.

Kazdin, A. E. (2003). *Research Design in Clinical Psychology* (4th edn). Boston: Allyn and Bacon.

Keller, M. B., Lavori, P. W., Friedman, B., Nielsen, E., Endicott, J., McDonald-Scott, P. & Andreasen, N. C. (1987). The Longitudinal Interval Follow-up Evaluation: a comprehensive method for assessing outcome in prospective longitudinal studies. *Archival of General Psychiatry, 44*, 540–548.

Kerlinger, F. N. & Lee, H. B. (2000). *Foundations of Behavioral Research* (4th edn). New York: Harcourt Brace.

Kiesler, D. J. (1967). A scale for the rating of congruence. In C. R. Rogers, E. T. Gendlin, D. J. Kiesler & C. B. Truax (eds), *The Therapeutic Relationship and its Impact: A Study of Psychotherapy with Schizofrenics* (pp. 581–586). Madison: University of Wisconsin Press.

Kim, D., Wampold, B. E. & Bolt, D. M. (2006). Therapist effects in psychotherapy: a random effects modeling of the NIMH TDCRP data. *Psychotherapy Research, 16*, 161–172.

King, M., Sibbald, B., Ward, E., Bower, P., Lloyd, M., Gabbay, M. et al. (2000). Randomised controlled trial of non-directive counselling, cognitive-behaviour therapy and usual general practitioner care in the management of depression as well as mixed anxiety and depression in primary care. *Health Technology Assessment, 4(19)*.

Kivlighan, D. M. & Goldfine, D. C. (1991). Endorsement of therapeutic factors as a function of stage of group development and participant interpersonal attitudes. *Journal of Counseling Psychology, 38*, 150–158.

Klein, M., Mathieu-Coughlan, P., Gendlin, E. T. & Kiesler, D. J. (1969). *The Experiencing Scales: A Research and Training Material* (Vols 1 & 2). Madison: Wisconsin University Press.

Klein, M., Mathieu-Coughlan, P. & Kiesler, D. J. (1986). The experiencing scales. In L. S. Greenberg & W. Pinsof (eds), *The Psychotherapeutic Process* (pp. 21–72). New York: Guilford Press.

Klerman, G. L., Weissman, M. M., Rounsaville, B. J. & Chevron, E. S. (1984). *Interpersonal Psychotherapy of Depression.* New York: Basic Books.

Knox, S., Hess, S. A., Petersen, D. A. & Hill, C. E. (1997). A qualitative analysis of client perceptions of the effects of helpful therapist self-disclosure in long-term therapy. *Journal of Counseling Psychology, 44(3),* 274–283.

Kopta, S. M., Howard, K. I., Lowry, J. L. & Beutler, L. E. (1994). Patterns of symptomatic recovery in psychotherapy. *Journal of Consulting and Clinical Psychology, 62(5),* 1009–1016.

Krupnick, J. L., Sotsky, S. M., Simmens, S., Moyer, J., Elkin, I., Watkins, J. et al. (1996). The role of the therapeutic alliance in psychotherapy and pharmacotherapy outcome: findings in the National Institute of Mental Health Treatment of Depression Collaborative Research Program. *Journal of Consulting and Clinical Psychology, 64,* 532–539.

Kuhnlein, I. (1999). Psychotherapy as a process of transformation: analysis of posttherapeutic autobiographic narrations. *Psychotherapy Research, 9(3),* 274–288.

Ladany, N., Friedlander, M. L. & Nelson, M. L. (2005). *Critical Events in Psychotherapy Supervision: An Interpersonal Approach.* Washington, DC: American Psychological Association.

Lambert, M. J. (ed.) (2004). *Bergin's and Garfield's Handbook of Psychotherapy and Behavior Change* (5th edn). New York: John Wiley.

Lambert, M. J. & Barley, D. B. (2002). Research summary on the therapeutic relationship and psychotherapy. In J. C. Norcross (ed.), *Psychotherapy Relationships that Work: Therapist Contributions and Responsiveness to Patients* (pp. 17–36). New York: Oxford University Press.

Lambert, M. J., Garfield, S. L. & Bergin, A. E. (2004). Overview, trends, and future issues. In M. J. Lambert (ed.), *Bergin's and Garfield's Handbook of Psychotherapy and Behavior Change* (5th edn, pp. 805–821). New York: John Wiley.

Lambert, M. J., Hansen, N. B. & Finch, A. E. (2001). Patient-focused research: using patient outcome data to enhance treatment effects. *Journal of Consulting and Clinical Psychology, 69(2),* 159–172.

Lambert, M. J. & Hill, C. E. (1994). Assessing psychotherapy outcomes and processes. In A. E. Bergin & S. L. Garfield (eds), *Handbook of Psychotherapy and Behavior Change* (4th edn, pp. 72–113). New York: John Wiley.

Lambert, M. J., Morton, J. J., Hattfield, D., Harmon, C., Hamilton, S., Reid, R. C., Shimokawa, K., Christopherson, C. & Burlingame, G. M. (2004). *Administration and Scoring Manual for the OQ® – 45.2 (Outcome Questionnaire).* Orem, UT: American Professional Credentialing Services.

Lambert, M. J. & Ogles, B. M. (1997). The effectiveness of psychotherapy supervision. In C. E. Watkins (ed.), *Handbook of Psychotherapy Supervision* (pp. 421–446). New York: John Wiley.

Lambert, M. J. & Ogles, B. M. (2004). The efficacy and effectiveness of psychotherapy. In M. J. Lambert (ed.), *Bergin's and Garfield's Handbook of Psychotherapy and Behavior Change* (5th edn, pp. 139–193). New York: John Wiley.

Lambert, M. J., Whipple, J. S., Smart, D. W., Vermeeresch, D. A., Nielsen, S. L. & Hawkins, E. J. (2001). The effects of providing therapists with feedback on patient progress during psychotherapy: are outcomes enhanced? *Psychotherapy Research, 11,* 49–68.

Lampropoulos, G. K. (2001). Bridging technical eclecticism and theoretical integration: assimilative integration. *Journal of Psychotherapy Integration, 11,* 5–19.

Larsen, D. L., Attkisson, C. C., Hargreaves, W. A. & Nguyen, T. D. (1979). Assessment of client/patient satisfaction: development of a general scale. *Evaluation and Program Planning, 2,* 197–207.

Lebow, J. (2006). *Research for the Psychotherapist: From Science to Practice.* New York: Routledge.

Lepper, G. & Riding, N. (2006). *Researching the Psychotherapy Process: A Practical Guide to Transcript-based Methods.* New York: Palgrave Macmillan.

Levitt, H., Butler, M. & Hill, T. (2006). What clients find helpful in psychotherapy: developing principles for facilitating moment-to-moment change. *Journal of Counseling Psychology, 63,* 314–324.

Levitt, H. M., Butler, M. & Travis, H. (2006). What clients find helpful in psychotherapy: principles for facilitating change. *Journal of Counseling Psychology, 53(3),* 314–324.

Lietaer, G. (1992). Helping and hindering processes in client-centered/experiential psychotherapy: a content analysis of client and therapist post-session perceptions. In S. G. Toukmanian & D. L. Rennie (eds), *Psychotherapy Process Research: Paradigmatic and Narrative Approaches* (pp. 134–162). Newbury Park, CA: SAGE.

Lietaer, G. & Neirinck, M. (1986). Client and therapist perceptions of helping processes in client-centered/experiential psychotherapy. *Person-Centered Review, 1,* 436–455.

Lilliengren, P. & Werbart, A. (2005). A model of therapeutic action grounded in the patients' view of curative and hindering factors in psychoanalytic psychotherapy. *Psychotherapy: Theory, Research, Practice, Training, 42,* 324–339.

Linden, D. E. J. (2006). How psychotherapy changes the brain – the contribution of functional neuroimaging. *Molecular Psychiatry, 11,* 528–538.

Llewelyn, S. P. (1988). Psychological therapy as viewed by clients and therapists. *British Journal of Clinical Psychology, 27,* 223–237.

Llewelyn, S. P. & Hardy, G. (2001). Process research in understanding and applying psychological therapies. *British Journal of Clinical Psychology, 40,* 1–21.

Luborsky, L. (1962). Clinicians' judgments of mental health. *Archives of General Psychiatry, 7,* 407–417.

Luborsky, L. (1984). *Principles of Psychoanalytic Psychotherapy: A Manual for Supportive-Expressive Treatment.* New York: Basic Books.

Luborsky, L., Barber, J. P., Binder, J. et al. (1993). Transference-related measures: a new class based on psychotherapy session. In N. E. Miller, L. Luborsky, J. P. Barber & J. P. Docherty (eds), *Psychodynamic Treatment Research: A Handbook for Clinical Practice* (pp. 326–341). New York: Basic Books.

Luborsky, L. & Crits-Cristoph, P. (1990). *Understanding Countertransference: The Core Conflictual Relationship Theme Method*. New York: Basic Books.

Luborsky, L. & Crits-Cristoph, P. (1998). *Understanding Countertransference: The Core Conflictual Relationship Theme Method* (2nd edn). Washington, DC: American Psychological Association.

Luborsky, L., Crits-Christoph, P., McLellan, A. T., Woody, G., Piper, W., Liberman, B. et al. (1986). Do therapists vary much in their success? Findings from four outcome studies. *American Journal of Orthopsychiatry, 56(4)*, 501–512.

Luborsky, L. & Luborsky, E. (2006). *Research and Psychotherapy: The Vital Link*. Lanham, MD: Jason Aronson.

Luborsky, L., Mark, D., Hole, A. V., Popp, C., Goldsmith, B. & Cacciola, J. (1995). Supportive-expressive dynamic psychotherapy of depression: a time-limited version. In J. P. Barber & P. Crits-Christoph (eds), *Dynamic Therapies for Psychiatric Disorders (Axis I)* (pp. 13–42). New York: Basic Books.

Luborsky, L., McLellan, A. T., Diguer, L., Woody, G. & Seligman, D. A. (1997). The psychotherapist matters: comparison of outcomes across twenty-two therapists and seven patient samples. *Clinical Psychology: Science and Practice, 4*, 53–65.

Luborsky, L., McLellan, A. T., Woody, G. E., O'Brien, C. P. & Auerbach, A. (1985). Therapist success and its determinants. *Archives of General Psychiatry, 42*, 602–611.

Luborsky, L., Singer, B. & Luborsky, L. (1975). Comparative studies of psychotherapies: is it true that 'Everyone has won and all must have prizes'? *Archives of General Psychiatry, 32*, 995–1008.

Luborsky, L., Woody, G. E., Hole, A. V. & Velleco, A. (1995). Supportive-expressive dynamic psychotherapy for treatment of opiate drug dependence. In J. P. Barber & P. Crits-Christoph (eds), *Dynamic Therapies for Psychiatric Disorders (Axis I)* (pp. 131–160). New York: Basic Books.

Macran, S., Stiles, W. B. & Smith, J. A. (1999). How does personal therapy affect therapists' practice? *Journal of Counseling Psychology, 46(4)*, 419–431.

Martin, D. J., Garske, J. P. & Davies, M. K. (2000). Relation of the therapeutic alliance with outcome and other variables: a meta-analytic review. *Journal of Consulting and Clinical Psychology, 68*, 438–450.

Martin, J. & Stelmaczonek, K. (1988). Participants' identification and recall of important events in counseling. *Journal of Counseling Psychology, 35(4)*, 385–390.

Maruish, M. E. (2004). *The Use of Psychological Testing for Treatment Planning and Outcomes Assessment* (3rd edn, Vols 1–3). Boston: Lawrence Erlbaum Associates.

McKenna, P. & Boyd, D. (1997). Longitudinal utilisation of mental health services: a timeline method, nine retrospective accounts, and a preliminary conceptualisation. *Psychotherapy Research, 7*, 383–395.

McLeod, J. (1999). *Practitioner Research in Counselling*. London: SAGE.

McLeod, J. (2001a). *Qualitative Research in Counselling and Psychotherapy*. London: SAGE.

McLeod, J. (2001b). Developing a research tradition consistent with the practices and values of counselling and psychotherapy: why *Counselling and Psychotherapy Research* is necessary. *Counselling and Psychotherapy Research, 1*, 3–11.

McLeod, J. (2003). *Doing Counselling Research* (2nd edn). London: SAGE. (First published 1994.)

McLeod, J. (2007, May). The impact and meaning of research for clients and counsellors. Paper presented at 13th Annual research conference of the British Association for Counselling and Psychotherapy, York, UK.

Mellor-Clark, J., Curtis Jenkins, A., Evans, R., Mothersole, G. & McInnes, B. (2006). Resourcing a CORE Network to develop a National Research Database to help enhance psychological therapy and counselling service provision. *Counselling and Psychotherapy Research, 6*, 16–22.

Meltzer H., Bebbington, P., Brugha, T., Farrell, M., Jenkins, R. & Lewis, G. (2003). The reluctance to seek treatment for neurotic disorders. *International Review of Psychiatry, 15*, 123–128.

Messer, S. B. (2001). Introduction to the special issue on assimilative integration. *Journal of Psychotherapy Integration, 11*, 1–4.

Miller, S. D., Duncan, B. L. & Hubble, M. A. (2005). Outcome-informed clinical work. In J. C. Norcross & M. R. Goldfried (eds), *Handbook of Psychotherapy Integration* (2nd edn) (pp. 84–102). New York: Oxford University Press.

Miller, W. R. (1983). Motivational interviewing with problem drinkers. *Behavioural Psychotherapy, 11*, 147–172.

Miller, W. R. (1995). *Motivational Enhancement Therapy with Drug Abusers.* Albuquerque, NM: University of New Mexico.

Miller, W. R. & Rolnick, S. (1991). *Motivational Interviewing: Preparing People to Change Addictive Behavior.* New York: Guilford Press.

Miller, W. R. & Rolnick, S. (2002). *Motivational Interviewing: Preparing People to Change Addictive Behavior* (2nd edn). New York: Guilford Press.

Morrow-Bradley, C. & Elliott, R. (1986). Utilization of psychotherapy research by practicing psychotherapists. *American Psychologist, 41*, 188–197.

Moyers, T. B. & Martin, T. (2006). Therapist influence on client language during motivational interviewing sessions. *Journal of Substance Abuse, 30*, 245–251.

Mullin, T., Barkham, M., Mothersole, G., Bewick, B. M. & Kinder, A. (2006). Recovery and improvement benchmarks in routine primary care mental health settings. *Counselling and Psychotherapy Research, 6*, 68–80.

Narrow, W. E., Rae, D. S., Robins, L. N. & Regier, D. A. (2002). Revised prevalence estimates of mental disorders in the United States: using a clinical significance criterion to reconcile two survey's estimates. *Archives of General Psychiatry, 59*, 115–123.

Nathan, P. E. & Gorman, J. M. (eds) (2007). *A Guide to Treatments that Work* (3rd edn). New York: Oxford University Press.

National Collaborating Centre for Mental Health & National Institute for Clinical Excellence (2007). *National Clinical Practice Guideline Number 23. Depression: Management of Depression in Primary and Secondary Care.* London: The British Psychological Society and Gaskell.

Nilsson, T., Svensson, M., Sandell, R. & Clinton, D. (2007). Patients' experiences of change in cognitive-behavioral therapy and psychodynamic therapy: a qualitative comparative study. *Psychotherapy Research, 17*, 553–566.

Nock, M. K. (2002). A multiple-baseline evaluation of the treatment of food phobia in a young boy. *Journal of Behavior Therapy and Experimental Psychiatry, 33,* 217–225.

Norcross, J. (ed.) (2002). *Psychotherapy Relationships that Work: Therapist Contributions and Responsiveness to Patients.* New York: Oxford University Press.

Norcross, J. C., Beutler, L. E. & Levant, R. F. (eds) (2006). *Evidence-based Practices in Mental Health: Debate and Dialogue on the Fundamental Questions.* Washington, DC: American Psychological Association.

Norcross, J. C. & Connor, K. A. (2005). Psychotherapists entering personal therapy: their primary reasons and presenting problems. In J. D. Geller, J. C. Norcross & D. E. Orlinsky (eds), *The Psychotherapist's Own Psychotherapy Patient and Clinician Perspectives.* New York: Oxford University Press.

Norcross, J. C., Geller, J. D. & Kurzawa, E. K. (2000). Conducting psychotherapy with psychotherapists: I. Prevalence, patients, and problems. *Psychotherapy, 37(3),* 199–205.

Norcross, J. C. & Goldfried, M. R. (eds) (2005). *Handbook of Psychotherapy Integration* (2nd edn) New York: Oxford University Press.

Norcross, J. C. & Grunebaum, J. D. (2005). The selection and characteristics of therapists' psychotherapies: a research synthesis. In J. D. Geller, J. C. Norcross & D. E. Orlinsky (eds), *The Psychotherapist's Own Psychotherapy Patient and Clinician Perspectives.* New York: Oxford University Press.

Norcross, J. C. & Guy, H. (2005). Prevalence and parameters of personal therapy in the USA. In J. D. Geller, J. C. Norcross & D. E. Orlinsky (eds), *The Psychotherapist's Own Psychotherapy Patient and Clinician Perspectives.* New York: Oxford University Press.

Ogles, B. M., Lambert, M. J. & Fields, S. A. (2002). *Essentials of Outcome Assessment.* New York: John Wiley.

Okiishi, J., Lambert, M., Neilsen, S. & Ogles, B. (2003). Waiting for Supershrink: an empirical analysis of therapist effects. *Clinical Psychology and Psychotherapy, 10,* 361–373.

Olk, M. E. & Friedlander, M. L. (1992). Trainees' experiences of role conflict and role ambiguity in supervisory relationships. *Journal of Counseling Psychology, 39,* 389–397.

Orlinsky, D. E., Botermans, J. M. F., Wiseman, H., Ronnenstad, M. H. & Willutzki, U. (2005). Prevalence and parameters of personal therapy in Europe. In J. D. Geller, J. C. Norcross & D. E. Orlinsky (eds), *The Psychotherapist's Own Psychotherapy Patient and Clinician Perspectives.* New York: Oxford University Press.

Orlinsky, D. E., Grawe, K. & Parks, B. K. (1994). Process and outcome in psychotherapy – noch einmal. In A. E. Bergin & S. L. Garfield (eds), *Handbook of Psychotherapy and Behavior Change* (4th edn, pp. 270–376). New York: John Wiley.

Orlinsky, D. E. & Howard, K. I. (1986). The psychological interior of psychotherapy. In L. S. Greenberg & W. Pinsof (eds), *The Psychotherapeutic Process* (pp. 477–502). New York: Guilford Press.

Orlinsky, D. E., Norcross, J. C., Ronnestad, M. H. & Wiseman, H. (2005). Outcomes and impacts of psychotherapists' personal therapy: a research review. In J. D. Geller, J. C. Norcross & D. E. Orlinsky (eds), *The Psychotherapist's Own Psychotherapy Patient and Clinician Perspectives.* New York: Oxford University Press.

Orlinsky, D. E. & Ronnestad, M. H. (2005). *How Psychotherapists Develop: A Study of Therapeutic Work and Professional Growth*. Washington, DC: American Psychological Association.

Orlinsky, D. E., Ronnestad, M. H., Gerin, P., Willutzki, U., Dazord, A., Ambuhl, H., et al. (1999). Development of psychotherapists: concepts, questions, and methods of a collaborative international study. *Psychotherapy Research, 9*, 127–153.

Paulson, B. L., Everall, R. D. & Stuart, J. (2001). Client perceptions of hindering experiences in counselling. *Counselling and Psychotherapy Research, 1*, 53–61.

Paulson, B. L., Truscott, D. & Stuart, J. (1999). Clients' perception of helpful experiences in counseling. *Journal of Counseling Psychology, 46*, 317–324.

Paulson, B. L. & Worth, M. (2002). Counseling for suicide: client perspectives. *Journal of Counseling and Development, 80*, 86–93.

Philips, J. P. N. (1986). Shapiro personal questionnaire and generalized personal questionnaire techniques: a repeated measures individualized outcome measurement. In L. S. Greenberg & W. Pinsof (eds), *The Psychotherapeutic Process: A Research Handbook* (pp. 557–590). New York: Guilford Press.

Piper, W. E., Joyce, A. S., McCallum, M. & Azim, H. F. (1998). Interpretive and supportive forms of psychotherapy and patient personality variables. *Journal of Consulting and Clinical Psychology, 66(3)*, 558–567.

Piper, W. E., Ogrodniczuk, J. S., Joyce, A. S., McCallum, M., Rosie, J. S., O'Kelly, J. G. & Steinberg, P. I. (1999). Prediction of dropping out in time-limited, interpretive individual psychotherapy. *Psychotherapy, 36*, 114–122.

Prochaska, J. O. & DiClemente, C. C. (1983). Stages and processes of self-change of smoking: toward an integrative model of change. *Journal of Consulting and Clinical Psychology, 51*, 390–395.

Prochaska, J. O., DiClemente, C. C. & Norcross, J. C. (1992). In search of how people change: applications to addictive behaviors. *American Psychologist, 47*, 1102–1114.

Prochaska, J. O. & Norcross, J. C. (2002). Stages of change. In J. C. Norcross (ed.), *Psychotherapy Relationships that Work: Therapist Contributions and Responsiveness to Patients* (pp. 303–313). New York: Oxford University Press.

Prochaska, J. O. & Norcross, J. C. (2003). *Systems of Psychotherapy: A Transtheoretical Analysis* (5th edn). Pacific Grove, CA: Brooks/Cole.

Prouty, A. M., Markowski, E. M. & Barnes, H. L. (2000). Using the Dyadic Adjustment Scale in marital therapy: an exploratory study. *The Family Journal, 8*, 250–257.

Psychotherapy Research (1994) Special issue, *4(3&4)*.

Reis, B. F. & Brown, L. G. (1999). Reducing psychotherapy dropouts: maximizing perspective convergence in the psychotherapy dyad. *Psychotherapy, 36(2)*, 123–136.

Rennie, D. (1990). Toward a representation of the client's experience of the psychotherapy hour. In G. Lietaer, J. Rombauts & R. Van Balen (eds), *Client-centered and Experiential Psychotherapy in the Nineties* (pp. 155–172). Leuven: Leuven University Press.

Rennie, D. (1992). Qualitative analysis of the client's experience of psychotherapy. In S. Toukmanian & D. Rennie (eds), *Psychotherapy Process Research: Paradigmatic and Narrative Approaches* (pp. 211–233). Newbury Park, CA: SAGE.

Rennie, D. (1994). Client's deference in psychotherapy. *Journal of Counseling Psychology, 41*, 427–437.

Rhodes, R. H., Hill, C. E., Thompson, B. J. & Elliott, R. (1994). Client retrospective recall of resolved and unresolved misunderstanding events. *Journal of Counseling Psychology, 41*, 473–483.

Rice, L. N. & Greenberg, L. S. (eds) (1984). *Patterns of Change.* New York: Guilford Press.

Rice, L. N. & Kerr, G. P. (1986). Measures of client and therapist vocal quality. In L. S. Greenberg & W. Pinsof (eds), *The Psychotherapeutic Process: A Research Handbook* (pp. 73–106). New York: Guilford Press.

Rice, L. N., Koke, C. J., Greenberg, L. S. & Wagstaff, A. K. (1979). *Manual for the Client Vocal Quality Classification System.* York: York University Counselling and Development Centre.

Rice, L. N. & Saperia, E. P. (1984). Task analysis and the resolution of problematic reactions. In L. N. Rice & L. S. Greenberg (eds), *Patterns of Change* (pp. 29–66). New York: Guilford Press.

Rogers, C. R. (1942). *Counseling and Psychotherapy: Newer Concepts and Practice.* Boston, MA: Houghton Mifflin.

Rogers, C. R. (1951) *Client-centered Counselling.* Boston, MA: Houghton-Mifflin.

Rosenberg, M. (1965). *Society and the Adolescent Self-image.* Princeton, NJ: Princeton University Press.

Safran, J. D. & Muran, J. C. (1996). The resolutions of ruptures in the therapeutic alliance. *Journal of Consulting and Clinical Psychology, 64*, 447–458.

Safran, J. D. & Muran, J. C. (2000). *Negotiating the Therapeutic Alliance.* New York: Guilford Press.

Sampson, H. (1986). Introduction to empirical studies of plan concept. In J. Weiss & H. Sampson (eds), *The Psychoanalytic Process: Theory, Clinical Observations, and Empirical Research* (pp. 221–240). New York: Guilford Press.

Schulte, D. & Hahlweg, K. (2000). A new law for governing psychotherapy for psychologists in Germany: impact on training and mental health policy. *Clinical Psychology: Science and Practice, 7*, 259–263.

Seligman, M. E. P. (1995). The effectiveness of psychotherapy: the consumer reports study. *American Psychologist, 50(2)*, 965–974.

Sexton, T. L., Alexander, J. F. & Mease, A. L. (2004). Levels of evidence for the models and mechanisms of therapeutic change in family and couple therapy. In M. J. Lambert (ed.), *Bergin's and Garfield's Handbook of Psychotherapy and Behavior Change* (5th edn, pp. 590–646). New York: John Wiley.

Sexton, T. L., Weeks, G. R., & Robbins, M. S. (eds) (2003). *Handbook of Family Therapy: The Science and Practice of Working with Families and Couples.* New York: Routledge.

Shapiro, D. A. (1995). Finding out how psychotherapies help people change. *Psychotherapy Research, 5*, 1–21.

Shapiro, D. A., Barkham, M., Rees, A., Hardy, G. E., Reynolds, S. & Startup, M. (1994). Effects of treatment duration and severity of depression on the effectiveness of cognitive-behavioral and psychodynamic-interpersonal psychotherapy. *Journal of Consulting and Clinical Psychology, 62(3)*, 522–534.

Shapiro, D. A., Rees, A., Barkham, M., Hardy, G., Reynolds, S. & Startup, M. (1995). Effects of treatment duration and severity of depression on the maintenance of gains after cognitive-behavioral and psychodynamic-interpersonal psychotherapy. *Journal of Consulting and Clinical Psychology, 63(3)*, 378–387.

Shea, M. T., Elkin, I., Imber, S. D., Sotsky, S. M., Watkins, J. T., Collins, J. F. et al. (1992). Course of depressive symptoms over follow-up: findings from the National Institute of Mental Health Treatment of Depression Collaborative Research Program. *Archives of General Psychiatry, 49*, 782–787.

Shrout, P. E. & Fleiss, J. L. (1979). Interclass corelations: uses in assessing rater reliability. *Psychological Bulletin, 86(2)*, 420–428.

Silberschatz, G. (1986). Testing pathogenic beliefs. In J. Weiss & H. Sampson (eds), *The Psychoanalytic Process: Theory, Clinical Observations, and Empirical Research* (pp. 256–266). New York: Guilford Press.

Silberschatz, G., Sampson, H. & Weiss, J. (1986). Testing pathogenic beliefs versus seeking transference gratifications. In J. Weiss & H. Sampson (eds), *The Psychoanalytic Process: Theory, Clinical Observations, and Empirical Research* (pp. 267–276). New York: Guilford Press.

Skovholt, T. M. & Jennings, L. (2004). *Master Therapists: Exploring Expertise in Therapy and Counseling.* Boston: Allyn and Bacon.

Skovholt, T. M., Jennings, L. & Mullenbach, M. (2004). Portrait of master therapist: developmental model of the highly functioning self. In T. M. Skovholt & L. Jennings, *Master Therapists: Exploring Expertise in Therapy and Counseling* (pp. 125–146). Boston: Allyn and Bacon.

Sloane, R. B., Staples, F. R., Cristol, A. H., Yorkson, N. J. & Whipple, K. (1975). *Psychotherapy Versus Behavior Therapy.* Cambridge, MA: Harvard University Press.

Smith, M. L. and Glass, G. V. (1977). Meta-analysis of psychotherapy outcome studies. *American Psychologist, 32*, 752–760.

Smith, D. P. (2004, June). Secularism, spirituality, and agnosticism: differences among psychotherapists' religiosity according to theoretical orientation and nationality. Paper presented at 34th annual conference of International Society for Psychotherapy Research, Rome, Italy.

Smith, M. L., Glass, G. V. & Miller, T. I. (1980). *The Benefits of Psychotherapy.* Baltimore, MD: Johns Hopkins University Press.

Snow, R. E. (1991). Aptitude-treatment interaction as a framework for research on individual differences in psychotherapy. *Journal of Consulting and Clinical Psychology, 59(2)*, 205–216.

Spanier, G. (1976). Measuring dyadic adjustment: new scales of assessing the quality of marriage and similar dyads. *Journal of Marriage and the Family, 38*, 15–28.

Speer, D. C. (1992). Clinically significant change: Jacobson and Truax (1991) revisited. *Journal of Consulting and Clinical Psychology, 60*, 402–408.

Speer, D. C. & Greenbaum, P. E. (1995). Five methods for computing significant individual client change and improvement rates: support for an individual growth curve approach. *Journal of Consulting and Clinical Psychology, 63*, 1044–1048.

Sprenkle, D. & Piercy, F. (eds) (2005). *Research Methods in Family Therapy.* New York: Guildford Press.

Stiles, W. B. (2002). Assimilation of problematic experiences. In J. C. Norcross (ed.), *Psychotherapy Relationships that Work: Therapist Contributions and Responsiveness to Patients* (pp. 357–365). New York: Oxford University Press.

Stiles, W. B. (2006). Case studies. In J. C. Norcross, L. E. Beutler & R. F. Levant (eds), *Evidence-based Practices in Mental Health: Debate and Dialogue on the Fundamental Questions*. Washington, DC: American Psychological Association.

Stiles, W. B., Barkham, M., Twigg, E., Mellor-Clark, J. & Cooper, M. (2006) Effectiveness of cognitive-behavioural, person-centred, and psychodynamic therapies as practiced in UK National Health Service settings. *Psychological Medicine, 36*, 555–566.

Stiles, W. B., Elliott, R., Llewelyn, S. P, Firth-Cozens, J. A., Margison, F. R., Shapiro, D. A. & Hardy, G. (1990). Assimilation of problematic experiences by clients in psychotherapy. *Psychotherapy, 27*, 411–420.

Stiles, W. B., Honos-Webb, L. & Surko, M. (1998). Responsiveness in psychotherapy. *Clinical Psychology: Science and Practice, 5*, 439–458.

Stiles, W. B., Shankland, M. C., Wright, J. & Field, S. D. (1997). Aptitude-treatment interactions based on clients' assimilation of their presenting problems. *Journal of Consulting and Clinical Psychology, 65*, 889–893.

Stiles, W. B. & Shapiro, D. A. (1994). Disabuse of the drug metaphor: psychotherapy process–outcome correlations. *Journal of Consulting and Clinical Psychology, 62(5)*, 942–948.

Stiles, W. B. & Snow, J. S. (1984). Counseling session impact as viewed by novice counselors and their clients. *Journal of Counselling Psychology, 31*, 3–12.

Strupp, H. H., Horowitz, L. M. & Lambert, M. J. (eds) (1997). *Measuring Patient Changes in Mood, Anxiety, and Personality Disorders: Toward a Core Battery*. Washington, DC: American Psychological Association.

Strupp, H. H. & Howard, K. I. (1992). A brief history of psychotherapy research. In D. K. Freedheim (ed.), *History of Psychotherapy: A Century of Change* (pp. 309–334). Washington, DC: American Psychological Association.

Tarrier, N., Kinney, C., McCarthy, E., Humphreys, L., Wittkowski, A. & Morris, J. (2000). Two-year follow-up of cognitive-behavioral therapy and supportive counseling in the treatment of persistent symptoms in chronic schizophrenia. *Journal of Consulting and Clinical Psychology, 68*, 917–922.

Task Force on Promotion and Dissemination of Psychological Procedures (1995). Training in and dissemination of empirically validated treatments: report and recommendations. *The Clinical Psychologist, 48(1)*, 3–23.

Timulak, L. (2005). *Současný výzkum psychoterapie*. Praha: Triton.

Timulak, L. (2007). Identifying core categories of client identified impact of helpful events in psychotherapy – a qualitative meta-analysis. *Psychotherapy Research, 17*, 305–314.

Timulak, L. & Lietaer, G. (2001). Moments of empowerment: a qualitative analysis of positively experienced episodes in brief person-centred counselling. *Counselling and Psychotherapy Research, 1*, 62–73.

Tingey, R. C., Lambert, M. J., Burlingame, G. M. & Hansen, N. B. (1996). Assessing clinical significance: proposed extensions to method. *Psychotherapy Research, 6*, 109–123.

Tjeltveit, A. C. (1999). *Ethics and Values in Psychotherapy*. London: Routledge.

Truax, C. B. (1967). A scale for the rating of accurate empathy. In C. R. Rogers, E. T. Gendlin, D. J. Kiesler & C. B. Truax (eds), *The Therapeutic Relationship and its Impact: A Study of Psychotherapy with Schizofrenics* (pp. 555–568). Madison: University of Wisconsin Press.

Varvin, S. & Stiles, W. B. (1999). Emergence of severe traumatic experiences: an assimilation analysis of psychoanalytic therapy with a political refugee. *Psychotherapy Research, 9(3)*, 381–404.

Wallerstein, R. S. (1992). The Menninger project. In D. K. Freedheim (ed.), *History of Psychotherapy: A Century of Change.* Washington, DC: American Psychological Association.

Walsh, R., Perruci, A. & Severns, J. (1999). What's in a good moment? A hermeneutic study of psychotherapy values across levels of psychotherapy training. *Psychotherapy Research, 9*, 304–326.

Waltz, J., Addis, M. E., Koerner, K. & Jacobson, N. S. (1993). Testing the integrity of psychotherapy protocol: assessment of adherence and competence. *Journal of Consulting and Clinical Psychology, 61*, 620–630.

Wampold, B. E. (1997). Methodological problems in identifying efficacious psychotherapies. *Psychotherapy Research, 7*, 21–43.

Wampold, B. E. (2001). *The Great Psychotherapy Debate: Models, Methods, and Findings.* Mahwah, NJ: Lawrence Erlbaum Associates.

Wampold, B. E. & Bolt, D. M. (2006). Therapist effects: clever ways to make them (and everything else) disappear. *Psychotherapy Research, 16*, 184–187.

Wampold, B. E. & Brown, G. S. (2005). Estimating therapist variability: a naturalistic study of outcomes in managed care. *Journal of Consulting and Clinical Psychology, 73*, 914–923.

Wampold, B. E., Lichtenberg, J. W. & Waehler, C. A. (2002). Principles of empirically supported interventions in counseling psychology. *The Counseling Psychologist, 30(2)*, 197–217.

Wampold, B. E., Mondin, G. W., Moody, M., Stich, F., Benson, K. & Ahn, H. (1997). A meta-analysis of outcome studies comparing bona fide psychotherapies: empirically 'All must have prizes'. *Psychological Bulletin, 122*, 203–215.

Ward, E., King, M., Lloyd, M., Bower, P., Sibbald, B., Farrelly, S. et al. (2000). Randomised controlled trial of non-directive counseling, cognitive-behavior therapy, and usual general practitioner care for patients with depression. I: Clinical effectiveness. *British Medical Journal, 321*, 1383–1388.

Waskow, J. E. & Parloff, M. B. (eds) (1975). *Psychotherapy Change Measures.* Rockville, MD: National Institute of Mental Health.

Watson, J. C. & Geller, S. (2005). The relation among the relationship conditions, working alliance, and outcome in both process-experiential and cognitive-behavioral psychotherapy. *Psychotherapy Research, 15*, 25–33.

Watson, J. C., Goldman, R. N. & Greenberg, L. S. (2007). *Case Studies in Emotion-focused Treatment of Depression: Comparison of Good and Poor Outcome.* Washington, DC: American Psychological Association.

Watson, J. C., Gordon, L. B., Stermac, L., Kalogerakos, F. & Steckley, P. (2003). Comparing the effectiveness of process-experiential with cognitive-behavioral psychotherapy in the treatment of depression. *Journal of Consulting and Clinical Psychology, 71*, 773–781.

Weiss, J. (1986). Two psychoanalytic hypotheses. In J. Weiss & H. Sampson (eds), *The Psychoanalytic Process: Theory, Clinical Observations, and Empirical Research* (pp. 22–24). New York: Guilford Press.

Weiss, J. (1993). *How Psychotherapy Works: Process and Technique.* New York: Guilford Press.

Weiss, J. & Sampson, H. (eds) (1986). *The Psychoanalytic Process: Theory, Clinical Observations, and Empirical Research.* New York: Guilford Press.

Weissman, M. M. & Brothwell, S. (1976). Assessment of social adjustment by patient self-report. *Archives of General Psychiatry, 33,* 1111–1115.

Weissman, M. M., Markowitz, J. C. & Klerman, G. L. (2000). *Comprehensive Guide to Interpersonal Psychotherapy.* New York: Basic Books.

Westen, D. & Morrison, K. (2001). A multidimensional meta-analysis of treatments for depression, panic, and generalized anxiety disorder: an empirical examination of the status of empirically supported therapies. *Journal of Consulting and Clinical Psychology, 69(6),* 875–899.

Westen, D., Novotny, C. M. & Thompson-Brenner, H. (2004). The empirical status of empirically supported psychotherapies: assumptions, findings, and reporting in controlled clinical trials. *Psychological Bulletin, 130,* 631–663.

Wheeler, S. (2003). *A Research on Supervision of Counsellors and Psychotherapists: A Systematic Scoping Search.* Rugby: BACP.

Whipple, J. L., Lambert, M. J., Vermeersch, D. A., Smart, D. W., Nielsem, S. L. & Hawkins, E. J. (2003). Improving the effects of psychotherapy: the use of early identification of treatment failure and problem-solving strategies in routine practice. *Journal of Counseling Psychology, 50,* 59–68.

Wilfley, D. E., Welch, R. R., Stein, R. I., Spurell, E. B., Cohen, L. R., Saelens, B. E. et al. (2002). A randomized comparison of group cognitive-behavioral therapy and group interpersonal psychotherapy for treatment of overweight individuals with binge-eating disorder. *Archives of General Psychiatry, 59,* 713–721.

Wise, E. A. (2004). Methods for analyzing psychotherapy outcomes: a review of clinical significance, reliable change, and recommendations for future directions. *Journal of Personality Assessment, 82,* 50–59.

Woody, G. E., Luborsky, L., McLellan, A. T., O'Brien, C., Beck, A. T., Blaine, J. et al. (1983). Psychotherapy for opiate addicts: does it help? *Archives of General Psychiatry, 40,* 639–645.

Worthington, E. L. & Roehlke, H. J. (1979). Effective supervision as perceived by beginning counselors-in-training. *Journal of Counseling Psychology, 26,* 64–73.

Worthington, E. L. & Sandage, S. J. (2002). Religion and spirituality. In J. C. Norcross (ed.), *Psychotherapy Relationships that Work: Therapist Contributions and Responsiveness to Patients* (pp. 383–400). New York: Oxford University Press.

Yalom, I. D. & Leszcz, M. (2005). *The Theory and Practice of Group Psychotherapy* (5th edn). New York: Basic Books.

Young, J. E. & Beck, A. T. (1980). *Cognitive Therapy Scale: Rating Manual.* Unpublished manuscript. Philadelphia, PA: University of Pennsylvania.

Zuroff, D. C., Blatt, S. J., Sotsky, S. M., Krupnick, J. L., Martin, D. J., Sanislow III, C. A. & Simmens, S. (2000). Relation of therapeutic alliance and perfectionism to outcome in brief outpatient treatment of depression. *Journal of Consulting and Clinical Psychology, 68,* 114–124.

Index

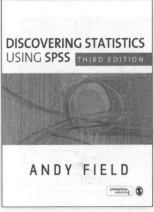
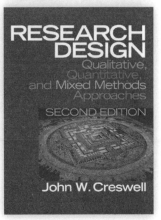

The Qualitative Research Kit

Edited by Uwe Flick

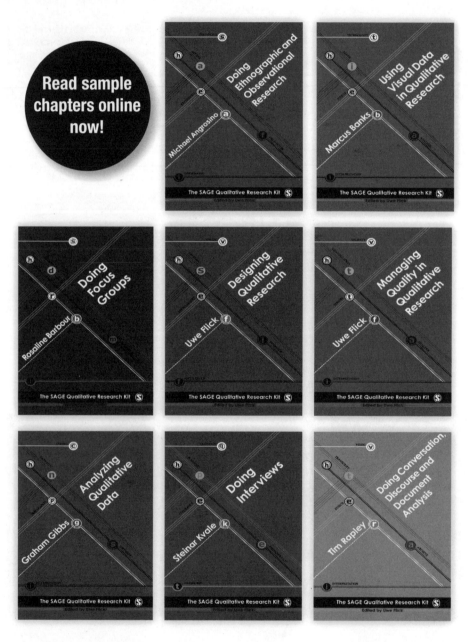

Read sample chapters online now!

Doing Ethnographic and Observational Research — Michael Angrosino — The SAGE Qualitative Research Kit — Edited by Uwe Flick

Using Visual Data in Qualitative Research — Marcus Banks — The SAGE Qualitative Research Kit — Edited by Uwe Flick

Doing Focus Groups — Rosaline Barbour — The SAGE Qualitative Research Kit

Designing Qualitative Research — Uwe Flick — The SAGE Qualitative Research Kit — Edited by Uwe Flick

Managing Quality in Qualitative Research — Uwe Flick — The SAGE Qualitative Research Kit — Edited by Uwe Flick

Analyzing Qualitative Data — Graham Gibbs — The SAGE Qualitative Research Kit — Edited by Uwe Flick

Doing Interviews — Steinar Kvale — The SAGE Qualitative Research Kit — Edited by Uwe Flick

Doing Conversation, Discourse and Document Analysis — Tim Rapley — The SAGE Qualitative Research Kit — Edited by Uwe Flick

www.sagepub.co.uk